211
G 57?

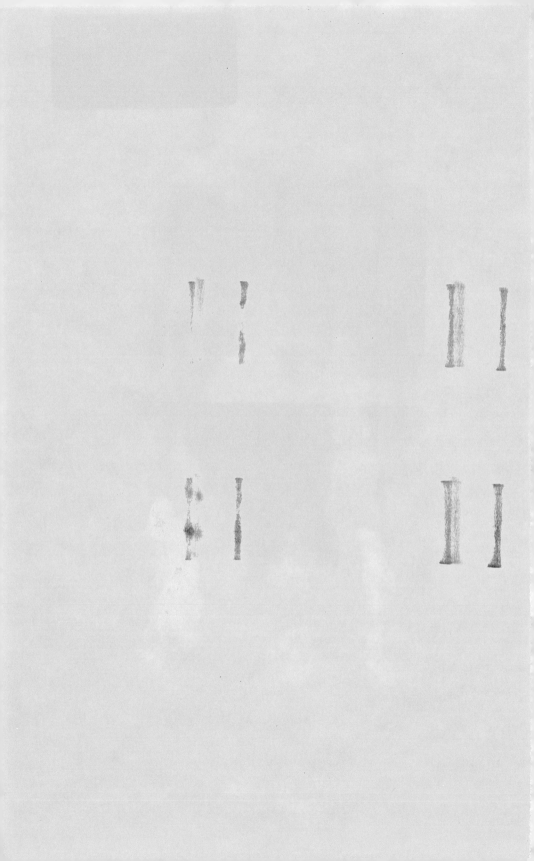

THE CONTEMPORARY DISCUSSION SERIES

GOD IN LANGUAGE

GOD
IN
LANGUAGE

EDITED BY
ROBERT P. SCHARLEMANN
AND GILBERT E. M. OGUTU

A NEW ERA BOOK

PARAGON HOUSE PUBLISHERS
New York

Published in the United States by
Paragon House Publishers
2 Hammarskjöld Plaza
New York, NY 10017

A New Ecumenical Research Association Book

Library of Congress Cataloging-in-Publication Data

God in Language.

(God, The Contemporary Discussion Series)
Chiefly essays presented at a conference arranged
by the New Ecumenical Research Association; held in
Seoul, Korea, Aug. 1984.
"A New ERA book."
Includes bibliographies and index.
1. Languages—Religious aspects—Congresses.
I. Scharlemann, Robert P.   II. Ogutu, Gilbert E. M.
III. New Ecumenical Research Association
(Unification Theological Seminary)   IV. Series.
BL65.L2G63   1987   211'.014   86-25412

ISBN 0-913757-12-8
ISBN 0-913757-13-6 (pbk.)

Contents

Contents

Preface

Language is both a tool and a medium. It is a tool in the sense that we can use words in order to do things. We can do things *with* language—we can bring about communication, make promises, give commands, state matters of fact, and so on. It is a medium in the sense that we do things not only *with* language but also *in* language; it is the medium, or the element, in which we do the act. Thus, when we state a fact or make a promise or the like we are doing something with language but we are also doing it in language. We have language as a tool at our disposal to the extent that we can make use of it to do things, but we are in language as our medium or element to the extent that it provides the environment in which we do those same things. We can say "It is raining" in order to call attention to the need to take an umbrella or in order to explain why we are putting on a raincoat. But when we say it, the whole English language from which the words are taken is the medium in which they make sense at all. The relation between saying the English words "It is raining" in the absence of the whole language and saying them in the medium of that language is like the relation between making the motions of a swimmer while on dry land and making those same motions in the water. The motions are the same, but whether swimming actually takes place depends upon whether they are made in the element of swimming, water; it is in the medium of water that the motions constitute swimming, or that, to put it almost tautologically, swimming is what it is. Similarly, the sounds of the words "It is raining" are the same whether one says them in a community where English is spoken and understood or in a community in which no one knows the English language. Whether the words do anything—give information, announce an intention, explain an action—depends, however, not just upon the material of the words (their sounds or appearances) but upon whether they are used as words in a language. Speaking or writing them as words in a language is like making the motions of swimming in water; the action is in its element. That is the sense in which language is both the medium in which and the means by which communication, as well as the other accomplishments of language, takes place.

There is another sense in which language is a medium, or a thing in the middle. If we make a basic distinction between subjects and objects, then language is midway between the two. A word is a kind of object because it is physically perceptible like chairs and tables; a spoken word can be heard and a written one seen. To the extent that it is thus perceptible, it is an object like other objects in the world. Yet there is a difference. For what distinguishes a word from a noise or a scribble is that it is a sign with a sense. If we did not understand a sense in a written or spoken word, it would not be a word at all but only a noise or a scribble. That words have a meaning (even if it can vary) makes them more like subjects than objects; they have a thought-content which is distinct from the physically sensible content of the auditory or visual figures. That they are intelligible things, or signs, makes them more like subjects than objects; that they are physically perceptible makes them more like objects than subjects. That they have both features is what places them midway between the subjective and the objective. In this sense, too, language is a medium. Does its being a medium mean that language limits reality, so that things become less than what they really are as soon as they are put into words? In one way, words are obviously less than things. The word "food" cannot satisfy hunger, only real food can. But in another way, language seems to be more than everyday reality because poetic words can create worlds that may appear to be more real than the world of the ordinary. Is the relation between the word "God" and reality like that between the word "food" and edible food or is it like the relation between poetic words and the world they create—or is it like neither or both?

The essays which have been brought together for this volume were written in response to the question of the effect that language as a medium has upon the knowledge of God. Language is undoubtedly something by means of which we can attain knowledge. That is true at least when we gain knowledge by communication— through books, teaching, conversation. But is there any importance to the fact that the knowledge is also attained *in* language as well as with language? This is the basic question to which the several authors have addressed themselves. Most of the essays were presented originally at a conference arranged by the New Ecumenical Research Association and held in Seoul, Korea, in August of 1984.

The essays reflect a range of answers to the question posed as well as different ways of understanding the question itself. For purposes of this volume, they have been placed into three groups: those treating of language and knowledge, those discussing aspects of language, and those investigating particular questions of current interest. The general question is answered most directly by Asa Kasher, when he argues that the medial character of language does not affect the knowledge of God because what knowledge means is independent of language. We do learn certain things by learning to speak a natural language (that is, a language like English, French, and Chinese in contrast to sign language or machine languages); but the substance of what goes into justifying assertions comes from a separate form of reasoning related to a particular "sphere of life." Frank Harrison addresses himself to the question whether acknowledging the embedding of logic in language and the plurality of languages must lead to relativism without restraint. He provides the outline of an answer—a "methodological program"—in a theory of language which sees it as a general structure composed of the three elements of syntax, semantics, and pragmatics; and he proposes that meaningful theological talk takes place within a descriptively adequate language, that is, a language which makes use of empirical predicates, not logical ones. According to this theory, the meaningfulness and truth of the assertion that God exists might then be shown if the proposition that God exists is a necessary condition for accepting the semantic foundations of descriptively adequate language. Francis D'Sa and Nona Bolin bring certain Heideggerian and post-Heideggerian themes into play; D'Sa with his analysis and interpretation, centering on such concepts as "dwelling," of the Gospel of John and Bolin with her recounting of the way in which the onto-theology of Western metaphysics (the identification of God with a supreme being and with being in general) has been called into question by Heidegger's "radical" phenomenology and by Derrida's grammatology or double writing.

A different kind of double writing, though still an illustration of Derrida's point that one cannot destrue—deconstruct or analyze—a writing without doing another writing, is the subject of Martin Jaffee's treatise: the writing of a commentary on the Mishnah. According to Jaffee's analysis, the exegetical procedure is one which uses the Misnah as pre-text (the text already there to be interpreted) and pretext (the text through which as well as for which the commentator's text speaks). Gilbert Ogutu, providing a specific illustration of the cultural and linguistic conditioning to which Harrison gives theoretical consideration, uses what the Luo of Kenya said of the supreme being, Nya-saye, in order to analyze the conception implicit in language. On that basis he raises the question, at the end, whether the existing translation of the Bible makes real sense in terms of that history. Shlomo Biderman provides an analysis of authority-claims in religious language in order to solve the apparent conflict between "autonomy" and "authority," or between morality and religion, which is expressed in Plato's *Euthyphro* in the question whether something is good because God chooses it or whether God chooses it because it is good. Biderman argues that, in monotheistic religions, seeing God as the authority does not necessarily involve acceptance of specific statements about God's existence and will.

In these discussions, Jaffee, Ogutu, and Biderman bring out three different aspects of language: the interplay between oral and written, commenting and original language; the function of language in mediating a knowledge of concepts; and the use of language to perform illocutionary acts. Two additional aspects are considered in the essays by Robert Scharlemann and Frederick Sontag. Scharlemann appeals to the "instantiating" capacity of the word "God" in order to show how, in Martin Buber's *I and Thou*, it is possible to tell the difference between the thou as such and the thou which Buber identified with God. Sontag considers the relation between speaking and silence, not only indicating how silence can remove the limits that words place but also suggesting that, in the contemporary world, it is through silence that God speaks, though it takes a discipline to hear what silence says.

The last group of essays is devoted to matters of current controversy: Wittgenstein's view of language, the relation of philosophy and religion in Duméry's philosophy of religion, anthropomorphism in religious language, and the utopian and sacred elements in language as such and in theology. In his essay, Michael Coughlan is concerned, in the first place, with the consistency of Wittgenstein's position on language. But he discusses the question in such a way as to bring up, from a different point of view, the issue of metaphysics that Bolin had treated. Henry Duméry's philosophy of religion presents Charles Courtney with the opportunity to consider language in the setting of the distinction between act and expression and to ask about the competence of philosophy to make critical judgments in religion. Frederick Ferré provides a defense of the much-maligned anthropomorphic features of religious language, arguing not only that anthropomorphism is unavoidable but that the interests of spirituality, which first give rise to its critique, can be served only by affirming a certain kind of anthropomorphism. Finally, in Gabriel Vahanian's article on the utopianism of language (words are no place, they can only take place), illuminated by a response from Lonnie Kliever, we can hear the overtones not only of the dialectical theology of Rudolf Bultmann but of the "otherness" that is a theme of so much current literature.

ROBERT P. SCHARLEMANN

Part One
LANGUAGE
AND
KNOWLEDGE

"What Effect Does Language as a Medium Have on Knowledge of God?" "In a Sense None."

ASA KASHER

There are different kinds of religious claims for knowledge of God, but in the present paper we are interested in just one kind of such claims, namely, of those made with respect to what is said when certain assertions are made, allegedly about God.

Let us mention some simple assumptions we all make with respect to such assertions. First, every standard assertion is made with words of a certain natural language. In a typical situation, we have an assertion A, a speech act performed by a felicitous utterance of some sentence S, the content of which is, under the circumstances of utterance, a certain proposition P. Secondly, and still obviously, some assertions have a true content whereas some others do not. In any case, the content of an assertion is always a putative subject of some knowledge claims, namely, claims that some person or other knows that the content of the assertion, that is to say, the asserted proposition, is true.

Thus, our prime question—"What effect does language as a medium have on knowledge of God?"—can be rephrased to read: "What effect does language as a medium have, when one of its sentences, S, is felicitously used to make an assertion A about God, on claims for knowledge that the asserted proposition P is true?"

Put in a nutshell, our answer to this question would be: "None"; that is to say, natural language as such does not have any special effect on such claims for knowledge. However, put more guardedly, our answer is that in a sense natural language as such does not have any special effect on claims for knowledge that certain asserted propositions, allegedly about God, hold true.

One of our starting points is part of the classical conception of knowledge in general. According to this conception, three conditions must obtain for a person to know that a proposition P is true. First, the proposition P itself must be true. Secondly, the person has to accept *P*, or, in other words, to believe that *P* is true. And, thirdly, that person has to be justified in believing *P* to be true. To be sure, this analysis of the concept of knowledge has been both criticized and repaired by contemporary philosophers, but the details are presently not of our concern. What seems to us to be particularly interesting, from our present point of view, is the third condition.

What does it take for a person *Alpha* to be justified in believing a proposition *P* to be true? Consider the following examples of challenged beliefs being defended:

(1) *Alpha:* I believe the baby is sick.
   Beta: What makes you think so?
   Alpha: Notice the following symptoms: . . .
(2) *Alpha:* I believe she was murdered by her grandson.
   Gamma: Why do you think so?
   Alpha: First, because he was the only person seen to enter her house during the night of the murder, and, secondly, because he was the single heir of his wealthy grandmother, and he is extremely greedy and crooked.
(3) *Alpha:* This typewriter is red.
   Delta: How do you know?
   Alpha: Well, I see that it is red. What else should I say?
(4) *Alpha:* 17 is a prime number.
   Epsilon: Is that so?
   Alpha: Yes, just try to divide it by 2 and 3 and see what happens.

Examples of religious beliefs, expressed, challenged, and defended will be discussed later.

There are a few observations that it might be helpful to make about these examples.

Notice, first, that there is nothing odd in challenges such as *Beta's*, in example (1), or *Epsilon's*, in example (4). Under ordinary circumstances, when a speaker *Alpha* asserts something, *P*, either by expressing it or by sincerely saying that he believes that *P*, *Alpha* is under a prima facie commitment to present, on appropriate demand, grounds for holding *P* to be true. Usually, when a speaker *Alpha* discloses a belief of his own, an appropriate request for justification of this belief will appear as a permissible turn in a natural conversation, whereas by letting such a challenge go unmet,

Alpha will be accused of having introduced some dissonance into an otherwise smooth exchange of words.

However, some challenges are seemingly odd. *Delta*'s request, in example (3), is a case in point. Now, the oddity of such cases does not qualify *Alpha*'s commitment to present on demand grounds for his holding true the belief under consideration. What renders *Delta*'s request odd is not the content of his request for information that would show *Alpha*'s being justified in holding some proposition true, but rather *Delta*'s request for information which seems to be at his disposal anyway. Usually, *Delta* would be aware of *Alpha*'s grounds for holding a belief as to the color of a present object, since *Delta* himself would be aware of, say, that typewriter's being red and also of *Alpha*'s being aware of it. What else could *Alpha* do in an ordinary attempt to justify his belief that the color of the present typewriter is red?

Generally speaking, processes of justification have natural end points. Under normal conditions, a challenge to my asserted belief that the present typewriter is red will be met and discarded by my pointing out that I see it redly, so to speak. Under less common circumstances, for example, when lighting conditions are special, the same challenge could be met and discarded by my showing that such lighting conditions do not cause a typewriter which is not red to seem red. On a still different occasion, the end point of the corresponding justification process will be different from the previously mentioned end points.

Clearly, every justification of an asserted belief, P, involves some evidence for P; call it E. What emerges from a comparison of examples (1) to (4) with each other is that they involve different types of evidence, that is to say, different conceptions of what should count as evidence E for the proposition P under consideration. Thus, a challenge to a mathematical assertion expressing *Alpha*'s accepting as true the proposition that 17 is a prime number can be met by nothing less than a specification of a proof of that asserted proposition. On such occasions, the required relationship between what is regarded as appropriate evidence and the asserted belief rests on the strong concept of proof, in a strict, formal sense of the term. On the other hand, a challenge to a medical assertion expressing *Alpha*'s belief that the baby is sick will not be met by *Alpha*'s presenting a formal proof which demonstrates that the baby is sick. Rather than be met by a deductive argument, such a challenge will be treated as an ordinary demand to present some particular facts which would confirm the belief that the baby is sick. Hence, *Alpha* meets that challenge by specifying an appropriate cluster of symptoms. Such a cluster of symptoms is considered a confirmation of *Alpha*'s belief that the baby is sick whenever the latter is the best available explanation of the former: the baby's being sick is the best explanation at *Alpha*'s disposal for the fact, say, that the baby keeps crying, though it is not a crybaby, nor has it been harmed or frightened by anybody or anything. All this is, indeed, on a par with the relationship which experimental data bear, on typical occasions, to scientific theories they help to confirm.

For our present purposes, it is important to note that there are contexts in which a proposition cannot be justified just by pointing out some facts which are best explained by it. A typical case in point can be found in some judicial proceedings. Consider *Alpha*'s justification of his asserted belief that she was murdered by her grandson, in example (2). Although the best available explanation for her being found dead is that her grandson murdered her, the circumstantial evidence *Alpha* has for his belief would not provide sufficient grounds for convicting that grandson of murder according to some systems of law, in the absence of reliable eyewitnesses.

There is no uniform method of justifying asserted beliefs about deities. One encounters different methods of justification applied to one and the same asserted belief, namely, that God exists. To understand that, consider two types of argument for the existence of God.

On many occasions, arguments of the ontological type are meant to be taken as proofs in some strict sense of the term. Thus, a remarkable feature of arguments of the ontological type is that they center upon conceptual analyses of notions such as 'perfection', 'existence', and 'necessity', in addition to some definition of 'God'. Hence, the belief that God exists is meant to be justified by an ontological argument, in the sense of its being shown to follow deductively from a few premises which, in turn, rest on some commonly acceptable conceptual mesh.

On the other hand, arguments of the teleological type are purportedly analogous to some scientific arguments. Recall William Paley's "Natural Theology, or Evidences of the Existence and Attributes of the Deity, Collected from the Appearances of Nature," where his argument from design rests on the case of the human eye, which produces sight in an intricate way. The existence of a supreme designer is, then, meant to serve as the best available explanation of the facts with respect to the structure and operation of the human eye. Consequently, the latter facts are regarded, by whoever espouses the related argument from design, as an adequate support of the former existential proposition and therefore as a justification for holding it true.

There is a third method of justifying asserted beliefs with reference to God, applied much more often in some religions. How does one go about justifying an asserted belief with reference to God's will, action, or commandment in a theological parlance which permits forming such asserted beliefs? The answer rests neither on any type of proof, in some strict sense of the term, nor on any kind of argument which is supposedly similar to some scientific reasoning. The method we have in mind is, rather, the one applied when a religious tradition or law directs its followers to the sacred writings of that religion for a justification of a belief with reference to acts or words ascribed to God.

Some allusions to sacred books or to other religious writings have a practical point. If the asserted belief is, for example, that according to what is referred to as God's will a certain person must not do a specific work during the seventh day of the week, it might be justified, within some religion, by alluding to a couple of verses of the Bible. Far from being formal or scientific in nature, such methods of interpretation are developed, applied, and transmitted in the same way as methods of argument in legal traditions.

We see, then, that there are completely different methods of justifying asserted beliefs, whether with reference to God or not. A competent speaker of a natural language knows how to apply an appropriate method of justification whenever an asserted belief of his has been properly challenged. Where does knowledge of how to justify one's own asserted beliefs come from? In answering this question we will reach an answer to the main problem of the present paper as well.

A competent speaker of a natural language has knowledge of different kinds. He knows the language, but obviously he knows much which is not part of the language. Knowledge of how to prove simple theorems is not part of the knowledge of a natural language, even if the latter is used in formulating the former. Knowledge of how to defend empirical claims is also outside the confines of a speaker's knowledge of his native tongue. Similarly, legal arguments are always phrased in some combination of Latin and the vernacular, but the legal customs or statutes which govern them do not form part of the body of grammar.

Thus, knowledge of how to justify one's own asserted beliefs has ingredients which do not belong to the knowledge of the natural language used for assertion. What does belong to the language itself, as part of the constitutive rules of the speech act of assertion, is knowledge of the commitment a speaker undertakes whenever he makes an assertion to present on demand an appropriate justification of the asserted belief. This is schematic knowledge, since the specification of what counts as an appropriate method of justification in a given context of utterance is not determined by language itself.

In other words, language does not provide us with justifications of asserted beliefs (excluding some simple tautologies), but it makes essential use of various methods of justification by which we form beliefs and defend them when the related assertions are challenged. The substance of each of these methods does not stem from language, but the restrictions imposed on a system of rules for it to constitute a method of justification do seem to us to stem from our concept of assertion, and, therefore, from our very concept of natural language.

To be sure, such schematic knowledge appears elsewhere in language as well. Consider, for example, indexical terms, such as 'she', 'here', or 'now'. When we use such a term in a speech act, we rely on our addressee's ability to determine the intended referent of that indexical term, but, of course, the addressee's method of identifying such referents is not as a whole part of his linguistic competence. Thus, for understanding sentences such as 'She is pretty', both an understanding of English and a method of locating at the context of utterance a salient woman (different from both speaker and addressee) is required. That the intended referent is a salient woman different from both speaker and addressee is known to the speaker through his knowledge of the meaning of the term 'she', but anything else which is incorporated within his method for identifying the intended referents of uses of the word 'she' is not part of linguistic knowledge, but rather biological, cultural, or what have you. The meaning of the term 'she' is, in a sense, a scheme.

The contribution of natural language as such to justification of asserted beliefs with reference to God is limited to a scheme, namely, a general specification of the conditions which a system of rules has to fulfil in order to qualify as a method of justification. The substance of any such method is contributed by some separable form of reasoning, usually a major ingredient of a certain human sphere of life, such as science or law. Religion is also a sphere of Life that provides people with some special forms of reasoning applied to assertions and beliefs with a reference to God. Now, the substance of a method of justification stemming from a certain religion is not contributed by the human faculty of language, nor by the details of a certain natural language. Hence, as far as justification methods of asserted beliefs are concerned, if knowledge of God, in the sense of knowledge that some assertions with reference to God are true, involves a special ingredient, the latter cannot be ascribed to language. From this point of view, language as a medium has no effect on knowledge of God in the mentioned sense.

We have been speaking about language as a medium, but a closer examination of the presupposition that language is a medium will reveal another angle of our negative answer to the main problem here under consideration. It is a basic tenet of a certain philosophical view of language that several kinds of linguistic rules are constitutive rather than instrumental. For instance, rules that characterize a certain speech act, such as assertion or command, do not specify an independently existing phenomenon, but rather constitute a sphere of activity that otherwise would not exist at all. To use a standard analogy, the rules governing a certain type of speech act are on a par with the rules of chess playing rather than with the regulations meant to govern the traffic. A medium being a middle entity, so to speak, one that is flanked by independently existing entities, such as a human being on the one hand and reality or God on the other hand, it is clear that a medium is instrumental. However, whatever forms a system of constitutive rules cannot be instrumental. Thus, discussion of effects that language as a medium has must be restricted to those parts or aspects of language which are, in some sense, of an instrumental nature.

The best candidate for playing the role of a medium within language is, indeed, reference. Roughly speaking, a referential term stands for something in the world. The reference-relation between terms in the language and things in the world is governed by certain rules of the language and our problem now is to find out what effect, if any, these rules have on knowledge of God in the sense under discussion here.

Since our discussion centers upon knowledge claims with reference to God, let us briefly consider the contribution of language to knowledge claims made by using proper names.

There are several philosophical theories of proper names in general. According to theories of one type, proper names have a sense, which is a uniquely satisfiable description (of the referent). For instance, the use of the proper name 'Aristotle' rests on some uniquely identifying description of a human being, who is also male, Greek, a philosopher, the author of certain books, the tutor of a certain king, etc. Clearly, knowledge that Aristotle was the tutor of Alexander the Great does not belong to anyone's knowledge of English. Thus, according to theories of this type, our natural language does not provide us with uniquely identifying descriptions of whatever is referred to in our language by a proper name, but since mastering our native tongue involves mastering the concept of a proper name, it is part of our linguistic knowledge that the use of any proper name must rest on an appropriate description. Again, the general conception as to what counts as an appropriate description is part of the language itself, but the details of a description on which the use of a particular proper name rests and the demonstration that that description is appropriate, under the circumstances, are beyond the confines of language. In the particular case in which a proper name is used in a natural language as referring to a deity, it is a religious tradition or theological analysis which provides one with some purportedly appropriate description sustaining the use of a proper name of the deity. Language, as a medium of reference, does not have any effect on the use of terms such as 'God', according to theories of the present type, beyond the very general restrictions it imposes on what counts as an appropriate description in a context of utterance.

According to causal theories of proper names, any use of the latter rests on a historical chain of communication. Each regular link in such a chain consists of a person's learning how to use the proper name for reference to what someone else has used the name to refer to. Such a chain starts with an act of "baptism," where an object is named by ostension or description. Such a theory poses some problems in understanding the term 'God' as a proper name, but whether such problems are solvable or not, such a theory of proper names does not lead us to any different answer as to what effect, if any, language, as a medium of reference, has on knowledge of God.

In conclusion of the present discussion, which has been mostly negative in nature, we would like to make a single positive remark. As it will turn out, our positive claim will also include a major ingredient of a negative nature.

What Effect Does Language Have on Knowledge of God?

We take it for granted, with respect to each of us, that one's native tongue shapes and rules one's thoughts. In most areas of contemplation, the limits of one's natural language are the utter limits of one's thought. Whatever can serve as the object of thought, knowledge, or belief can be the object of speech as well. And the more powerful a language turns out to be, the richer is the related realm of possible thoughts.

If it is assumed that a language can be extended in a way which broadens one's selection of asserted beliefs with reference to God, one would be justified in assuming that the selection of thoughts one can entertain with reference to God has thus also been extended. If so, one might argue, language does have an effect on our knowledge of God, through its effect on our possible objects of knowledge with reference to God.

Here I confess myself to be an adherent of a certain *via negativa* in theology. Purported assertions with reference to God are actually assertions about everything on earth. Thus, asserting that God is perfect is tantamount to asserting that everything on earth is imperfect, and the claim that God should be worshiped is equivalent to a claim that nothing on earth should be worshiped.

Hence, the effect our language has on our thought about the world might be taken, through such a *via negativa*, to be an effect our language has on knowledge of God. Some might argue that this is an effect our language has, not on knowledge of God, but rather on ignorance of God. For some, even the latter formulation with reference to God is much too strong, but this is a topic for another discussion.

2

Language, Knowledge, and God

FRANK R. HARRISON, III

Today there are severe and critical challenges to any religion viewed as a viable and important element in the life of the individual and society. Rampant materialism and a quickly spreading, highly sophisticated technology have combined to make religion seem a moot issue to be discussed amongst intelligent people. There are, of course, specifically more academic challenges which are in keeping with, and reinforcing of, the general tenor of the day. Two such challenges, especially in current western thought, bring into question the meaning and truth of religious claims. These challenges are not unrelated. For instance, it seems reasonable to suppose that if religious claims are meaningless, then they are neither true nor false. However, if one holds that religious claims are true—or false, for that matter—then, in some way, these claims must be accepted as meaningful. Furthermore, purportedly true religious claims would appear to be knowledge claims couched in a particular language. *Meaning, truth, knowledge,* and *language* become intertwining strands of a complicated arras in intelligible discussions of religious claims.

These introductory comments are intentionally, and unavoidably, vague and ambiguous. They are as vague and ambiguous as the concepts *religion, meaning, truth, knowledge,* and *language* used in making them. Yet, it is impossible at this point in my essay to define these concepts with much clarity without prejudicing further discussion. One major difficulty in clarification of, and agreement on, the use of these concepts is that they are learned, insofar as they are learned, as interrelated elements of a specific language reflecting diverse cultural dimensions and stances. General cultural backdrops form part of the very understanding and application of the concepts religion, meaning, truth, knowledge, and language. The Confucianist, for example, may disagree with several of the suggestions of the previous paragraph. He might maintain that there is a fundamental religious meaning far exceeding specific discursive discourse couched in a particular language. Nor might he agree that truth is a property of particular propositions corresponding to equally particular events in his World. The meaning and truth of the Confucianist is discovered only by transcending the realm of particulars. This meaning and truth is beyond particular languages, particular concepts, particular truths and falsehoods, particular religions.

There are two views of knowledge paralleling what may loosely be called the "eastern" and "western" stances to which I have alluded. The westerner is prone to inquire whether a particular sentence, such as "God exists" or "God is infinite," is meaningful and, if so, whether true or not. The easterner is more inclined to speak of a path—a method—to be followed leading to non-propositional enlightenment. Certainly the knowledge claims of the mystic, speaking of direct encounter, becoming one with what is utterly transcendent, are not unknown in the west. But these claims are typically seen as an embarrassment to the propositional view of meaning, knowledge, and truth that is more generally held in the west. This is not so in the eastern tradition where knowledge is a matter of enlightenment achieved, if achieved, by dedication to a path subordinating, and eventually overcoming, the illusion of the reality of the particular individual.[1]

There is more than a temptation for each—westerner and easterner—to look upon the other as wrong-headed. For each by his own criteria judges the other to be incorrect, if not a fool.[2] How else but by using my own criteria can I come to know, understand, and evaluate some position foreign to me? In order to come to know, understand, and evaluate anything, there must be a great deal which I hold fast as already known, as beyond doubting. Yet, in attempting to know, understand, and evaluate a religion which is enmeshed in a culture so radically different from mine, so much of what I hold fast must be abandoned that one time familiar concepts knowledge, understanding, and evaluation become quite unintelligible to me. But, it is exactly this—what is held fast by one side—that is brought into serious doubt by the other.[3]

Not only are there the challenges of the meaning and truth of viable religion, there is also a third challenge of cultural relativism. I address each of these challenges in this essay. In doing so I have not attempted primarily to present a set of theses to be defended. Rather, I have suggested a methodological program to be developed and carried out. The application of this method—this path—admittedly must begin in specific cases of differing cultures reflected in particular languages. Yet, while each of us must begin in precisely the cultural dimensions reflected in our own language, we need not necessarily remain there. Further, as is the case with any methodology, there are some underlying doctrinal assumptions. The acceptance of these assumptions, however, does not rest on the prior acceptance of particular cultural insights or religious views. The assumptions made in this essay are general and universal. I have not fully developed my program in this paper, nor could I have done so in the space allotted. Nonetheless, I hope that some fruitful steps have been taken.

Language

From the human viewpoint, what is commonly referred to as linguistic activity comprises one of the most complicated, and important, sorts of human functions. There is little doubt that different uses of language determine how a person perceives, evaluates, and reacts to his world. Seemingly, it is only within specific linguistic practices that one comes to appreciate and accept what is to count as a decision, a reason, a justification, an argument for something or another. Even what is to count as true or false, real or not, is revealed in specific linguistic activity. How a person and his society relates with another individual, society, and his world is fashioned in no small part by linguistic practices. However, for all of its importance and central control in the life of individuals dwelling in particular societies, this extremely important human function of linguistic activity is more often than not taken for granted. Indeed, using a particular language becomes "transparent" for the fluent practitioner of that language.

These observations tend to suggest that language is the sum of various practices carried out by individuals in numerous cultural contexts. The view adopted in this paper, however, is that language is not to be equated with such human activities making use of concrete items such as written marks, spoken sounds, or body behavior in particular contexts. Rather, language is primarily understood as an abstract structure which may be concretely expressed through particular uses of concrete items in given contexts. In general, an abstraction is not identical with that from which it is abstracted. *The* game, backgammon, for example, is made up of differing rules, definitions, conventions, and general forms of practices combining together to govern how specific activities are to be carried out in relation to one another in particular cases by means of concrete paraphernalia. *A* game of backgammon, on the other hand, is precisely a datable, instantiation of *the* game backgammon. The same distinction is drawn between language and particular datable cases of speaking or writing a language. Even the sum of all cases of speaking and writing, say, Italian, would not be the same as the language, Italian.

Language, viewed as an abstract system, is composed of a limited number of "signs," that is, types to be replaced eventually with specific tokens, combinable in an indefinitely large number of ways in accordance with a limited number of rules, definitions, conventions, general practices, and the like. I refer to these rules, definitions, conventions, and even general practices, as the "semiotic foundations" of a language. It is the various results of combinations of signs in accordance with the semiotic foundations of a language which may be given particular uses at particular times and places by particular language users in order to achieve particular goals. In sum, then, by language I understand—minimally a set of signs coupled with the means for correctly arranging those signs and interpreting them for particular use by some sign user. A full-fledged language, therefore, displays a triadic relation consisting of (1) a concatenation of signs, (2) an interpretation of those signs, and (3) some use to which those signs are placed. All of this— concatenation, interpretation, and use—is accomplished by means of sign users appealing to the semiotic foundations of the language.

Such a view is reminiscent of a position taken by Carnap in his *Introduction to Symbolic Logic and Its Applications.* Here Carnap calls the general study of language "semiotic," and divides it into three separate and quite distinct parts, namely, syntax, semantics, and pragmatics.[4] Carnap says:

A pragmatic description of, say, the French language tells how this or that language usage depends on the circumstances of the speaker and his context. Certain modes of expression are used in one period but not another; or they are used when the speaker has certain feelings and images, and evoke from the hearer certain feelings and images; or they are used when the whole situation—comprising speaker, hearer, and environment—satisfies certain conditions. All this is disregarded by the semantics of the French language, which presents (in, say, the form of a dictionary) the relation between French words and compound expressions on the one hand and their designata on the other. Thus, whereas pragmatics includes consideration of historical, sociological and psychological relations within the language community where French is spoken, semantics confines itself simply to giving an interpretation of this language. The semantical description of French contains all the specifications necessary to understand this language and to use it correctly. The syntactical description of the French language, on the other hand, contains still less than the semantical; the syntactical description specifies rules by which it can be decided whether or not a given sequence of words is a sentence of the French language (without it being presupposed that the sentence is understood). Beyond this, as we shall see, syntax may include rules which determine certain logical relations between sentences, e.g., the relation of derivability.[5]

The sharp Carnapian separation of syntax, semantics, and pragmatics usually associated with Positivistic views of language is not adopted in my essay.[6] Nonetheless, I do maintain that language, as an abstract system, is best grasped as a triadic structure in which there is much interplay amongst its distinguishable areas. It is in this more fluid sense that I employ the terms *semiotic, syntax, semantics,* and *pragmatics.*

Knowledge

Until recently in the history of western philosophy, knowledge in its broadest propositional sense has usually been understood as justified true belief. While this use, traceable to Plato's *Theaetetus,* closely relates knowledge with belief, they are not equated. To believe something to be the case is not the same as to know something is the case. One may legitimately say, "I believe that-p, but I could be wrong." On the other hand it makes no logical sense to say, "I know that-p, but I could be wrong." The rules of logic, broadly conceived, are equally ruptured in uttering, "I know that-p, but I do not believe it." Thus, while belief is taken as a necessary condition for knowledge, it is not viewed as a sufficient one.

In order to speak of having propositional knowledge, one must be able to give justifications for one's beliefs, and not merely state what one thinks, hopes, or believes to be the case.[7] Thus, what is to count as justification for knowledge claims cannot be merely the subjective opinions of some individual. Justifications must be completely objective. It is not sufficient that beliefs be justified in order to qualify as knowledge, they must also be true. At one time, for instance, it was held, and objective justifications were given for the claim, "The earth is flat." Of course, this justified belief is not now held to be true even though it did fit at one time, without contradiction, into a large overall system of other beliefs. Not only are there the general Cartesian requirements that veridical knowledge claims must be justified and true, they must be certain. That is, the concept *certain* becomes an essential part of the definition of the concept *knowledge*. Admittedly, it is difficult to ascertain just what this epistemic requirement of certainty demands. There appear, however, to be at least four ways in which one can use *certain* in connection with *knowledge*.

There is, first, the psychological sense of certain. A person slams a fist on the table exclaiming, "I am absolutely certain that he is an evil person even though I can give you no reasons for saying this, and even though much of what he does seems to suggest otherwise." Then, second, in philosophical discussions the concept certain is used in the sense of incorrigible. Typical examples are "I have a toothache," "I am seeing, right here and now, a red color patch," or "I seem to hear a door closing." The certainty of such claims follows from the logical point that the truth of the propositions is guaranteed by the fact that they are held to be true by the person asserting them. In the general quest for certainty to guarantee justifications of knowledge claims, a great deal has been made of this use of certain in incorrigible propositions.[8] Third, by certain it may be understood that the denial of what is claimed to be known would yield a formal contradiction. In this sense the formal propositions of logic and mathematics are said to be known with certainty. More recently in western philosophical literature a fourth use of certain has been introduced by Wittgenstein. We are certain of our knowledge claims when, in particular circumstances, we cannot reasonably be said to doubt what we are asserting.[9]

What of these multiple uses of certain? There is general agreement amongst western philosophers that the psychological use of certain is of no philosophical interest. For one to shout "I am certain of it," does nothing whatsoever to justify, to establish, to defend whatever it is of which a person is claiming certainty. However, there has been a great deal of debate concerning the second and third uses of certain, both of which are found in the writings of Descartes. The Rationalist, in speaking of knowledge claims, holds that propositions making assertions about one's own immediate mental states, intuitions, and sensory perceptions are certain. In such cases it is logically impossible for the person making the assertion to be mistaken. Incorrigible propositions represent one form of certainty. Further, those propositions, the denial of which yields a contradiction—formal propositions—are also certain. Any other proposition is certain only insofar as it is derivable from one, or both, of these two types. The Empiricist in speaking of knowledge claims is in general agreement with the Rationalist concerning the certainty of incorrigible propositions. The Empiricist also agrees with the Rationalist concerning the certainty of formal propositions. Nonetheless, he disagrees with the Rationalist in saying that formal propositions make no assertions whatsoever about our world. Rather, formal propositions are held to be certain solely because of the ways in which their terms are arbitrarily defined. For the Empiricist, then, only incorrigible propositions are both certain and assertive.

Much of the history of post-Cartesian western philosophy may be understood as an extended debate between the Rationalist and Empiricist concerning the certainty and assertiveness of formal propositions as placed in the overall discussion of knowledge as justified true belief. Combining elements in this discussion of language and knowledge, one can begin to appreciate the many stances which, each with their own nuances, may be taken in responding to the question, "What Effect Does Language as a Medium Have on Knowledge of God?" Grant, for instance, that knowledge is justified true belief expressed in propositions, the truth of which must be certain in the sense that the denial of these propositions would yield a formal contradiction. Couple this assumption with an emphasis on the syntactic aspects of language. Within such a conceptual frame, one has conditions favoring the development of ontological arguments for the existence of God. Or, perhaps one wishes to emphasize the concept certain in terms of incorrigible, again maintaining that propositional knowledge is justified true belief. Couple this viewpoint with an emphasis on the semantic aspects of language and one has conditions favoring the development of radical Empiricism in which any talk about God is dubious at best. Or, perhaps, the pragmatic aspects of language are underscored, coupled with a rejection of any legitimate Cartesian use of certain. In these cases it would not be surprising to hear, for example, that the concept 'God' is culturally bound, having no universal content at all. Then, some type of "Wittgensteinian Fideism" might be seen to emerge.[10]

Paralleling the triadic structure of language represented in the distinguishable, but not distinct, areas of syntax, semantics, and pragmatics, one may also speak of the triadic structure of knowledge. Knowledge is the expression of reality as various particular worlds are being established out of reality.[11] In that reality is the permanent possibilities of becoming and experience, one may wish to stress this in metaphysical knowledge. This sort of knowledge is the expression of what is permanent in any possible World. If, on the other hand, the particular elements of a particular world are to be stressed, empirical knowledge is brought into focus. Empirical knowledge is the expression of what is held to be existent to a particular world. Furthermore, there are two types of empirical knowledge. There is that type which necessarily holds fast for one particular world, but perhaps not for another. Then there is empirical knowledge in the sense that such knowledge is contingent within a particular world.[12] Finally, one may wish to emphasize the establishing of a world out of reality by means of some nexus. In that case the third aspect of knowledge, axiological knowledge, is being brought into focus. Axiological knowledge is the expression of the process of order being optimized in variety.[13] One of several aspects of knowledge, therefore, may be brought into focus for particular purposes at particular times, later to become part of a general epistemic backdrop for what then is being focused.

God

To say the term 'God' is vague and ambiguous is not novel, but it is important. The Hindu use of 'God' in referring to the Gods of his pantheon is not the use of the ancient Greek. Yet, perhaps the God of Hinduism and ancient Greek religions have more in common with one another than the use of God in the Judeo-Christian tradition. On the other hand, the God of Judaism, while similar to, is distinct from the Christian use. Even within what may loosely be spoken of as a single religious tradition, the uses of God are anything but clear. The stern judgmental God of hard-core Protestantism has many characteristics uncommon to the more merciful God of Catholicism. Nor is the God of Saint Thomas the same as the God of Professor Whitehead, although both are currently embraced by different Christian theologians. There are many religions, many theologies, many views of God, or the Gods. Each of us, in fact, comes from some tradition in which the term 'God' is used in some manner other than secular or profane. Just what is specifically considered the correct use of God will have great bearing on individual responses to the question, "What Effect Does Language as a Medium Have on Knowledge of God?"

While these observations should not be particularly surprising, how to understand them and what to do with them are difficult issues with which to deal. Historically two extreme positions have been taken. One of these may be called "Cultural Relativism," and the other, "Cultural Tyrannicalism." It may be held that the only meaning of the concept 'God' is that which is placed on it through the sundry uses of the word God in a particular culture.[14] Given the position of Cultural Relativism, everyone is correct in his views of the Deity for there is no objective right or wrong. Other people, however, have been tempted to say, "We have the true concept of the Deity. We, above all others, know." Justifying such claims, there may be appeals to divine revelations, to the writings in a book considered holy, to a particular living person, or the like. Given the stance of Cultural Tyrannicalism, everyone is wrong except the Tyrant. Such challenges of cultural ambiguity will be addressed more specifically at the end of this essay.

There is also a grammatical ambiguity associated with the term 'God.' While this problem of ambiguity is familiar, it is well to be reminded of it, as it is to remember cultural ambiguities. The term 'God' may be used in propositions such as "Apollo is an ancient God." In this example, God is being used as a general term indicating a specific property—being a God—which may, or may not, be correctly predicated of an indefinitely large number of individuals. On the other hand, one might say "God is infinite." In this case God is being used as a proper name of a specific individual uniquely selected from, by the use of that proper name, an indefinitely large number of individuals. The distinction is important. For instance, if God is being used as a general term indicating a property, then it is appropriate to ask for some sort of definition of that term. This is not the case, however, if God is being used as a proper name. Then it is appropriate to seek a definite description of that individual, God. Thus, at this juncture in the discussion, there are two distinct routes which one might take. In this paper the term God is to be understood as the proper name of a specific individual.[15]

A proper name is not defined; it is attached to a definite description of an individual. A definite description is a linguistic means of pointing out a specific individual from a group of individuals. It functions linguistically somewhat as a photograph functions pictorially. Now, any individual has an indefinitely large number of attributes, or properties. Many of these attributes may also be possessed by other individuals. Yet, some of the attributes of the individual in question may be consistently listed in conjunction such that this particular conjunction uniquely specifies this individual as opposed to that one. It is important to stress that in order to accomplish this specification it is not necessary to list consistently in conjunction all of the indefinitely large number of attributes of an individual. Indeed, it is altogether unclear what such a requirement for completeness could possibly mean.[16] However, while a definite description could never be complete, it must be consistent. This requirement is demanded by the logico-metaphysical principle that nothing in reality—and, hence, nothing in any world—can, logically speaking, correspond to a contradiction.[17]

Assuming "God" is the name of a specific individual, can a consistent definite description be given for that individual?[18] The first step in attempting this would be to ascertain what are some of the attributes of this individual. What properties is He said, in some particular language, to have? To answer this question one may turn to what the theologian says. It has already been emphasized that there are many religions, many theologies, many views of God, or the Gods. Nevertheless, in order to proceed with an example of the general program being suggested, consider the divine attributes suggested by St. Thomas. In Part One, Questions III–VII, of the *Summa Theologica*, St. Thomas says that God is simple, perfect, good, and infinite.[19] How are these attributes to be understood? This question introduces the second step in constructing a definite description for the individual, God. Whatever that definite description is, it must be meaningful to us. If we, as sentient sign interpreters, are finally to understand divine attributes, and thus to understand the definite description of God, then those attributes need to be characterized in terms of the most general empirical predicates of that language in which the proper name, God, is being used. Thus, understanding the proper name, God, would be guaranteed exactly to the extent that one understands those empirical predicates used in any meaningful—true or false—empirical proposition of the particular language in question.

Very well. Consider the divine attribute, infinite. St. Thomas says:

After considering the divine perfection, we must consider God's infinity, and His existence in things; for God is said to be everywhere, and in all things, inasmuch as He is boundless and infinite.[20]

God is, therefore, viewed as being omnipresent in the sense of being everywhere at once, but nowhere in particular to the exclusion of any other place. Certainly this is only a rough approximation of the attribute of omnipresence. It should not be, for example, taken as suggesting a pantheistic view in which God is identified with the sum total of the spaciotemporal order. But, to maintain that omnipresence is a synonym for infinite is not that helpful in clarifying our understanding of the divine attribute of being infinite.[21] Greater clarity can be achieved, as suggested, by seeking fundamental, general empirical predicates of the language being used to make assertions about the nature of the Deity while defining "omnipresent" in terms of those empirical predicates.

For instance, consider "(1) is a part of (2)," or "P (1) (2)," as a dyadic, empirical predicate in that language being used to make assertive claims about God. P (1) (2) is either defined by means of other predicates in the language in which it functions, or it is not. Suppose that P (1) (2) is not defined within the language; it is a primitive in the language. In this case it is necessary to seek the semiotic foundations governing the use of P (1) (2). Some of these foundations may be expressed axiomatically as

1. (x) Pxx
2. (x) (y) $[(Pxy \cdot Pyz) \supset Pxz]$
3. (x) (y) $(Pxy \supset Pyx)$

"P (1) (2)" displays total reflexivity, transitivity, and symmetry within the language.

Given "P (1) (2)," another dyadic, empirical predicate, "O (1) (2)," may be introduced as nonprimitive in the language. This predicate, read "(1) overlaps (2)," is defined as

$$\text{"Oxy"} = \text{df. "}(\exists z) (Pzx \cdot Pzy)\text{"}$$

For x to overlap y, there is some z such that z is a part of both x and y.

The divine attribute of omnipresence can now be expressed of God as

$$\text{"God"} = \text{df. "}(\sigma x) \{ (y) [Oxy \cdot (z) (Ozy = Ozx)] \}\text{"}$$

This is to say, God is that unique individual which is everywhere at once and nowhere in particular.

To continue, the same program would have to be carried through for the other divine attributes supplied by the theologian such that the final definite description of God would be both consistent and establish His uniqueness in terms of the empirical predicates used in formulating meaningful empirical propositions about our world.

Given the discussion, to this point, concerning language, knowledge, and God, the last section of this essay is now ready to be introduced. In this installment the previous discussions will be brought together and expanded. Finally, as a methodological program suggested for further amplification, comments will be more specifically related to the general question, "What Effect Does Language Have on Knowledge of God?"

Talk about God

This section begins with the introduction of the concept, *language adequate to describe our world*, where language is understood as an abstract system of signs governed by diverse semiotic foundations.[22] A language is said to be adequate to describe our world and our experiences of it if the following conditions are met:

1. The various semiotic foundations—axioms, rules, general practices—of the language may be clearly set forth, albeit not all at once;

2. The language is consistent in the formulation and use of its semiotic foundations;

3. The semiotic foundations of the language permit descriptions;

4. The semiotic foundations of the language permit the formulation of empirical theories having a high degree of confirmation substantiated by observation, thus allowing successful predictions;

5. The semiotic foundations of the language permit the formulation of those axioms and definitions needed to develop mathematics;

6. And the semiotic foundations of the language permit the meaningful normative evaluations and comparisons of multiple domains of discourse acceptable in the language.[23]

It is within the framework of a descriptively adequate language that meaningful theological discussions take place, if they take place at all. As an example, consider the typical claim, set within the Judeo-Christian tradition, "God exists." Within more-or-less traditional Judeo-Christian theologies, "God exists" is viewed as a meaningful, assertive and necessarily true proposition. There is, it is claimed, some consistent definite description of a particular individual named God. And, further, there is also some consistent concept, *existence*.[24] Within these boundaries, it is being claimed as true that not only does God exist, but it is logically impossible for Him not to exist. It is precisely this combination of claims that has been denied by Empiricism in its various modern and contemporary stances. These are positions tracing their heritage back to the Cartesian understanding of *knowledge* as justified true belief, in the sense of certain knowledge. If, so the cant of the Empiricist goes, a proposition is both meaningful and assertive, but not incorrigible, then it cannot be certain in the sense that its denial would yield a formal contradiction. That is to say, a meaningful, assertive and non-incorrigible proposition, if true, must be contingently true. On the other hand, a proposition which is not incorrigible, but is certain, cannot be assertive. Rather its certainty—the denial of the proposition producing a formal contradiction—rests simply on arbitrary definitions given to the several terms in that proposition. So, no proposition, other than an incorrigible one, can be both certain and assertive. If "God exists" counts as a meaningful proposition, but not incorrigible, then it must be either assertive and contingent, or necessarily true but not assertive. Neither alternative is acceptable within the Judeo-Christian tradition. Thus, according to the Empiricist, the sentence, "God exists," is not a meaningful proposition within that tradition.

Deep seated ambiguities lurk, however, in the very foundations of this attack of Empiricism. Uncovering some of these confusions will be helpful in also setting forth more clearly the general methodological program being suggested in this essay. To begin, one might inquire, for example, what is it for a proposition to be necessarily true and assertive? Addressing this question more clearly, the concepts *a priori, a posteriori, analytic,* and *synthetic propositions* are introduced.[25]

First, *a priori* and *a posteriori* draw a distinction within the general realm of pragmatics. As Bowman Clarke suggests:

What is important here is that this distinction is made in terms of what will be allowed in the determination of the truth or falsity [of a proposition]; that is, in terms of what we would allow to count in the justification for accepting or holding the statement [proposition] as true or false.[26]

An *a priori* proposition is one such that its actual truth-value is not determined by an appeal to any particular features in our world. An *a posteriori* proposition, on the other hand, is one such that its actual truth-value is determined by appeals to particular items in our world. How particular items of the world stand is not relevant in determining the truth-value of *a priori* propositions; they are relevant in ascertaining the truth-value of *a posteriori* propositions.

Second, *analytic* and *synthetic* draw a distinction in the general realm of semantics. Again quoting Clarke:

Although Kant's manner of distinguishing between analytic and synthetic judgments is of little use in contemporary logic, I think it could justifiably be claimed that it is an attempt to make, in contemporary terminology, a distinction at the level of semantics, for his distinction has to do with meaning in the sense of the interpretation of the symbols [in a proposition].[27]

Within the context of semantics, then, an analytic proposition is one such that its truth-conditions depend entirely on the laws of the Truth Functional Calculus, the First Order Predicate Calculus, the Calculus of Identity and/or particular definitions.[28] Any proposition not fulfilling this criterion is synthetic.

An analytic proposition is *a priori*, for neither its truth-conditions nor its truth-value is determined by resorting to any sort of empirical observations of specific items in a particular world. But, it does not follow that every *a priori* proposition is also analytic, as is claimed by the Empiricist. Now, analytic *a priori* propositions are held to be necessarily true in the sense that the denial of any such proposition would yield a formal contradiction. However, the Empiricist contends that necessarily true propositions are true, not because they assert something specific about our world, but merely because of the ways in which one arbitrarily defines the symbols used in them.[29] But what is to be understood by the claim of the Empiricist that an *a priori* proposition asserts nothing about our world? In addressing this question one might ask what is it for any proposition to assert something about our world? Consider empirical propositions.

It is reasonable to suggest that an empirical proposition tells us something about this particular item of our world in contrast to that particular item. To justify an empirical claim one investigates the specific happenings in his world. But "asserts something about our world" may be understood in another way. A proposition may make an assertion about our world in general as contrasted to pointing out a particular item of it. For example, consider the proposition, "Given any two events, if one precedes the other, then the second does not precede the former," or "(x) (y) (Pxy ⊃ ∼ Pyx)." This proposition is not deducible from the Truth Functional Calculus, the First Order Predicate Calculus, or the Calculus of Identity—with or without any definition of "x preceding y" which preserves the empirical content of this relation.[30] Here is an example of a proposition which is not analytic. It is synthetic. The proposition does have empirical content. Is it, therefore, *a posteriori*? Is its truth-value determined by making appeals to specific items in our world? No. What is asserted about our world by "Given any two events, if one precedes the other, then the second does not precede the former," is not something about this particular pair of objects as contrasted with that particular pair. Consequently, the truth-value of the proposition is not determined by any particular empirical observations. Particular observations of specific items in our world are simply not to the point in this, and similar, cases.

The phrase "asserts something about our world" may be understood in one of two ways—as either synthetic *a posteriori* or as synthetic *a priori*. In neither case could such a proposition be deduced from the laws of the calculi previously mentioned; nor would its denial produce a formal contradiction. Both types of empirical propositions assert something about our world. However, the truth-value of the synthetic *a posteriori* proposition is established by examining particular items in our world, whereas the truth-value of the synthetic *a priori* is not. The general upshot of this is that another use of *necessity*—and the correlative concept, *certain*—begins to emerge. This new concept, necessity, is not to be identified with analytic *a priori* propositions.

The point of the above distinction is important. Language makes use not only of relations belonging to the technical vocabulary of logic, such as "x is identical with y," in order to be descriptive and adequate. A descriptively adequate language must also use predicates which are not part of logic, but which are the empirical predicates of that language. These empirical predicates are either definable by other empirical predicates or they are not. If they are not definable, then they must be considered primitives of the language in which they are used. In that case their use in a descriptively adequate language is determined by the synthetic semiotic foundations of the language in question. Or, if these empirical predicates are definable by other empirical predicates, then these predicates must be definable by still other empirical predicates or not. If the language is adequate, this process must eventually cease in a set of synthetic *a priori* foundations governing the use in the language of primitive, empirical predicates.

These remarks are a result, in part, of the characterization of both an *adequate* descriptive language and an adequate *descriptive* language. Indeed, for a language to be descriptive it must make use of empirical predicates. In order to have empirical content, that is, in order to be able to describe the world, definitions of empirical predicates must come to an end in those synthetic *a priori* semiotic foundations governing the uses of such predicates. Such synthetic *a priori* foundations are synthetic because they are not deducible from the laws of logic. They are foundational because they are not deducible from anything. They have empirical content in that they govern the uses of the empirical predicates in a descriptively adequate language. These semiotic foundations are also *a priori* because no appeal to any observational tests is relevant in establishing their truth-value. Rather, it is on the assumption of, and commitment to, such synthetic *a priori* foundations that one can even meaningfully speak of particular cases of confirmation or falsification. More precisely, a necessary condition for any synthetic *a posteriori* proposition to count as meaningful and assertive is that the use of its empirical predicates is ultimately regulated by synthetic *a priori* foundations incorporated into the syntactic, semantic, and pragmatic dimensions of a descriptively adequate language.

Because synthetic *a posteriori* propositions are not deducible from the synthetic *a priori* foundations of a language, the acceptance of these foundations does not guarantee the truth of any particular synthetic *a posteriori* proposition. Whether such a proposition is actually true or not is a contingent matter depending upon relevant observations, tests, and the like. However, any proposition which is deducible from the synthetic *a priori* foundations of a descriptively adequate language will itself be synthetic *a priori.* Such a proposition will be meaningful, assertive and necessarily true.

Suppose "God exists" could be deduced from the synthetic *a priori* foundations of a descriptively adequate language. Every deduction, of course, may be re-expressed as a hypothetical proposition such that the conjunction of all the premises becomes the antecedent of that hypothetical, while the conclusion becomes the consequent. Further, the antecedent of such a hypothetical represents a sufficient condition for the consequent, while the consequent represents a necessary condition for the antecedent. Then, if "God exists" could be deduced from the synthetic *a priori* foundations of a language, it would be not only meaningful, assertive, and true, but also a necessary condition for the acceptance of the semiotic foundations of that language. On the other hand, the very acceptance of the semiotic foundations of the language would be logically sufficient to demand the acceptance of "God exists."[31]

I have distinguished between reality and world. Within this distinction I wish to maintain that what is, is. One does not change or create reality by means of, or through, the language that one does in fact use. Indeed, it is reality which sets the most general boundaries of what is sayable in any world. However, many different things are said in a language. In large part it is through a particular language—what can be, and is, said in that language—that some world is established in which the language users dwell. In such a particular language not only are the users bound by reality, they are also committed to various things which are held fast—held to be necessarily the case in their world—states-of-affairs which are expressed in the synthetic *a priori* propositions of the language. Within the combined frames of that which holds for any world and that which holds for a particular world, the language users assert what would count as individual facts and, of these, which obtain and which do not.

Now, a language cannot be used which commits one to asserting that such and such exists and at the same time denying the existence of that such and such without contradiction. Quine has ably made this point in reference to debates over the existence of classes.[32] The same principle holds in discussions concerning the existence of God. If someone accepts a language which commits him to the existence of God, here understanding God in the Judeo-Christian tradition, and at the same time denies His existence, then that person is snared in a contradiction. If a language adequate for descriptive discourse is also adequate for the formulation of a definite description of God and for establishing that "God exists" is meaningful, assertive, and necessarily true, then either (1) this theological consequence must be accepted, (2) the adequately descriptive language rejected, or (3) the principle of noncontradiction cast aside, in which case (4) the remaining language would not be adequate for descriptive purposes.

Talk about God, proofs of His existence, and so forth are always relative to the language in which such activities are embedded. But so are any talk and any proofs of anything at all. It should not be surprising to anyone to note that if something is said, it must be said in a particular language. From this rather humble observation, however, there are many who would march into some form of Cultural Relativism. My view attempts to guard against this by bringing into play two essential notions. First, there is reality—the permanent possibilities of becoming and experience—shared in, to some degree or another, by all language users. Second, there is descriptively adequate language which, while flexible in its application, is nonetheless a guideline determining any language which is useful in both scientific and theological discussions. Within these boundaries there are the semiotic foundations of particular languages. And while these foundations of different languages are not identical in every respect, even here there are great overlaps especially in, first, the area of syntax, second the area of semantics, and lastly even in the area of pragmatics. On the other hand, one should not rush from Cultural Relativism headlong into Cultural Tyrannicalism. My view attempts to guard against this by allowing full measure to the flexibility of the concept, descriptively adequate language. My position also strongly acknowledges the concept, pragmatics, which takes account of the numerous and rich variety of ways the semiotic foundations of a language can be formulated and applied in specific cases of human activity.

In this essay I have not attempted to construct any definite description for God. Nor have I offered any proof for the existence of such an individual. It was not my intention to do either. Indeed, the main thrust of this essay has been methodological. I have attempted to suggest, in very broad terms, a way to avoid several challenges to viable religion—challenges mentioned earlier in this paper. In doing this, I have also suggested certain elements which need to be woven into this proposed methodology. And in no instance have I attempted to come down on the side of any particular religion to the exclusion of others. Yet whether such a program is workable may only be ascertained by attempting it in detail.[33]

Ad majorem gloriam Dei

═══════════NOTES═══════════

1. Underlying such distinctions is the general western focus on the individual, the particular, as that which is, in some sense, truly real. Even the God of the western tradition is seen as a particular individual. This is not so in the general eastern tradition. There the individual, the particular, is seen as illusionary and to be overcome. Of course, this east-west dichotomy is in part academic and, hence, should not be pushed too far. Plato certainly has elements of both stances in his writings. And even the more hard nosed Aristotle must finally come to grasp the Unmoved Mover through contemplation. Nor should one forget Wittgenstein kicking away his *Tractatus* ladder—to mention a very few western examples.

2. Cf.: Ludwig Wittgenstein, trans. Denis Paul and G. E. M. Anscombe, *On Certainty* (Oxford: Basil Blackwell, 1969), § 611.

3. Peter Winch, *The Idea of a Social Science* (New York: Humanities Press, 1958).

4. Rudolf Carnap, *Introduction to Symbolic Logic and its Applications* (New York: Dover Publications, Inc., 1958), 78–80.

5. *Ibid.,* 79.

6. Notice, for example, the English sentence, "I ain't got none of 'em," which means, "I do not have any of them." If one were to consider this example strictly from the view of English syntax, it would be discarded as meaningless. Yet, the sentence has use, bears meaning, in many spoken contexts. The interplay between syntax, semantics and pragmatics is far stronger and more subtle than imagined by Carnap in his *Introduction*.

7. Especially in post-Cartesian epistemology, reflected in theology, the stress has been on knowledge as that which is expressed in true propositions. One makes a knowledge claim, that is, utters a particular proposition purported to be true. If that single proposition is verified or confirmed, then it becomes a bit of knowledge to be added to the list of other such bits of knowledge. This position presupposes, minimally, an atomistic view of knowledge. It also gainsays as nonsensical other forms of knowledge such as tacit knowledge, aesthetic knowledge, and so forth. Such limitations of what is to count as acceptable forms of knowledge permit a bit of legerdemain to be performed right before our academic eyes; a sleight of hand based on very questionable assumptions concerning the criteria governing the concept, knowledge. See, for instance, my a) "Epistemic Frames and Eschatological Stories," *The Return of the Millennium,* ed. Joseph Bettis and S. K. Johennesen (Barrytown, NY: New ERA Books, 1984). Consider especially pages 63–67. b) "Knowing God," in *Philosophy Today,* 9, no. 3/4 (Fall 1964):200–210. c) "Talk About God," *The Iliff Review,* 21, no. 1 (Winter 1964):49–54.

8. This is especially so in what may loosely be called the empirical tradition, as growing out of the works of David Hume, when analyzing empirical propositions as understood in that tradition. For a critical analysis of this position, see: D. M. Armstrong, *A Materialist Theory of Mind* (London: Routledge & Kegan Paul, 1968), 100–113.

9. Wittgenstein, *On Certainty.*

10. Post-Cartesian philosophy traces, as does much of contemporary western thought, its heritage into mechanistic and individualistic conceptual frames of the Renaissance. Convoluted though it may be in the many doctrines it has spawned, in this tradition one generally finds underscored and orchestrated concepts such as efficient and material causality, empirical observation, factuality, objectivity, verification, coupled with the search for certainty in knowledge. Dichotomies such as certainty-doubt, fact-value, knowledge-belief, and objective-subjective are also hallmarks typical of this Renaissance tradition. These concepts and dichotomies are now very deep-seated in western views of the world. And it has been within the boundaries formed by the conceptual frames employing these concepts and dichotomies that much modern and contemporary moves, and countermoves, in theology and philosophy of religion have been—and are still being—made.

    Today different forces, both in science and philosophy, are being mounted against this Renaissance tradition. Einstein and Heisenberg are examples in science that quickly come to mind. The later Wittgenstein, Polanyi, and the general movements of phenomenology and American pragmatism are amongst those examples important in the arena of philosophy. And, indeed, I am in general sympathy with the overall dissatisfaction with the ontic and noetic frames emerging out of the Renaissance.

    Yet, the responses to these objective views are not without their own shortcomings and dangers. As an example of this, albeit only one, I submit what is known as "Wittgensteinian Fideism." Different forms of life, different language games, different logics are introduced and discussed. But these apparently lead to fragmented views of ourselves, our worlds, and our relationships to those worlds. Eventual intellectual schizophrenia, cultural relativism, and the like seem to be amongst the fruits of abandoning objectivity, certainty, and knowledge in their Renaissance tradition.

    In "On Hearing God" in *The Defense of God*, ed. John K. Roth and Frederick Sontag (New York: Paragon House Publishers, 1985), pp. 68–83, I develop further the view of language and knowledge introduced in my essay, "Epistemic Frames and Eschatological Stories" (see above: note 7). This stance is also assumed in this current paper, "Language, Knowledge and God." Language and knowledge are introduced in terms of the basic concepts: reality, world, nexus of a world, and person. Here reality is understood as the permanent possibilities of becoming and experience as they exist independently, in themselves. World, on the other hand, indicates the establishing of an ordered selection, by a sign interpreter, of diverse elements of experienced reality. Nexus of a world suggests those structures by which the selecting of the various elements of experienced reality takes place, thus establishing a world in which the sign interpreter dwells. And by person the notion of a self-reflexive intersection of reality, world and nexus of a world is introduced into the overall conceptual frame.

11. Note that I do not wish to identify expression with propositional expression. Propositions are only one vehicle by means of which knowledge may be expressed. Simply for the purposes of this essay, however, I do focus on propositional knowledge. A more expanded paper would also have to discuss tacit knowledge against which propositional knowledge must be set.

Language and Knowledge

12. In more technical jargon a distinction is made in empirical knowledge between (1) synthetic *a priori* and (2) synthetic *a posteriori*. Since the time of Kant, it has been convenient—if ofttimes not misleading—to introduce four characteristics which, seemingly, may be predicated in several combinations of "judgments" (i.e., propositions): (1) analytic, (2) synthetic, (3) *a priori*, and (4) *a posteriori*. Since the logical (much less the metaphysical, etc.) functions of these terms are often convoluted, I wish to make a few comments about them. I begin by reminding the reader of the tripartite division of semiotic previously discussed in this essay. In examining a language we may speak of its syntactic rules, that is the rules governing the purely formal relations holding between the signs of a proposition of the language; its semantic rules, that is the rules governing the meanings of the illogical signs of the language; and its pragmatic rules, that is the rules governing how the language is related to the language user, his multitudinous practices, commitments, etc. Within this set of distinctions, the terms analytic and synthetic are semantic concepts dealing with the question of how the signs within a proposition are defined. On the other hand, *a priori* and *a posteriori* are pragmatic concepts dealing with such questions as what we, the language users, would accept as making a given proposition true or false.

I now offer the following characterizations to clarify further a central position taken in this essay. Nor are these characterizations arbitrary, but rather are suggested by the history of philosophy itself. (1) A proposition is analytic if it is true solely in terms of The Truth Functional Calculus, The First Order Predicate Calculus, The Calculus of Identity and/or a set of definitions. (2) A proposition is synthetic if it is not analytic. (3) A proposition is *a priori* if its truth-value is not justified by any appeal of the language user to particular experiences, observations, "facts in the world," or the like. (4) A proposition is *a posteriori* if it is not *a priori*.

Consider some proposition, '*p*'. We may now inquire which of the following four combinations are sensible: (1) *p* is analytic *a priori*; (2) *p* is analytic *a posteriori*; (3) *p* is synthetic *a priori*; or (4) *p* is synthetic *a posteriori*. Traditionally in the literature, (1) and (4) find general acceptance, although what is being accepted has often been altogether murky. (2) is universally discarded as a contradictory combination of terms. If the truth-conditions of '*p*' are simply a matter of the ways in which the signs of that proposition are defined, then its actual truth-value could not be determined by any appeal to particular experiences, observations, etc., in our world. Since any analytic proposition is true solely in terms of The First Order Predicate Calculus plus a set of definitions, no empirical observations on the part of the language user could ever be relevant to determining the truth or falsity of '*p*'. It is over (3) that fiery battles rage. And it is precisely this battle in which I shall engage as my essay unfolds.

13. Note, I wish to speak of optimizing order in variety—not of maximizing order, as I did in "Epistemic Frames and Eschatological Stories." This switch of terms does not represent any change in view, but is merely an attempt to be more clear. The concept, to maximize, carries with it quantitative implications, for instance, which I do not intend to suggest.

14. Or some equivalent word such as "theos," "deus," "dios," "Gott," and so on.

15. This choice may appear arbitrary and, given my tradition, perhaps it is. But, again, while each of us must start somewhere, if we are to begin at all, it does not follow that that is the only starting point or that all starting points must necessarily lead to quite different destinations. Paths sometimes do merge, as I hold that they eventually do in the case of this juncture.

16. What could a complete list of an indefinitely large number of items be? One might have a rule, or a procedure, to continue a list. One might have a rule, or a procedure, to determine for any possible item suggested for a list whether or not that item is a legitimate member of that list. But, this is not to have a complete list of an indefinitely large number of entries.

17. This is a key "assumption" in my essay. The quote marks just used indicate a peculiar use of the term assumption. It is an odd use because it is difficult to picture logically what a meaningful and articulatable alternative to this assumption could be. Furthermore, granting that it is not the case that anything can possibly exist corresponding to a contradiction entails some commitment to a meaningful use of "not," that is to the concept, *logical denial*. Given these two points, namely (1) the logico-metaphysical assumption and (2) logical denial, then one is faced with the twin assumption that corresponding to a necessarily true proposition—the denial of a contradiction—something must necessarily exist.

18. Permit me to remind my kind and patient reader again that no attempt is made in this paper to construct such a definite description. I am not presenting a specific theological position. Rather, I am suggesting a general methodological program to be considered for possible execution—a program which will, hopefully amongst other things, address itself to the sundry challenges of the viability of religion mentioned in this essay. In sum, my paper is in philosophy of religion; not theology.

19. Anton C. Pegis, *Basic Writings of Saint Thomas Aquinas*, vol. 1 (New York: Random House, 1944), 25–62.

20. *Ibid.*, 56.

21. Willard Van Orman Quine, "Two Dogmas of Empiricism," *From a Logical Point of View* (Cambridge: Harvard Univ. Press, 1953), 20–37.

22. The discussion of the concept language has been limited in this essay to the human context of sign interpreters and users. I have done this for convenience and to avoid needless complications. However, sunflowers, for instance, are also correctly said to experience reality, to dwell in their world, and to be sign interpreters. Moreover, in a fuller treatment of language, I should, amongst other things, draw distinctions between sign and symbol.

23. It may be argued that these criteria are too vague to be of much use in determining whether a particular language is—yes or no—descriptively adequate. However, to admit a degree of vagueness is not to admit that these criteria are useless. They do provide flexible boundaries for saying of some language that it is descriptively adequate. It is exactly this sort of flexibility which is needed in order to apply these criteria to particular cases of language in attempting to carry out the general program being presented in this essay.

24. It is not being suggested here that existence is some sort of empirical predicate

within the descriptively adequate language. "God exists" may be symbolized as "(∃x) x = God." Then, of course, a definite description of God is needed to which the proper name God may be attached.

25. While these concepts are most notably found in the writings of Kant, no commitment to either his metaphysics or his epistemology is being suggested here. See above: note 12.

26. Bowman L. Clarke, *Language and Natural Theology* (The Hague: Mouton & Co., 1966), 70. Those familiar with the work of Clarke will recognize his influence in my essay. They will also recognize how far I have moved from his position.

27. *Ibid.*, 71.

28. Thus, "It is not the case that if it is raining, then it is not raining" is analytic because its truth-conditions are determined by the laws of the Truth Functional Calculus. "All bachelors are men" is also analytic because of the laws of the First Order Predicate Calculus coupled with a definition of bachelor as un-married man.

29. Outside of possible exceptions in what have been called artificial languages—itself a queer expression considering that any human language is an artifact of some sort—for instance, mathematics and logic, the term arbitrary has a peculiar ring to it in the claims of the Empiricist. In general, neither I, nor anyone else, arbitrarily defines the words used in one's native language except for very special purposes in quite limited cases. I simply learn my language and use it. See my "Necessarily True Statements and Linguistic Convention-alism," *The Journal for the Indian Academy of Philosophy*, 22, no. 2 (1973):17–23.

30. Nor does the denial of this proposition—that is, "$\sim$ (x) (y) (Pxy $\supset$ $\sim$Pyx)"—produce any formal contradiction, as can be seen by inspecting "(∃x) (∃y) (Pxy • Pyx)."

31. The meaningfulness of the proper name God, as previously discussed, is guar-anteed by constructing a consistent definite description of God in terms of the most general empirical predicates of that language in which a proof is being offered.

32. Willard Van Orman Quine, *Methods of Logic* (New York: Henry Holt & Com-pany, 1959), 196–252.

33. Finally—but by far not the least important—I wish to thank most sincerely all those who generously offered comments, criticisms and suggestions con-cerning an earlier version of this paper discussed in Seoul, Korea.

3

The Language of God and the God of Language[1]

The Relation between God, Human Beings, World and Language in St. John

FRANCIS X. D'SA

Introduction

Whenever human beings discourse consciously, they do so because of what they know experientially. If this experience focuses on a practical, informative state of affairs, their discourse transmits information. The center of attention then is the field of perception. Such discourse is based on experiences common to the discourse-partners. The world of common experiences is the world of the elements, their compounds and aggregates. Whatever water, for example, may mean to an Eskimo, to someone in the Rajasthan desert, and to one living on the banks of the Ganges, water is the element common to all of them. This commonality enables them to speak of their different manner of perceiving water and of the different meaning each of them links with water.

It is on experiences like these that another function of language, namely, that of transformation is built up. For we communicate not merely information; sometimes through information we wish to say something more than that. Thus someone may speak of the living water: "I am the living water." There is information in such an utterance; that, however, is not its main aim since through the information it purports to evoke an experience at a deeper level. In an utterance such as this the information points to a depth level that is beyond information but is all the same intimately connected with it. "I am the living water" is surely communicating some information, but equally surely we understand something more through this information. This something more of meaning is not outside of the information; it is closely connected with it, though obviously it is not identical with it. Such a function of language is more in line with transformation than information and expresses itself through metaphor.[2]

For the purposes of this essay it is important to note the distinction between metaphor and figure of speech. The latter is purely decorative and ornamental and therefore basically dispensable; the former is of the essence of the experience that it purports to evoke. For metaphor is born from an experience of symbol.[3] We have experience of symbol when the body (of the symbol) becomes so transparent that it manifests its soul. Any body when it reveals its soul is experienced as symbol. When the body remains opaque, it is experienced as a mere object. In such a case our understanding of it has remained at the object level and our expression of it will not be more than descriptive. When, however, we experience and understand its soul (i.e., its depth-dimension) what we have is knowledge of the body as symbol.

Such knowledge of symbol expresses itself (presses itself out, as it were) in the language of metaphor. And metaphor, we said, is born from symbol-experience. Its *raison d'être* is to evoke in the listener a similar knowledge of the symbol. Thus symbol-knowledge gives birth to metaphor and metaphor evokes in the hearer the symbol-knowledge from which the metaphor itself has emerged.[4]

When a thing is known as symbol it means that the thing has become meaningful to the knowing person. This meaningfulness or significance is not reducible to any of the body-qualities of the symbol though it is true that it is through the body-qualities that the knowledge of significance is mediated. Anything in our world can become meaningful to us. The something more of meaning is not restricted to any one particular kind of objects or events or persons. This implies that the whole world is potentially meaningful. Now, this potential meaningfulness of the world is, I believe, the center around which any holistic understanding of language has to rotate. For significance is given to, not made by, us and is radically different from any type of emotional attachment or response which evaporates when the emotion has disappeared. Such significance transforms us totally and gives meaning to our lives; from significance we receive courage to face difficulties and risk ourselves in dangerous situations; suffering and sorrow become bearable and are unable to crush us. Significance makes selflessness self-explanatory and obvious, and selfishness comes to be seen as irrational and ultimately meaningless.

No one single encounter with significance enlightens the whole of our lives. That is why we thirst for more. In itself significance is not partial since it is a realm. Our access to it is partial because we merely partake in the totality of significance—and in the process we ourselves become significant.[5]

For such an understanding of language the Gospel of St. John offers tempting possibilities. In John's Prologue we are told that God speaks eternally and that the world comes to be through this speaking. The language of God through whom (!) everything exists is the reason for our being and existence. He it is who en-light-ens all that is since He is the life and light of all. Everything in the world is (and can be) ultimately meaningful because He gives light and life (significance) to everything. Because the language of God dwells in everything and speaks through everything, human beings can speak. For we speak only when we hear this voice of significance in the world. We speak when persons and events and things become significant to us. Our speaking is but a response to the language of God incarnate in the world. This speaking can become ultimately coherent only when we learn to understand the language of God accurately and authentically and so understand the God of language. Since the world is the concretization of God's language, to know the world holistically is to know God's language and to know God's language is to know the God of language. It is from such a stance that I have attempted a study of the relation between God, human beings, world, and language.

The Prologue, John I and John II-XX

Though the Prologue may have originated differently from the rest of John's Gospel, the Gospel as a whole, I suggest, forms a unity that is as remarkable as it is relevant. In this essay I have a twofold aim: first, to indicate a certain organic unity by drawing attention to a definite thematic development that can be traced in the Prologue, in John I, and in the rest of the Gospel. I am not suggesting that the kind of unity I indicate here was necessarily suggested by the evangelist. I merely point to its existence in the text as we have it now, in which the three units I have mentioned do indeed form this sort of organic whole. Second, the unifying theme of this organic whole is, I believe, a hermeneutical key for the reading of the Gospel and for an understanding of the nature of our world. At its simplest this hermeneutically significant theme would read: to believe in Jesus is to see him as the symbol of God's Word and World. Because God's language dwells in him, Jesus is the hermeneutical key through which we can understand the depth-meaning of a world that is always symbolic. This because it too has been called into being by the language of God. This theme will emerge clearly as we study the meaning structure of the Gospel as a whole, and then go on to examine in detail, from our specific perspective, each of the three sections—the Prologue, John I and the rest of the Gospel—of which this meaning structure is composed.

The Meaning Structure of the Gospel of John

The thrust of John's Gospel can be said to be summed up in the climactic expression of the Prologue (1:14) "the Language of God *(ho logos tou theou)* became flesh and dwelt among us." That is, in Jesus the language of God has become flesh. He is the paradigm from whom we learn to understand how God speaks. Hence he alone knows and speaks this language authentically and accurately. For God's Spirit dwells on him (1:32). His works and his words disclose who and what he really is. From him we also learn about the real nature of the world. We discover that the things of this world are symbols *(semeia)* of God's language of love, symbols of God's indwelling.[6] For things come to be and happen only when God speaks.

From John's Prologue we derive the principle: the world is because of, in, and through God's Logos (1:1–5). And Jesus, the Christ, is shown to be the conscious concretization of this principle (1:9–18). Aware of God's presence and power in himself, he could discern and proclaim God's presence and power in the world process. John's Gospel attempts to make the reader aware of the reality of God's Word speaking in and through the world. It is a holistic vision that is being offered and awareness of it is possible on one condition: the reader must learn to dwell with Jesus, that is, he must make his home with Jesus, assimilate his values and his vision, and accept and make his own Jesus' commitment and commission. The reader, like the two disciples of the Baptist, must actively search for Jesus' dwelling and only then, he too, like them, will begin to see where Jesus dwells (1:35–42). Dwelling with Jesus is the beginning of one's history of salvation. From then on one will begin to look at the world differently, one will go out of one's way to testify to this new world (1:19–37), and to this new language speaking concretely through this world. The culmination of this salvific process is the discovery that Jesus is the New Israel, the meeting point between heaven and earth (1:43–51).

Such is the programmatic perspective of the first chapter of the Gospel. The rest of the Gospel (traditionally called the Book of Signs) illustrates how the paradigmatic principle put forward in the Prologue (that the language of God dwells and speaks in Jesus) helps us to discover the nature of this world. For the *semeia* which Jesus works in John's Gospel proclaim that God's language dwells in and speaks through persons, events, and things of this world.

We thus come to know in this Gospel about the eternal abode of the *logos tou theou* in the bosom of the Father, about his temporal address in this world ("Jesus of Nazareth, the son of Joseph"), and finally his tempiternal dwelling in Jesus, the New Israel. To go back to our text, the Prologue enunciates the principle that the Logos is at the root of all that has come to be; and Chapters II-XX speak of this world as containing a depth-dimension. But it is Chapter I that shows how to connect this world with its root, namely, the Logos. The access to this Logos, we are told, is Jesus, the Symbol of the world, the unique being, that is, that was fully conscious of his Author and of his own authority.

Table 1. The Meaning Structure of John

Prologue	John I	John II-XX
LOGOS	JESUS	WORLD
root of all reality	paradigmatic symbol	universe of symbols

The function of the Prologue is to enunciate the process of the downward movement through which things come to be:

1. God

2. speaks eternally *(logos)*

3. and the world comes to be in time.

John I aims at illustrating the salvific movement operative in the belief that the world has come into being through God's language:

1. Dwelling with Jesus

2. enables the disciples to experience the Symbol-Jesus

3. and thus to become familiar with the language of God.

John II-XX is an implementation of the principle of the Prologue and of the salvific movement of Chapter I and hence narrates different attempts to discover where Jesus dwells.

1. Dwelling with Jesus

2. leads to a holistic experience of the world that has come into being through God's language (experience of symbol)

3. and expresses itself in beliefs (metaphors).

The Prologue: the Language of God Dwelling in Jesus (I:1–18)

The very first words of John's Gospel "in [the] beginning was the Logos" (I:1) are in striking contrast with "this beginning of his *semeia* Jesus did at Cana of Galilee" (II:11). The distinction between these two beginnings is of vital importance in understanding John's *semeia*-language. The first beginning is the *a priori* condition of possibility for the second. This implies that no temporal beginning is possible without the first principle which dwells with God in the beginning. For a thing to be, to become, to begin to be, the language of God has to mediate. The Logos (language, not a particular language but the source of all intelligibility and thus of all language) is in the beginning of anything and everything. There is no beginning whatever without language. Every beginning whether ontological or chronological has to do with language.

The Logos dwells with God, is in his presence, and is divine (I:1–2). However one interprets *pros ton theon* and *kai theos ēn ho logos,* there can be no doubt that language is, as it were, at the beck and call of God, and belongs to the realm of the Divine. Thus to come in contact with language is to encounter the God of language. For it is through the Logos that God creates and sustains the world. So to know a thing in its fulness is to discover language at its root. Hence to know anything real-ly is to know language as well. And to know language is to know God.

Furthermore, all that came to be, was alive with his (language's) life, and that life was the light of human beings (I:3–4). The life of every being is from language. Whenever human beings come to know this life, they become en-light-ened. It is this life which is at the heart of all things. It manifests itself through things like light. Whenever one is enlightened by the significance of a thing, one is in fact being enlightened by this light.[7] But often things and persons

40

and events do not mean much to us; their significance does not strike us. This is a symptom of our blindness, of our refusal to accept the light (I:9–11). But those who see and accept this light of Significance, receive power to become God's children (I:12–13). To see this light is to know things wholly, holistically; and knowing things thus means going to the very root of things. This refers to going to the significance of things from the viewpoint of Ultimate Significance. Only God's children, that is, those who participate in God's nature, see things from the viewpoint of Ultimate Significance. In fact, what the Prologue is saying is that only those who see the Ultimate Significance of things are really God's children. For accepting the light of language implies recognizing it in the first place.

God always and continuously speaks, and so his Language always and continuously becomes flesh, that is, it becomes transformed and translated into the *semeia*-world. But God's language is of a peculiar nature. God speaks in such a way that he says what he means and means what he says. This is the only instance where utterance, meaning, and event are perfectly identical. In our case it is a different matter altogether. We can say things that we do not mean, and thus we bring forth not words but sterile sounds. God's language, however, is without exception authentic. When he speaks he puts his heart, as it were, in his words; that is why he dwells in his words. Hence another principle of John's Gospel is God's dwelling in this world through his language. From this angle it is clear why believing means for John recognizing and accepting this language dwelling in the *semeia*-world. It is therefore understandable why in certain contexts believing is for John synonymous with true seeing and vice versa.[8] For seeing things in their fulness and totality is equivalent to believing that God through his language dwells among us and in all things.

Throughout all this one must keep in mind that it is only in and through Jesus that one comes to such a belief. Knowing Jesus as the paradigm of God's language we learn the language that God speaks through the world and its multifaceted history, above all, through our lives.

John I: Witnessing and Dwelling

It is possible to know about the symbol-nature of the world only through the testimony of someone who knows the symbols of reality and the reality of symbols. Just as in the world of the blind, discourse on color is possible only if someone blessed with vision speaks of it, so, too, discourse about the symbol-nature of the world is possible through the testimony of one who sees the depth-dimension of persons, things, and events. If John's Gospel devotes more than one-third of its first chapter to the testimony of John the Baptist (I:6–9; 19–37) and then works out the ripple effects of this testimony in its description of the calling of the first disciples, to almost the very end of the chapter (I:35–50), this is not merely in order to stress the role of testimony in authenticating the *kerygma* of Jesus; it is to point to the essential function of testimony where revelation is concerned. For what light is to the eye, testimony is to revelation. This is because religious knowledge having to do with the depth-dimension of things expresses itself by its very nature in symbol-language, and this is opaque without the testimony of someone who knows the significance of the symbols in question. Without the testimony about the depth-dimension of things, our knowing would be confined to the pragmatic dimension. Water, for example, can be seen as what quenches thirst or irrigates our fields or makes navigation possible. This requires no special revelation. But to believe that it can become the means to eternal life requires experience, or testimony based on experience of the living water. The same could be said of bread and other necessities of life. Thus, it is only through the testimony of people like John the Baptist that we discover that the prime necessities of earthly life are indispensable preliminaries to eternal life.

John Witnesses to Jesus' Dwelling (I:1–18)

John the Baptist explicitly witnesses to the light (I:6–7); to the one "who comes after me, but takes rank before me" (I:15,30); to the one "who stands among you, whom you do not know, who is to come after me" (I:26–27); to the "spirit coming down from heaven like a dove and dwelling upon him" (I:32), to "God's Chosen One" (I:34); and to "the Lamb of God" (I:36). Implicitly, however, John is all the while testifying to the language of God with whom (!) he has come in touch, and who is the life and light of all (I:4,6–9). John twice asserts that he did not recognize Jesus (I:31,33). What he probably meant is that he did not see anything more in Jesus than his contemporaries did. But the moment when He who sent him to baptize said to him, "When you see the Spirit coming down upon someone and dwelling upon him, you will know that this is he who is to baptize in Holy Spirit" (I:33), John began to see the total reality that Jesus was. In Johannine vocabulary, once John saw where (with whom) Jesus dwelt, he recognized who Jesus was. Out of this recognition sprang forth his testimony of Jesus. Seeing where Jesus dwells, John began to speak God's Language.

The pattern at work in John's knowledge and proclamation is as follows:

1. John *hears the testimony* of the one who sent him to baptize with regard to Jesus who was to baptize in Holy Spirit (I:33).

2. John *accepts* this testimony (I:17).

3. He *sees* where (with whom) Jesus dwells (I:32).

4. Out of this experience gushes forth his proclamation (testimony) about Jesus, that is, *he begins to speak the language of God* (I:7,15,34,36).

The Disciples Learn Where Jesus Dwells (I:35-51)

Whatever may be the historical meaning(s) of the metaphor "Lamb of God," its contextual meaning is clear. The Lamb of God is the one who takes away the sin of the world (I:35). For John the sin of the world is nothing other than the inability to believe, to believe that Jesus has the power to take away sin, and so the inability to see in him his divine Sonship. His power to take away sin, and his divine Sonship, are different ways of expressing the truth that he dwells with the Spirit. And because he dwells with the Spirit, he alone can baptize in Holy Spirit (I:35).

Because the disciples of John understood his testimony ("Behold the Lamb of God") in some such vague manner, they asked him about his dwelling (I:36,38). Their question "Where do you dwell?" is clearly a theological, not a topographical, query. To dwell *(menein)* is a theological (almost a technical) verb in John's Gospel. The same verb occurs in connection with Jesus' dwelling with the Father (XIV:10; XV:10), our dwelling with Jesus (XV: 4-7), the branches dwelling in the vine (XV:14), dwelling in the Spirit (XIV:17). Indeed, to understand and realize this word is the methodological master key with which the reader can unravel the secrets of Jesus' *semeia* to which the rest of the Gospel witnesses. For, if one has not learned to dwell with Jesus, then the Gospel narratives could at best be interesting, but would not inspire.[9]

The Significance of Dwelling

Fundamental to our discussion of the first chapter of John is the structure of its triple narrative (I:19–39) which is built on the three interconnected questions "Who are you?" (I:22), "What are you seeking?" (I:38), and "Where do you dwell?" (I:38). The focus is on dwelling, since the first question leads to the search for Jesus' dwelling, and since the metaphor of dwelling is one of the major themes of John's Gospel. Though dwelling ("Where do you dwell?"), self-knowledge ("Who are you?"), and inner quest ("What are you seeking?") are three aspects of one integral experience, they all have different, if related, formal objects. Self-knowledge leads to a genuine openness, an openness to change and conversion which results in the absence of self-deceit and self-defence and thus prepares the way for the inner quest. The inner quest comes to rest only in the presence of a Thou, and in the presence of an absolute Thou, the rest is absolute. Such a communion of subjects is another name for dwelling. But this is only a logical way of looking at the process. Existentially the order is reversed. It is from our dwelling that we realize what we are after and who we are. It is such knowing that makes clear to us the content of our inner quest and of our self-knowledge. The objection might be raised that such an understanding of dwelling is anachronistic and therefore foreign to the world in which Jesus lived. This, I think, is not true. Such an understanding derives from Jesus' own self-understanding, though it is true that we are expressing it differently. For by dwelling with the Father (symbolically represented by the Father's Spirit dwelling upon Jesus—I:32), Jesus became conscious of who he was and what he was seeking. This made him aware of his identity and his mission. Because of this, he was authentic in his dealings with those around him, open to all who came his way, and to all that happened to him. His commitment to freedom, fellowship, and justice were not mere accidents in his life; rather they were the main fruits of his dwelling with his Father.[10]

Dwelling and Dhvani

To dwell somewhere or with someone, one has to be alive to the Dhvani-dimension of reality.[11] *Dhvani* is that function of language which reveals to us the depth-dimension of things, events, and persons by making them point through themselves but beyond themselves to that reality of which they are the manifestation. According to the testimony of Jesus, for example, bread broken in a specific context points to the Bread of Life, and water used in a specific manner opens our eyes to the Living Water. It is the simple reality of daily bread that leads a mystic poet like Jesus to the knowledge of the deeper reality that is the Bread of Life. The bread that we eat is merely one aspect of the total reality called bread. This includes both the bread and the Bread of Life aspects. However, the discovery of real Bread would be impossible without our daily bread. Conversely, we too, like our fathers in the desert, will die unless we discover the Bread of Life.

Now, in order to be able to view things from the Dhvani point of view one has to realize that the "eyes are blind; one sees with the heart." Such seeing is a holistic way of perceiving, for it is not so much a seeing as a vision, a depth-vision. A vision like this is given to a few and these are the mystical poets. From them we learn to see in bread the Bread of Life. Without the pioneering perspective of the poets, we would have to content ourselves with the bread that perishes.

However, it is important to note that the poet is neither projecting nor fantasizing; he is perceiving at the depth-level. In that sense he is discovering a dimension that is not accessible to the usual act of perception. The Dhvani way of knowing does not add to our information at the perception level; it does not bring in a new meaning. Rather, it introduces a new meaningfulness that was not perceived before. The same bread does not become more bread; it merely becomes more meaningful. The significance of bread increases in the context of the communion of God, world, and human beings.

How can one discover the Dhvani-dimension of reality? There are, I think, no rigid methods through which one can do this, just as there are no fixed prescriptions on how to become a poet. But we can begin by appropriating the discoveries of the mystics and poets. It is here that Dhvani-theory can come into the picture. For our dormant poetic sensibility can be activated so that we can learn to make use of the treasures that poets have uncovered; perhaps, in the process, we too can get started on a voyage of discovery. Hence, Dhvani-theory is of help to all who wish to cultivate a sense for the Dhvani-dimension of reality.

The theory of Dhvani is as simple to explain as it is difficult to execute.[12] There are different types of Dhvani; most of them, however, are mere figures of speech. Genuine Dhvani, however, belongs to the realm of symbols and metaphors.[13] Whereas one can dispense with figures of speech since they are mere ornamentation, one cannot dispense with symbols and metaphors. A symbol is of the essence of the depth-knowledge which it mediates. Bread, known the Dhvani-way, is of the essence of the Bread of Life. Here one may ask: How does one distinguish a merely intellectual notion of the Bread of Life from the real knowledge of the Bread of Life? The answer is: From the *rasa* (flavor, taste, the sap or juice, hence, also the essence) that such an experience produces. And how does one come to such an experience? It is here that the Gospel of John gives us an answer with his "Where do you dwell? Come and you will see!" (I:38–39). To the testimony of the poet and the prophet must correspond our hearing ("The two disciples heard him speak and they followed Jesus"—I:37). This hearing has to lead us to a seeking and a searching ("What are you seeking?"—I: 38). This will entail a putting aside of all that hinders our following of and following after what is beckoning us. "Come and you will see" is both a command and a promise! To follow is to assimilate the values of the one we are following. (Cf. "Seek first the Kingdom of God and his justice and all the rest will be given to you!"—Mt VI:33).

To move from bread to the Bread of Life one has to follow Jesus who proclaims that bread, when shared with others, especially the needy, will feed both our body and our soul. Jesus' life and death will reveal to us the specific perspective that enabled him to discover in bread the Bread of Life. Bread will then disclose to us its real and full nature which consists primarily of that quality which can feed not only the body but the whole being. For bread, like Jesus, is the meeting point, the communion between God, world, and human beings. Both nature and human beings are involved in the making of bread. Bread comes to be bread because neither the seed nor the soil hold on to their identity, but give themselves up so that something new might appear. In this giving up of themselves in order that others might live is the quintessence of communion, for seed and soil continue to live in a new fashion in the life that springs from them. When we break bread remembering the seed, the soil, and the sweat that watered them, we shall experience the depth-dimension of bread. (That is to say, this experience will evoke in us the same mind that was in Jesus who, being in the form of God, did not hold on to it but gave himself up for others—Phil II:6–7). Eating such bread in this manner is eating the Bread of Life. Briefly, then, to have a Dhvani-experience with regard to the symbols that Jesus discovered, it is necessary to make our own his values and his vision. This will not only open our eyes to the deeper reality which was accessible to him when he encountered it; it will make our hearts burn within us as he opens the Scriptures to us.

Dwelling in John I

Dwelling is one of the fundamental themes of John's Gospel, not only because the Gospel begins with this theme; not only because the whole of chapter one deals with it explicitly or implicitly; but because only the experience of dwelling where Jesus dwells can unravel the secrets of the Gospel.

The Gospel begins with the language of God dwelling with God in the beginning (I:1), and then proceeds to proclaim that this same language dwells among us (I:14), without, however, ceasing to be the One who is "nearest to the Father's heart," as the New English Bible puts it; or, according to the Revised Standard Version, is "in the bosom of the Father" (I:18). Further, when we come to John's testimony we realize that it was his participation in Jesus' dwelling that was both the source and the substance of his witness. "I myself did not know who he was; but the very reason why I came, baptizing in water, was that he might be revealed to Israel" (I:31). What should not escape our attention is a dual factor: the one whom John did not know at first came to be known (to John) as the One over whom the Spirit of God dwells and it is this One that John came to reveal to Israel. And when John says, "I saw it myself and have borne witness. This is God's Chosen One" (I:34), what he is in effect saying is that he has seen the Spirit dwelling on Jesus and thus constituting him as the Chosen One.

The experience of Jesus' dwelling leaves an indelible mark on John. For it is this experience that qualified him to be the bridegroom's friend who stands by and listens to him and who is overjoyed at hearing the bridegroom's voice (III:29). John is so much at peace with himself that he is not threatened even when his disciples leave him and follow Jesus. Finally, the source of his courageous testimony in the face of sure death is to be traced back to the fact that he had learnt to dwell where Jesus dwelt. On the other hand, the effect of this experience on John is seen not only in his works but also and above all in his language. It was John the Baptist who first testifies to Jesus as the Light (I:6–7), as the One who already was before John was born (I:15), as the Lamb of God who takes away the sin of the world (I:29), as the One whom John came to reveal to Israel (I:31), as the One on whom the Spirit descends and dwells (I:32), as the One who is to baptize in Holy Spirit (I:33), and as the Chosen One of God (I:34). John did not know Jesus but because of his experience of Jesus' dwelling, all of a sudden, Jesus now begins to mean so much to him that he speaks the language of God in diverse ways.

In the narrative about the two disciples of John, the motif of dwelling becomes thematic (I:35–39). When John proclaims Jesus as the Lamb of God (I:36), he is probably making use of an apocalyptic metaphor of the Lamb dwelling with God (Rev XIV:4; XV:3; XXI:22; XXII:1,3). Again, John, like the author of Revelation, speaks of Jesus as the bridegroom (Rev XIX:7,9; XXI:9) showing the affinity of the metaphor-language employed by John and the author of Revelation. Whatever else the expression Lamb of God might have meant, dwelling with God is probably implied in it. Our guess is further strengthened by the disciples' question to Jesus (put after they have heard John testify that Jesus is the Lamb of God—I:29), "Rabbi, where do you dwell?" (I:38). Without some earlier reference to dwelling, the question appears strange, sudden, and out of place. Because of this it seems probable to me that the substance of John's testimony was about Jesus' dwelling, whether expressed explicitly by the descent and dwelling of the Spirit on Jesus or implicitly by the expressions "Chosen One of God" and "Lamb of God."

The type of dwelling we have been speaking about fits in well with the Gospel narrative. The disciples are not in search of Jesus; they have seen and found him already. They are searching for something more. They want to know where he dwells. Obviously it cannot be Jesus' postal address, as it were, that they are after. They are intent on a type of dwelling that cannot be so much described as seen and experienced. Hence Jesus' answer: "Come and you will see!" What is important is that the disciples follow Jesus. 'Follow' too in John's Gospel has a theological meaning. Once one follows Jesus one begins to see. When the disciples go with Jesus they see where he dwells and they dwell with him that day. It was about the tenth hour, the hour of fulfilment; it was like heaven on earth.[14] It was only a glimpse, not a vision. When the disciples got acquainted with Jesus' dwelling, they came in touch with God's language. Jesus becomes for them now the Messiah.

"We have found the Messiah" (I:41). The One who before was Jesus is now proclaimed as the Messiah, the Christ. The selfsame reality (Jesus), seen in its depth-dimension, leads to fulness of faith and significance.

Interestingly, we find the theme of the pericope of the two disciples (I:29–39) spilling over into the next pericope, too (I:40–42). Here too we have testimony arising from experience, leading to experience and again resulting in testimony.[15] Thus Andrew, one of the two disciples who comes to know Jesus' dwelling, proclaims to his brother Simon Peter: "We have found the Messiah," and takes him to Jesus. Jesus looks at him and says, "You are Simon son of John. You shall be called Cephas" (that is, Peter, the Rock).[16] Jesus enlightens Simon about his hidden potential; the new name reveals his future relationship to the Church, wherein dwells the saving action of God in Jesus. Here again we see two instances where God's language is recognized: when Andrew speaks of Jesus as Messiah, and when Jesus speaks of Simon as Cephas, the Rock! In the first instance, it is a discovery for Andrew and in the second, it is a promise for Peter by Jesus.

In the final narrative about Philip and Nathanael (I:43–50) we have the two themes of God's dwelling and God's language skillfully woven into a concluding unit. "We have met the man spoken of by Moses in the Law, and by the prophets; it is Jesus son of Joseph, from Nazareth" says Philip (I:45). Philip's witness combines three elements: with the help of Jesus' temporal address he speaks of the eternal dwelling by employing the new language ("the man spoken of by Moses in the Law, and by the prophets"). His "come and see" is in the light of his own experience equivalent to "come and dwell." And as seen in the case of Simon Peter, Jesus reveals to Nathanael his genuine worth. "Here is an Israelite worthy of the name; there is nothing false in him" (I:47). When Nathanael is surprised at this, Jesus reassures him, "I saw you under the fig tree before Philip spoke to you" (I:48). Though the meaning of the symbolic expression is unknown to us, its evocative power should be gauged from the fact that Nathanael's confession is overwhelming. He discovers not only a sense of identity, but as a true and genuine Israelite, a deep sense of belonging—to the New Israel: "Rabbi, you are the Son of God; you are the King of Israel" (I:49). Nathanael, too, has learned to dwell with Jesus; he too has learned the language of God because he has discovered in Jesus the Son of God, the King of Israel!

Jesus' response to Nathanael is meant for all those who have been initiated with regard to his eschatological dwelling: "And he said to him [singular]: 'Truly, truly, I say to you [plural!], you [plural] will see heaven opened, and the angels of God ascending and descending upon the Son of Man' " (I:51). The concluding statement is a masterly fabric woven from the warp of Jesus' dwelling ("the angels of God ascending and descending upon the Son of Man") and the woof of the Language of God (Jesus is explicitly called the Son of Man; at the same time he is symbolized as the new Jacob, the New Israel). The real Israel where heaven and earth meet is the person who reveals in his words and his works that paradise is not a new place but a new perspective; a perspective that turns a house into a home, earth into heaven, and human beings into Children of God. One who has learned the language of God will see the Father when he looks at Jesus, and will dwell in the New Jerusalem while still living in this vale of tears. Such a one is a true Israelite. The rest of John's Gospel is an illustration of this.

John II-XX: Symbolic Actions in a World of Symbols

The purpose of chapters two to twenty is clearly summed up towards the end of the Gospel: "Now Jesus did many other symbolic actions (*semeia*) in the presence of his disciples, which are not written in this book; but these are written that you may believe that Jesus is the Christ, the Son of God, and that believing you may have life in his name" (XX:30–31). This is far from being an unfamiliar theme since already in chapter two after the changing of water into wine at Cana, it was thematically asserted that "this was the first of the symbolic actions that Jesus did and thus manifested his glory" and that "his disciples believed in him" (II:11). The symbolic actions that Jesus did aim intrinsically at evoking the belief that Jesus is the language of God become Man, the Son of God who dwells with the Father. Hence it will not be out of place to spell out the interconnection between the symbolic actions that Jesus performed and belief in him.

The symbolic actions of Jesus were an outpouring of what he was, namely, the language of God that became flesh and dwelt among us. He is the paradigm through whose help we learn the language of God. In him we see how God speaks: It is not as if God began to speak only in Jesus. God always speaks, since the

Logos dwells with him "in the beginning." The effect of this is that the world comes into being. The world, too, is the phenomenal form, as it were, of God's speaking, God's language. But it is only in and through Jesus that we come to know that this is so. It is first and foremost in him that we learn that God speaks and speaks thus! Dwelling with Jesus, we learn that we, too, like him, are children of the Father. From him we imbibe a specific way of looking at the world of human beings. This world is not a mere conglomeration of objects but is the body, the real symbol, of God's language. To know the body truly is to know the soul.

The First of His Symbolic Actions (II:1–12)

The Book of Symbolic Actions commences with the pericope of the wedding at Cana where the Mother of Jesus was present and Jesus and his disciples were invited. What is striking about this passage is the abundance of the symbolic at work. It is almost as if the Evangelist were impatient to realize his implicit theology of language, and in the process was not overly worried about the coherence of the diverse symbolic expressions he is dealing with. The narrative begins with the expression "on the third day there was a marriage" (II:1) giving us a discreet clue that the spirit in which the Book of Symbolic Actions is written (and consequently is to be read) is the Spirit of the "third day," the day of the Resurrection, of the new creation.[17] Simultaneously it takes us (by way of the Old Testament) to the theme of the pericope: the wine that Jesus gives abundantly to his followers is the Spirit that dwells over him. It is this Spirit that turns a marriage ceremony into a wedding feast. For both wine and wedding feast are metaphors for the messianic days.[18] The marriage to which Jesus is invited becomes the metaphor of the eschatological wedding feast where he alone is the real bridegroom. As the historical bridegroom recedes into the background, the real bridegroom, Jesus, in whom the definitive marriage between God and human beings takes place, is revealed.

But before proceeding further let us first cast a glance at the *dramatis personae* and their theological significance. There is, first of all, the Mother of Jesus who sizes up the situation. "They have no wine" (II:3). Now neither these words nor the reply of Jesus ("Woman, what to me and to you?"—II:4) seems to have been satisfactorily explained by commentators. Actually the pericope is attempting a delicate balancing act between *Historie* and *Geschichte*.

The lack of wine, probably historical, is the starting point of a theological conversation between Mother and Son. Thus the Mother, taking the lack of wine as an occasion, refers to the absence of and the need for the Spirit. "They have no wine" is a remark, not a request, and refers at one and the same time both to the actual situation (no wine), as well as to its theological dimension ("They do not have the Spirit"). For wine, we said, was for the Jews a reminder of the messianic days when the Spirit would be given in abundant measure. That the Son so understood his Mother is shown by the fact that he takes up the subject of the Spirit in reply. He begins with a familiar Semitism, "Woman, what to me and to you?" (II:4), meaning "This is no concern of ours," and continues "My hour has not yet come" (II:5). Jesus is obviously referring here to the hour of his glorification when the Spirit will be given. The flow of thought will become clear if we paraphrase this theological dialogue thus:

Mother: They do not have the Spirit.
Son: This is really no concern of ours. For when the Spirit will be given is determined only by the Father. My hour, the hour when I shall be glorified and the Spirit will be poured out in abundant measure, has not yet come.

The meaning of this utterance is quite clear to the Mother. For she tells the servants (diakonoi), "Do whatever he says" (II:5). This is not to be understood as a gesture of petty insistence, as if Mary were determined to get her will done, nor as a gracious remark through which she hoped to escape an ungracious situation. Rather, it shows that Mary has understood well her Son's words as announcing that the abundance of the Spirit is to be experienced only after going through his 'glorification,' but has realized, too, that such glorification would take place only when we follow Jesus and do whatever he says. It is possible that she may have understood the words of Jesus, "My hour has not yet come," as meaning "my glorification has begun but not yet reached its culmination." In any case, she has realized that the way to the glorification and to the reception of the Spirit is to do whatever he says.

This brings us to the diakonoi, who from this point onwards become the focus of the story. Indeed, they play a central role in the narrative—first, since they are called diakonoi, not douloi; secondly, because they are the ones whom the Mother of Jesus initiates into the secret of the wine by addressing them with the second (and last) word she utters in John's Gospel; thirdly, because they are the instruments through whose services water becomes wine; fourthly, because it is to them that Jesus gives the command to bring the good wine to the master of the feast; and, finally, because they, and not the master of the feast, know whence *(pothen)* the good wine came. It is consoling to realize that both Jesus and his Mother deal with the *diakonoi*, with the result that the latter alone know the secret of the water turned into wine. They have seen how God speaks. Henceforth it will be their task to offer the good wine to people like the master of the feast. For those who serve are really the symbols of the Spirit at work in the world.

In addition to the *diakonoi* there are "the six jars . . . for the Jewish rites of purification, each holding two or three measures" (about 120 to 160 gallons, i.e., 600–800 liters!). This exaggeration, like the number of jars, is symbolic of the Spirit that will be poured out without measure! The mediating Mother of Jesus, the attentive and efficient *diakonoi*, and the six Jewish jars form the context in which Jesus works his *semeion* wherein water becomes wine.

The Mother who has dwelt long years with her Son knows how to dwell with him (cf. "If you keep my commandments, you will dwell in my love just as I have kept my Father's commandments and dwell in his love!"—XV:10). This secret she discloses to the *diakonoi* when she advocates total, unconditional following of her Son. The openness of the *diakonoi* to Jesus' words and their promptness in executing them as well as the readiness of the 'full-filled' jars to subserve another function and purpose—all these make up the details of the recipe for changing water into wine. For to those who are open to Jesus and are determined to follow him fully, giving up whatever might be a hindrance to discipleship, daily life becomes a marriage feast and the humdrum water of tradition turns into the 'good wine' of the feast which will "give our souls a pure draught, that they may become possessed by that divine intoxication which is more sober than sobriety itself."[19] But it is through the *diakonoi* (that is, people who do what Jesus says in order to serve others) that water becomes wine, and life becomes a feast. Service is the secret of ultimate success; and servers are saviours.

Our pericope is replete with symbolic references, but it is not our task here to expatiate on this, but merely to point out the direction of the total symbolic action of Jesus, namely, to learn from the paradigm of Jesus how God speaks in and through the persons and events of our lives; concretely how in this new (post-Easter) age one can, through service, discover in the water of drudgery the wine of the wedding feast. This, with the help of the alchemic formula "Do whatever he says," given us by the Mother of Jesus, who herself had learnt it by dwelling with her Son.

Jesus Did Many Other Symbolic Actions (XX:30)

John's chapter on the marriage feast at Cana is a sample of the implied relationship between God, world, and language. But most of the symbolic actions that are narrated after this pericope are much simpler in structure and consequently more effective in their evocation. John, of course, is fully conscious that he is using symbol-language. See, for instance, the cleansing of the temple (II:12–22) where Jesus speaks of the temple and the Evangelist adds helpfully that "he spoke of the temple of his body" (XX:21). When speaking of being born anew Jesus makes it clear that he is speaking of being born of the Spirit (III:5). To bring out more forcefully the symbol-character of Jesus' language, the Evangelist repeatedly resorts to a literary device: one of the characters usually interprets the words of Jesus literally. This gives the Evangelist the chance to underscore the symbolic nature of his language. Nicodemus, for instance, interprets literally the new birth Jesus is speaking of. "How can a man be born when he is old? Can he enter a second time into his mother's womb and be born?" (III:4). This happens, too, in the case of the Samaritan woman who misunderstands the nature of water that Jesus gives: "Sir, give me this water, that I may not thirst nor come here to draw" (IV:15). Similarly, the Jews are puzzled with regard to the Bread of Life: "How can this man give us his flesh to eat?" (VI:52).

It is by introducing a literal interpretation of the symbol-language of Jesus that the Evangelist corrects such misunderstandings of the nature and function of the specific symbol that is being employed in the context. In the symbol-language of John's Gospel, birth means being born of the Spirit (III:5 ff.); water means living water (VII:39), the water welling up to Eternal Life (IV:10 ff.); bread refers to the Bread of Life (III:5 ff.); light means Light of the world (VIII:12); blindness means blindness to the Light of the world, and seeing means believing that Jesus is the Light of the world (IX:5 ff.); one who lays down his life for his sheep is a good shepherd and Jesus is the Good Shepherd (X:11 ff.); one who does the works of God is a Son of God; Jesus is such a one (X:36 ff.); death is life if one believes in Jesus as the Resurrection and the Life, and life is death if one does not so believe (XI:25 ff.); Lord and Master is one who washes the feet of his brethren (XIII:12 ff.); the way refers to Jesus, the way to the Father (XIV:4 ff.); to see Jesus is to see the Father (XIV:9 ff.), and, finally, to keep Jesus' commandments is to dwell in the Father's love (XV:9 ff.).

But These are Written That You May Believe . . . (XX:31)

Jesus seems, in John's Gospel, to be conscious of himself as the language of God and is portrayed as being aware of the significance of God's language:

I have given them the words *(rhēmata)* which you gave me and they have received them and know in truth that I came from you; and they have believed that you have sent me (XVII:18).

I have given them your Language *(logos)* (XVII:14).

And they have kept your Language (XVII:6).

Sanctify them in the truth; your Language is truth (XVII:17).

Whom God has sent utters the words of God, for it is not by measure that he gives the Spirit (III:34).

It is the Spirit that gives life, the flesh is of no avail; the words that I have spoken to you are Spirit and life (VI:62).

Lord, to whom shall we go? You have the words of Eternal Life; and we have believed, and have come to know that you are the Holy One of God (VI:68).

Why do you not understand my discourse *(lalia)?* Because you cannot hear my Language *(logos)!* (VIII:43).

He who is of God hears the words of God; the reason why you do not hear them is that you are not of God (VIII:47).

If anyone hears my words and does not keep them faithfully, it is not I who shall condemn him, since I have come not to condemn the world, but to save the world; he who rejects me and refuses my words has his judge already; the Language that I have spoken will be his judge on the last day. For what I have spoken does not come from myself; no, what I was to say, what I had to speak was commanded by the Father who sent me and I know that his commands mean Eternal Life. And therefore what the Father has told me is what I speak (XII:47–50).

The words that I say to you I do not speak as from myself; it is the Father, living *(menōn)* in me, who is doing this work (XIV:10). If anyone loves me he will keep my Language *(logos)*, and my Father will love him, and we shall come to him and make our home with him. Those who do not love me, do not keep my words. And my Language is not my own; it is the language of the One who sent me (XIV:23–24). If you dwell in me and my words dwell in you, you may ask what you will and you shall get it (XV:7).

The Book of Symbolic Actions is the Semantics and Semiotics needed to understand the language of God concretized in the symbols of this world. "Now Jesus did many other symbolic actions in the presence of his disciples, which are not written in this book; but these are written that you may believe that Jesus is the Christ, the Son of God, and that believing you may have life in his name" (XX:30–31). Looking at this world Jesus could cry out, "Abba, Father," and at the same time experience a deep sense of sonship and belonging. Believing that Jesus is the Christ means looking at the world as he did, as the language of God made flesh, and experiencing, like Jesus, a sense of fellowship and belonging, a sense of sonship. For from Jesus we learn that the earth is our home and the beginning of heaven.

Once we have been struck by the symbol-character of this world, we shall also become aware of all that destroys symbols and reduces them to things that pass away. Our task then will be to promote authentic action so that we work for the hungry in such a way that together we shall be eating the Bread of Life, and for the thirsty so that together we shall be drinking living water. For a theology of language does not mean inventing concepts and categories about God; rather, it will be the attempt to see how and what God is speaking through the events of our times and to articulate this. The evil of our world today consists not so much in the absence of God as in the absence of genuine bread, the bread of belonging, and genuine water for the wayfarer. Our bread is kneaded in blood and exploitation and our water is polluted by our profit-mentality. Such bread cannot ever become the Bread of Life and such water is surely not living water. The task of an authentic theology of language would be to spread awareness about the stones that are being proffered where bread is needed, and the poison that is being given in place of water. The final fruit of such a theology of language would be the spirit of discernment: the spirit that distinguishes the chaff of inauthenticity from the wheat of genuine living.

1. By "Language of God" I mean two things: primarily the language which God speaks and secondarily the language which speaks about God. By "God of Language" I am referring both to the source of language and the goal towards which language impels the whole world.

2. I am speaking of metaphor somewhat differently than, say, Paul Ricoeur does (cf. "Biblical Hermeneutics," *Semeia*: An Experimental Journal for Biblical Criticism 4, Society of Biblical Literature, [Scholars Press, Univ. of Montana, 1975], 29–148, esp. 75 ff.). Whereas Ricoeur stresses the aspect of tension between the literal meaning and the metaphorical meaning, I think that this tension is not, and therefore need not be, always explicit. While I admit almost all that Ricoeur says, I broaden my understanding of metaphor to all those expressions that point to a depth-dimension. Thus, when Jesus proclaims that he is the way, the truth, and the life, the tension between the literal and the metaphorical meanings is implicit, the statement is nonetheless metaphorical. Moreover, there are instances, I believe, where the tension is not apparent at all. Such is the case with seminal metaphors like Jesus' "Abba, Father!" In instances too where one confesses to another, "You are my happiness and joy," the tension is not evident. To identify a metaphor one has to find out if there is a pointing to and an evocation of a depth-dimension, a pointing beyond the literal meaning, and an evocation of something beyond the literal meaning. We have metaphor when the expression refers to a thing in its fulness and totality. The word bread is a metaphor when it is employed in such a manner that it is understood to feed not merely the body but to nourish the whole person. The pointer-function of a metaphor is usually apparent in the context where probably also the tension that Ricoeur speaks of manifests itself. Metaphors like "Abba, Father!" are seminal because from and through them other metaphors ("All human beings are brothers and sisters") take their origin. In these derived metaphors the tension-character is more evident, I think.

3. For a profound understanding of symbol see Karl Rahner, "Zur Theologie des Symbols," *Schriften zur Theologie*, Bd. 4 (Benziger Verlag, Einsiedeln, Zürich-Köln, 1962³), 275–311.

4. Metaphors arise from an experience of symbol. A symbol is a thing, any thing which discloses its depth-dimension. An experience of such disclosure expresses itself in metaphor. When, e.g., a believer saw Jesus and, seeing him, saw the Father, then in that case Jesus is the symbol and the expressions that the believer brings forth ("You are the Christ, etc.") are metaphors. Just as a symbol gives rise to diverse metaphors, the metaphors themselves in their turn can be interpreted in diverse and diverging ways. Another view on the relationship between symbol and metaphor is to be found in P. Ricoeur, "Metaphor and Symbol," *Interpretation Theory*: Discourse and the Surplus of Meaning (Texas Christian Univ. Press, Fort Worth, 1976), 45–69.

5. Significance is not a new meaning, it is the soul of meaning. It is that aspect which makes any meaning meaningful. We understand many things and events and persons but few of them are meaningful to us, that is, there does not emerge any personal relationship between them and us. When and if such a

relationship does arise, this is so because we have encountered the soul of their meaning. Such an encounter can take place both at the symbol as well as at the metaphor level. When we encounter a person (or an event or thing) in this manner we express it through metaphor, the quality of the metaphor depending both on the depth of the encounter and on the linguistic ability of the person. When we encounter a metaphor, another metaphor could be born. The significance that is the soul of everything is what I am referring to when I speak of the language of God incarnate in this world.

6. In translating the Greek word *logos* as "language" (Sprache), instead of using the more familiar "Word" (Wort), I am following Hans-Georg Gadamer. Gadamer begins his essay "Mensch und Sprache"—published in his *Kleine Schriften* I (J. C. B. Mohr [Paul Siebeck], Tübingen, 1976), 93–101—with the explicit affirmation: "Es gibt eine klassische Definition des Wesens des Menschen, die Aristoteles aufgestellt hat, wonach er das Lebewesen ist, das *Logos* hat. In der Tradition des Abendlandes wurde diese Definition in der Form kanonisch, dass der Mensch das *animal rationale*, das vernünftige Lebewesen, d.h. durch die Fähigkeit des Denkens von den übrigen Tieren unterschieden sei. Man hat also das griechische Wort *Logos* durch Vernunft bzw. Denken wiedergegeben. In Wahrheit heisst dieses Wort auch und vorwiegend: Sprache" (p. 95).

7. When persons, events, or things 'strike' us, a kind of personal relationship develops which transforms and in some way enlightens us. Try as we might, we shall never succeed in reducing this relationship to mere qualities of space and time, though this relationship develops and manifests itself through space-time qualities. What I am suggesting is that this kind of relation is based on and emerges from the language of God, "this real light which enlightens every Man."

8. Cf. Ferdinand Hahn, "Sehen und Glauben im Johannesevangelium," *Neues Testament und Geschichte. Historisches Geschehen und Deutung im Neuen Testament*, hrsg. von Heinrich Baltensweiler und Bo Reicke (Theologischer Verlag, Zürich; J. C. B. Mohr [Paul Siebeck], Tübingen, 1972), 125–141.

9. The calling of the first disciples of Jesus is described by John with a minimum of dialogue and with no word about what they saw at Jesus' dwelling when they responded to his invitation to "come and see." This confirms our opinion that the Gospel here is proposing a methodological principle, not describing an enquiry into Jesus' home address! Both the technique of narration as well as the narrative itself make it highly unlikely that the disciples were looking for Jesus' house. A literal understanding of their question, "Where do you dwell?" is not only pointless; it would make it difficult for us to explain satisfactorily why John should have placed this pericope about the search for Jesus' dwelling precisely at the beginning of the Gospel.

10. See George Soares-Prabhu, S. J., "The Kingdom of God: Jesus' Vision of a New Society," *The Indian Church in the Struggle for a New Society*, ed. D. S. Amalorpavadass, (National Biblical, Catechetical and Liturgical Centre, Bangalore, 1981), 579–608.

11. Cf. the informative and lucid article of Anand Amaladass, "Dhvani Theory in Sanskrit Poetics," *Biblebhashyam* 5:4 (Kottayam, India, 1979), 261–275.

12. Cf. my "Dhvani as a Method Interpretation," *ibid.*, 276–294. Most of the

studies on Dhvani fail to give sufficient importance to real Dhvani, that is, *rasa-dhvani*. It is usually translated as suggestion, a play on words. But *rasa-dhvani* is anything but a play on words and essentially belongs to the realm of metaphor. The use of Dhvani is not to be gauged from one particular word or even a sentence but from the whole of the immediate context in which it occurs. Hence though we speak of "Bread of Life" and "I am the living water" as examples of Dhvani, it would be more precise to state that these are only the focus of Dhvani—as a matter of fact, Dhvani requires an elaborate context and so it never could function in a mere word or just in a sentence. It is the whole context that prepares for the working of Dhvani and it is the whole context that makes its working palpable. Take the proclamation of Jesus: "I am the bread of life" (VI:36), and see how it is at home in the whole narrative (VI:24-69).

13. Cf. P. Ricoeur, *op. cit.*, esp. 77 ff.

14. Of all the commentaries on John that I have been able to consult, only Rudolf Bultmann's sees a special significance in this mention of the tenth hour. It is, he says, "die Stunde der Erfüllung." Cf. his *Das Evangelium des Johannes* (Vandenhoeck & Ruprecht, Göttingen, 1941), 70.

15. See a similar pattern at work in John's experience and expression mentioned on p. 12 in section 4.2.

16. Seeing and looking are important elements in the process of learning to dwell. Every mention of dwelling or learning to dwell in John I is found referring to seeing, beholding, noticing, etc. Cf. 1:14, 18, 29, 33, 34, 35, 36, 38, 49, 50, 51! Though scholars are not agreed as to the exact shades of meaning conveyed by these terms, they surely mean more than merely physical seeing. Cf. Raymond E. Brown, *The Gospel According to John* (Anchor Bible, New York, Doubleday, 1966), I:501-503; Edwin A. Abbot, *Johannine Vocabulary*: A comparison of the Words of the Fourth Gospel with Those of the Three (Adam and Charles Black, London, 1905), 1597-1611; and G. J. Phillips, "Faith and Vision in the Fourth Gospel," in F. L. Cross (ed.), *Studies in the Fourth Gospel* (Mowbray, London, 1957), 83-96. Oscar Cullmann's approach in his "Der johanneische Gebrauch doppeldeutiger Ausdrücke als Schlüssel zum Verständnis des vierten Evangeliums," *Theologische Zeitschrift* (Theologische Fakultät der Universität Basel), 4 Bd. (1948), 360-362 is interesting but in my opinion it is hermeneutically inadequate.

17. Cf. John Marsh, *The Gospel of St John*, Pelican Books, 1968, 141 ff.

18. Cf. Raymond E. Brown, *The Gospel According to John*, I:104-105.

19. Philo Alexandrinus, Legum Allegoriae, III.79, quoted in C. H. Dodd, *The Interpretation of the Fourth Gospel* (Cambridge Univ. Press, Cambridge, 1953), 298.

Deconstruction and Onto-Theological Discourse

NONA R. BOLIN

Here do I sit and wait, old broken tablets around me and also new half tablets. When cometh mine hour?—The hour of my descent, of my down-going. . . . Behold, here is a new tablet; but where are my brethren who will carry it with me into the valley and into hearts of flesh.

(Thus Spake Zarathustra)

I

Heidegger conceives traditional metaphysics as a forgetfulness of the question of Being. Onto-theology has cast the question of Being in a causal, visual, subjective manner. Being-constantly-present-at-hand is metaphysically depicted through visual imagery entrenched in a discourse that has as its center a regarding spectator that assures its own permanence, stability, and intelligibility.

Theology/philosophy is, for Heidegger, essentialist and subjectivist in that all beings are interpreted in relation to a Being/Knower. The Knowing Subject of theology to whom all beings are disposed is simply the eternal counterpart for all knowing subjects to whom things are disposed in the humanistic thought of Plato, Aristotle, Descartes, and Kant. This unfolding of subjectivism is tantamount to the presencing of Being and it is the complicity between theology and philosophy that makes possible the present historical configuration of the Age of Man and Technology.

Metaphysics, the way Being has been understood/misunderstood, includes under its domain all language that speaks with a Platonic voice; thus Heidegger calls all metaphysics "Platonism." Being appears in Plato's writing as idea *(eidos)*, but ideas violate beings, according to Heidegger, through a conceptual grasp. In metaphysics, subjectivism becomes the vehicle whereby truth shifts from disclosure *(aletheia)* to correspondence, accuracy, and correctness. The myth of the cave provides the Platonic paradigm wherein hiddenness and darkness are forced into revelation and light through correct vision. This priority of reason instills into Western thought the primacy of the subjective, and the centrality of *eidos* subverts temporal presencing in favor of the permanently present. The agreement of ideas and objects becomes the true model of Truth.

Aristotle's concept of *ousia* retains some traces of the Heraclitean notion of withdrawal and unconcealment. However, Aristotle's ties with *aletheia* are severed, according to Heidegger, once *ousia* is interpreted as substance and comes to embody the basic traits of necessity, selfsameness, and permanency. "By substance we can conceive of nothing else than a being which *is* in such a way that it needs no other being in order to be."[1]

As Aristotle conceives physical substance it is the ground of all physical attributes, a substance capable of change within its very constitution. It is this Aristotelian conception of physical presence that has become the model by which beings have been thought in the philosophical tradition.

Although Aristotle does not continue the Platonic emphasis on *eidos*, his inquiry into *kinesis* and *ousia* is conceived in terms of constant presence *(Anwesen)*. Consequently, the object becomes the means of interpreting knowing consciousness, namely, as a substance that contains unity and permanence. Given that *ousia* is inherently intelligible and such intelligibility demands a rational agent, the substantial ground of knowing takes on a centrality that dominates western metaphysics as Heidegger describes it.

Heidegger interprets Descartes as lagging behind the scholastics in his evasion of the question of Being.

This evasion means that Descartes leaves the meaning of being contained in the idea of substantiality. . . . The meaning was unclarified because it was held to be "self-evident."[2]

Descartes conceives of the subject as the self or *cogito* possessing the capacity of providing the idea of its own necessary existence. This idea of existence must issue from an actual existence based in Descartes' implementation of Aristotelian causality, and it is this idea that insures the self-certainty of the cogito.

Descartes' understanding of the *res cogitans* is essentially that of *res extensa*—substantiality. It is his failure to separate the ontic and the ontological understanding of substance that amounts to "the failure to master the fundamental problems of Being."[3]

In Descartes, Man becomes sovereign, for, as Heidegger sees it, it is Descartes who brings to subjectivity a new configuration in his centralization of the *cogito*. But Cartesianism has gone amiss in its conclusion of the duality of man and the world. It prescribes how beings should be rather than describes how they are. The initial encounter of beings and world is passed over, but this concealing is a forgetting, not an error or a matter of chance. Concealment is indicative of an essential kind of being, of being-in-the-world, and with this concealment of Being comes a progressive subjectivization of all being and a preoccupation with the appropriation of beings.

Kant, like Descartes, passes over the question of Being and the world. His participation in the subjectivist turn follows the traditional model of treating consciousness as a subject, a substantial entity in the manner of the *res cogitans*. Thus he maintains the dualisms of appearance and reality, finitude and absolutivity, immanence and transcendence. Nonetheless, Heidegger discerns a tension throughout Kant's work. He maintains *The Critique of Pure Reason* implicitly recognizes finitude as determining the categories of understanding.

When Kant questions how knowledge is possible such that things can present themselves as objects of consciousness, Kant treats/mistreats subjectivity as a modification of the *res cogitans*. The transcendental unity of consciousness is Kant's idealistic attempt to ground metaphysics for all time, but, as Heidegger interprets it, the transcendental ground that makes knowledge possible is essentially a finite process or finitude itself. But Kant's failure of nerve in explaining the implications of the finite character of transcendence forces him to couple transcendence with such apodictic necessity. Kant falls back upon a metaphysics that will not think contradiction and is incapable of recognizing the centrality of finitude. Kant's idealism prevents him from explicitly recognizing the primacy of finite transcendence conceived within the horizon of temporality.

Even though Kant overcomes the idea of self as substance in an Aristotelian sense, nonetheless Kant's transcendental subject is worldless and impervious to historical modification. Kant's idealistic epistemology, in complicity with the metaphysical tradition, inverts the meaning of Being by making subjectivity the ground and possibility of all experience.

In *Being and Time* Heidegger asks how it is possible to ask Kant's question: "How is knowledge possible?" But Heidegger proposes to ask the question without reductionistic reference to a *cogito*, a transcendental ego, consciousness or any other mode of subjectivity. It is to ask how the tradition can be overcome. Since Heidegger considers his method of overcoming to be phenomenological rather than voluntaristic, it is important to understand just how Heidegger conceives anew the very question of the meaning of Being. Unlike Husserl's phenomenology, which is an epistemological analysis of the immanent structures of consciousness, Heidegger is engaged in radical phenomenology which speaks a fundamental ontology that makes possible all epistemological analyses. He breaks with Husserlian methodology in his rejection of transcendental idealism and what he calls twentieth-century Cartesianism. Husserl emphasizes the intentionality of consciousness, but in *Being and Time* Heidegger avoids subjectivist connotations of consciousness and speaks of the intentional features of comportment. Through a non-egoistic rendering of comportment, Heidegger hopes to avoid a subject/object model of static consciousness. Instead Heidegger ventures an ontological reduction (rather than a transcendental reduction) whereby the old structures of understanding break down and the tradition is overcome. But how is this overcoming to be effectuated?

In order to understand what Heidegger means by overcoming it is first necessary to understand how he regards the tradition. Clearly it cannot be treated as an object of epistemic analysis, for subjectivity is concomitantly entreated. Epistemology is only possible within a fundamental ontology and the epistemic subject can never detach itself from a belongedness to Being. That which the tradition has concealed persistently calls in its unsaidness. But this disclosiveness is possible only if there is an understanding of Being.

It would be fundamentally mistaken to assume that Heidegger is attempting to overthrow the tradition by reaching a new theory of Being. Banishing old values in favor of new ones (a task he wrongly attributes to Nietzsche) is only a new form of concealment. Heidegger believes philosophy understands itself as having advanced through a series of questions which yield positive answers in such a way that progress is gauged in terms of solutions. But Heidegger's overcoming project is nonprogressive, for he does not propose new answers but a new questioning of questions.

Being and Time occurs in Heidegger's initial question of Being, which discloses the primary structure of the being for whom Being is an issue. *Da-sein*, the being that is determined by its belongedness to Being, belongs to Being in a way that can never be literalized or made fully explicit. Nonetheless, Heidegger seeks an intelligibility to speak the very ground of intelligibility which inevitably reveals itself as recalcitrant to conceptualization. But how is such a disclosure, one that radically redirects the question of Being, to be conceived? Heidegger's provisional analysis in *Being and Time* leads to an unspoken disclosure of the rupture of all metaphysical discourse, even his own discourse. The inevitable retreat is silence. Hence the unspoken proclamation of *Being and Time* is its own collapse on its own terms. In this sense Heidegger's text forecasts and enacts its own failure.

The breakdown of reflective analysis accelerates the decentralization of the epistemic subject, but since *Being and Time* continues to speak the language of onto-theology, it contains remnants of subjectivity. Consequently, *Being and Time* (with its *Da-sein* centeredness) leaves unspoken the relatedness of understanding to the meaning of Being. The concealment of Heidegger's own discourse allows a fundamental discourse that echoes its own inevitable silence in that *Being and Time* cannot speak the conditions of its own occurrence.

Heidegger's movement towards the unity of *Da-sein* betrays an atemporal, ahistorical notion of identity which reveals Heidegger's reluctance to think difference as disruption. Just as Aristotle, Descartes, Kant, and Husserl are concerned with the comprehensiveness of human existence, Heidegger participates in the misadventure of totality. In his desire for the cohesiveness of *Da-sein*, Heidegger displaces Being for being-in-the-world.

The relatedness of the historical finitude of *Da-sein's* disclosure of Being and *Da-sein's* own disclosive occurrence is left unanalyzed in *Being and Time*. For the most part it is left unexplored in his later work. But Heidegger never abandoned his engagement with decentering the configuration of subjectivity.

The common name subjectivity immediately and all too stubbornly burdens thinking with erroneous opinions which interpret every relation of Being to man, or even to his egoness, as a distinction of objective Being, as if objectivity in all its essential traits did not have to remain caught in subjectivity.[4]

II

For Jacques Derrida the discourse of deconstruction would not be possible without Heidegger's ontico-ontological difference. The logocentrism of traditional metaphysics takes its prominence in axiological oppositions: light/dark, mind/body, male/female, positive/negative, truth/error, etc. The master/slave relatedness of these oppositions is masked by pretenses of equality, harmony, and complementarity, but the master term is consistently identified with perfected, autonomous existence while the slave term functions/dysfunctions only derivatively as fallen other. These binary oppositions allow no peaceful coexistence, for the subject/object relation is inevitably one of domination.

Traditional metaphysics' logocentrism is also a phonocentrism, a privileging of speech over writing. For Derrida, this phonocentrism is even voiced in Heidegger's texts.

. . . [P]honocentrism merges with the historical determination of the meaning of being in general as 'presence,' with the subdeterminations which depend on this general form and which organize within it their system and their historical sequence (presence of the thing to the sight as the *eidos*, presence as substance/essence/existence. . . . The self-presence of the cogito, consciousness, subjectivity, the co-presence of the other and the self, . . . and so forth).[5]

Metaphysics understands writing to be twice removed from the realm of presence. Onto-theology distinguishes signifier from signified. Voice is closest to the signified and enjoys a proximity to being from which writing is exiled. As a series of physical marks that function in the absence of voice, writing is a mediation of a mediation. Hence, writing is exterior, mimetic, and has no constitutive meaning of its own. "This notion remains therefore within the heritage of that logocentrism which is also a phonocentrism, absolute proximity of voice and being, of voice and the meaning of being, of voice and the ideality of meaning."[6]

Grammatology breaks with phono-logocentrism through a deconstruction of the speech-writing dichotomy. From the standpoint of onto-theology, the temporality and physicality of writing are indicative of its errancy when contrasted to divine spiritual writing.

Natural writing is immediately united to voice and to breath. Its nature is not grammatological but pneumatological. It is hieratic, very close to the interior holy voice of the Profession of Faith, to the voice one hears upon retreating into oneself: full and truthful presence of the divine voice to inner sense. . . .[7]

The divine book, the quintessence of spiritual writing, is understood to represent ultimate reality, the house of the logos become corporal. Even the secular book is understood to be an indivisible entity, a unity preceded by what it signifies, constituted by an author. But, if the very corporality of the corpus severs meaning from presence, the signifier and the signified are endlessly separated in textuality, a writing to infinity. The text is the destruction of the book. It erases distinctions between subject and object, author and work. The text disavows all origins and closures. The text is anonymous. As it is for Heidegger, subjectivity is, for Derrida, a manifestation of presence; and the author, one who puts marks on a page, is a substitute for logos. The absence of the author is the absence of the central authority. Writing is orphaned speech. "The question of writing could be opened only if the book was closed."[8]

Derrida writes writing with two hands. With the right hand he writes the classical writing that presumes itself in the service of the logos, a writing of realism and representation. In its allegiance to structure, this writing regards itself as transparently reflecting the real, progressing from concept to concept in an ordered system that leads from logos back into logos. It is the pretentious writing of Man, ". . . the name of man being the name of that being who, throughout the history of metaphysics or of onto-theology—in other words, throughout his entire history—has dreamed of full presence, of reassuring foundations, the origin and the end of play."[9] Derrida's writing with the left hand is *écriture*, the play of signs. This writing disrupts classical writing and displaces its conceptual order. It venerates neither original nor eschatological presence. It is its own transgressive event and speaks neither a theism nor an atheism. It is a discourse that refers only to itself in a repetitious weaving of ciphers and disinherited signifiers.

This dissimulation of the woven texture can in any case take centuries to undo its web: a web that envelopes a web, undoing the web for centuries, reconstituting it too as an organism, indefinitely regenerating its own tissue behind the cutting trace, the decision of each reading.[10]

Double writing provokes the reversal of the metaphysics of presence. This doubling constitutes a fold between the text that issues its own undoing and the enactment of an other text, a text that writes the deconstruction of the original ". . . by means of this double play, marked in certain decisive places by an erasure which allows what it obliterates to be read, violently inscribing within the text that which attempted to govern it from without."[11]

Double writing demands a return to the book. Writing must exceed the book by bursting through its conceptual boundaries. Redoubling ruptures the self-identity of the book, alienating it from itself. Redoubling casts into relief the difference between presence and presence, word and word. Although "nothing has budged" and neither sign nor thing is perceivably changed, alterity displaces identity in a duplicity of eternal reoccurrence.

Deconstruction is not itself disruption. It locates the sites of the always already disrupted. Derrida seeks out the self-referential cracks in the text that allow the uncanny junctures between one discourse and another. But in that there is no discourse which is a complete alternative to the language of metaphysics, the double gesture is always indeterminate. Derrida works in the margins of metaphysical discourse, for just as metaphysics is paradoxically caught within the circle of needing that which it excludes, deconstruction is sustained only through the play of presencing and absencing in metaphysical discourse. Derrida seeks the incision inscribed within the fabric of onto-theology that can only point to itself because it has no voice to speak and no name to write,

. . . something that *could not be presented* in the history of philosophy, and which moreover, is *nowhere* present, since all of this concerns putting into question the major determination of the meaning of being as "presence," the determination in which Heidegger recognized the destiny of philosophy.[12]

The undoing of Greco-Christian theology/philosophy is not an eradication of religious forms, for these forms are reinscribed in a capriciousness of difference. In deference to difference, Derrida speaks what he calls a negative atheology that escapes the bindings of the book for the openness of the text. Negative atheology takes its place in a non-place, a site that is always elsewhere. Negative theology is still located within the oppositions of presence and absence while hierarchizing absence over presence. Negative theology is still theology in its longing for the absent center, nonetheless a center. The center is the condition for the intelligibility of the totality, and knowledge of the matrix must always refer back to the center. For Derrida, theology, positive or negative, is the succession of the metaphors that have formed and named the center, the determinacy of being as presence or absence in its various forms.

Negative atheology affirms the discord of difference without nostalgia or resentment.

Negative atheology is not a set of beliefs that may come upon the scene at some future time. It always already is possible only because the tablets have been broken. Amongst the fragments of the shattered laws, in the margins of the book, the suppressed takes root and flourishes. These gaps are the sites of play where the writer dances "with the feet, with concepts, with words: do I still have to say that one has to be able to dance with the *pen*—that *writing* has to be learned?"[13]

III

For Heidegger and Derrida, onto-theology is a metaphysics of power and violence. The discourse of presence, as an "absolute will-to-hear-oneself-speak"[14] is incapable of respecting the other as its own finite occurrence. Its violence is expressed in a discourse that exhalts the triumph of knowledge and love through denial, degradation, and death. The domain of onto-theology's power is a hierarchically structured totality. It is a domain which theology/philosophy struggles to unite into a universal kingdom under the banner of Truth. The will to Truth is the zealous will that strives for conformity in all dimensions of expression and experience, the subordination of difference to Sameness. The religious will and the philosophical will are co-conspirators in their mutual thrust toward ultimate meaning and this complicity is inevitably manifest in domination.

The ancient clandestine friendship between light and power, the ancient complicity between theoretical objectivity and technico-political possession . . . would make common cause with oppression and with the totalitarianism of the Same.[15]

Will the deconstruction of onto-theology deliver the death blow to theology, or will it open up a new space for a nonmetaphysical configuration of religious commitment? Heidegger and Derrida predictably give no predictions and few directions. Their own participation in transgressive writing only echoes the discordance of the breaking tablets. While we may be sceptical that theology will turn away from origins and eschatons, the religious affirmation of difference beyond God and Man is not precluded. Can the religious/philosophical will release its longing for the security of presence in a Nietzschean affirmation of a joyful wisdom without regret? Or are these very questions misconceived, resonant remnants of subjectivity? According to the deconstructionist it is not a matter of choice. Says Derrida:

I do not believe that today there is any question of choosing—in the first place because we are in a region where the category of choice seems particularly trivial, and in the second, because we must first try to conceive the common ground. . . . Here there is a kind of question, let us call it historical, whose conception, formation, gestation, and labor we are only catching a glimpse of today. I employ these words, I admit, with a glance toward the operations of childbearing—but also with a glance toward those who, in a society from which I do not exclude myself, turn their eyes away when faced by the yet unnamable which is proclaiming itself and which can do so, as whenever a birth is in the offing, only under the species of the nonspecies, in the formless, mute infant, and terrifying form of monstrosity.[16]

=====NOTES=====

1. Martin Heidegger, *Being and Time*, trans. Joan Stambaugh (manuscript as yet unpublished), 201.

2. *Ibid.*, 203.

3. *Ibid.*, 204–205.

4. Martin Heidegger, *Basic Writings*, ed. David Farrell Krell (New York: Harper and Row, 1977), 46.

5. Jacques Derrida, *Of Grammatology*, trans. Gayatri Chakravorty Spivak (Chicago: Univ. of Chicago Press, 1981), 12.

6. *Ibid.*, 11–12.

7. *Ibid.*, 17.

8. Jacques Derrida, *Writing and Difference*, trans. Alan Bass (Chicago: Univ. of Chicago Press, 1981), 294.

9. *Ibid.*, 292.

10. Jacques Derrida, *Dissemination*, trans. Barbara Johnson (Univ. of Chicago Press, 1981), 63.

11. Jacques Derrida, *Positions*, trans. Alan Bass (Chicago: Univ. of Chicago Press, 1981), 6.

12. *Ibid.*, 7.

13. Friedrich Nietzsche, *Twilight of the Idols*, trans. R. J. Holingdale (New York: Penguin Books, 1968), 66.

14. Jacques Derrida, *Writing and Difference,* 51.

15. *Ibid.,* 91.

16. *Ibid.,* 293.

BIBLIOGRAPHY

Derrida, Jacques. *Dissemination.* Trans. Barbara Johnson. Chicago: University of Chicago Press, 1981.

———. *Of Grammatology.* Trans. Gayatri Chakravorty Spivak. Chicago: University of Chicago Press, 1981.

———. *Positions.* Trans. Alan Bass. Chicago: University of Chicago Press, 1981.

———. *Writing and Difference.* Trans. Alan Bass. Chicago: University of Chicago Press, 1981.

Heidegger, Martin. *Basic Writings.* Ed. David Farrell Krell. New York: Harper and Row, 1977.

———. *Being and Time.* Trans. Joan Stambaugh. Manuscript as yet unpublished.

Nietzsche, Friedrich. *Twilight of the Idols.* Trans. R. J. Holingdale. New York: Penguin Books, 1968.

Part Two

THE MEDIUM
OF LANGUAGE:
TEXT, TALK,
AND SILENCE

5

The Pretext of Interpretation: Rabbinic Oral Torah and the Charisma of Revelation

MARTIN S. JAFFEE

The Oral Torah in Rabbinic Judaism

From the early centuries of the common era until our own day, Rabbinic Judaism has constituted the religion of most Jews. At the center of the imaginative and intellectual life of this Judaism stands the concept of Oral Torah. To Rabbinic ears the words "Oral Torah" convey at least two senses. On the one hand, they call to mind a coherent narrative of events surrounding revelation—a myth, in critical jargon. On the other hand, these words designate a traditional mode of exegetical thinking—a system of interpretation by which the meaning of revelation is made present and available to the faithful. The present essay discusses this second sense of Oral Torah in great detail. But insofar as the mythic sense in which the term is understood subserves the hermeneutical, some preliminary comments about the former are perhaps in order.

As far as historical research can determine, the notion that Moses received on Sinai a Written and an Oral Torah is associated with the early centuries of the Rabbinic movement (ca. 70–300 C.E.).[1] It is difficult to pinpoint the earliest versions of this idea, but it is quite clear that it comes to fullest expression as a polemic on behalf of the authority of a distinctive literary work. This work is the Mishnah, a code of ritual and civil law redacted ca. 200 by Rabbi Judah, Patriarch of Roman Palestine, and a major figure in the consolidation of Rabbinism in the second century.

As an explanation of the Mishnah's origins, the myth of Oral Torah legitimates the Rabbinic extension of the Jewish canon to include, in addition to the ancient Scriptures, a post-prophetic, self-consciously innovative work which claims to provide definitive guidance in the fulfillment of Israel's covenantal obligations to its God. It is in the earliest post-Mishnaic works of Rabbinism—in compilations of Biblical exegesis and in commentaries on the Mishnah—that we begin to find the explicit assumption that, when

Moses returned from Sinai, he brought with him not only two *tablets*, but two *Torahs*. One Torah, Holy Scripture, is immutably preserved as Written Torah, originally a unique gift to Israel, but now the possession of the nations. The second, the Mishnah and its attendant traditions of exegesis, is the Oral Torah, that body of knowledge, preserved in the memory, which sustains the covenantal relation between Israel and the Lord of All Worlds. Passed on by word of mouth from God to Moses, from Moses to Joshua, from Joshua to his disciples, and from them on to successive generations of spiritual heros, the Oral Torah has been preserved and embellished until Rabbi Judah the Patriarch himself arranged for its publication and dissemination to all Israel.[2]

The critical importance ascribed to the Mishnah by its designation as Oral Torah is nowhere better conveyed than in the following passage from a seventh-century collection of homilies, the *Pesikta Rabbati* (ed. M. Ish-Shalom, 14b):

Said R. Judah, the son of R. Shalom: Moses wanted the Mishnah to be written [as was Scripture]. But the Holy One Blessed Be He foresaw that the [gentile] nations would translate the [Written] Torah and read it in Greek. And they would say, "They [i.e., the Jews] are not Israel [for we have the Torah in our possession]!"

Said the Holy One Blessed Be He to Moses: O, Moses! The [gentile] nations will say, "We are Israel! We are the sons of the All Present!" And Israel, too, will say, "We are the sons of the All Present!" . . .

Said the Holy One Blessed Be He to the [gentile] nations: "You claim to be my sons, but I recognize him alone who holds my mysteries in his hands. He alone is my son!"

They said: "And what are these mysteries of yours?"

He said to them: "That is the Mishnah!"

The passage offers remarkable insight into Rabbinism's response to the Church's claim to find the fulfillment of the "Old Testament" promise in the life and death of Christ. Here the Mishnah is made to function precisely as the New Testament does in the theology of Christian supersessionism. That is, only from the perspective of a second revelation is it possible to begin to understand what is really at issue in the archaic revelation at Sinai. For Christians, that revelation is the New Testament, the product of renewed prophecy in the latter days. For Rabbinic Judaism, it is the Mishnah, the Oral Torah, as old as Sinai itself.

The foregoing exploration of the mythic dimension of Oral Torah places us now in a position to confront the real interests of this essay—the extent to which this Rabbinic myth of revelation informs the concrete methods by which Rabbinic exegetes unveil the meaning of the Mishnah. If, that is, Rabbinic exegetes of the Mishnah believe *it* to be Oral Torah and *themselves* to be the sole heirs to that Torah, are such beliefs reflected in the production of actual texts of Mishnaic exegesis? We move, then, from the mythic dimension of Oral Torah to a phenomenology of its texts, from sacred story to sacred hermeneutic.

If such Mishnaic exegesis as we find in early Rabbinism is indeed informed by the Oral Torah myth, the primary evidence for this must be sought in the Talmud Yerushalmi, or Palestinian Talmud, composed anonymously in Galilee during the late fourth century.[3] This Talmud, the fruit of nearly two centuries of post-Mishnaic Rabbinic exegesis, brings to the Mishnah a vast program of sustained comment, treating it—no less than Scripture itself—as a holy book. A description of the Yerushalmi's procedures for interpreting this holy book shall occupy us here.[4]

The Talmud Yerushalmi and the Expansion of Oral Torah

Our inquiry is confined to the example of a single, rather typical tractate of the Talmud Yerushalmi, Tractate Maaserot ("Tithes").[5] A commentary on the Mishnaic tractate of the same name, Yerushalmi Maaserot (hereafter, Y.) is an extensive discussion of the latter's tithing laws. It addresses the following issues, outlined by the Mishnah itself: (1) definitions of types of produce subject to Scripture's various commandments to remove priestly gifts and other offerings from crops harvested in the land of Israel; (2) the point in the ripening and/or harvest of produce at which its tithes and priestly dues must be separated for the use of their rightful recipients; (3) various restrictions regarding the consumption of untithed produce by its grower, purchaser, and their dependents. Insofar as the Yerushalmi raises issues extraneous to the Mishnah's interests, it invariably attempts to demonstrate that its own concerns are implied in the Mishnaic passage on which it comments. As I shall argue, however, the Yerushalmi's apparent submission to Mishnah Maaserot (hereafter, M.) regarding facts of law and theme obscures a fundamental freedom from the literary constraints of the Mishnaic text. A description of this freedom and an interpretation of its meaning is the task at hand.

The thesis of this study is that Y.'s exegetical discourse is mounted in service of a fundamental and indispensable pretext. This is so in two senses. In the first place, we may quite literally describe the Mishnah as the "pre-text" of the Yerushalmi. That is, the very existence of this Talmud is contingent upon the Mishnah, a text which precedes the commentary temporally and supersedes it in putative authority. The text of the Mishnah, therefore, is the *raison d'être* of the Talmud's own text of interpretation. Thus the discourse of Talmudic exegesis constitutes itself in sole reference to the discourse of the Mishnah, the pre-text which participates in the charisma of the central event of Israel's history—revelation.

There is a second, more fundamental sense in which the discourse of Y. is grounded in what I have called a pretext. The following discussion will point out that the methods by which Y.'s editors organize the literary materials of their commentary and correlate them to selected Mishnaic dicta bespeaks an implicit judgement that the Mishnah can speak as Torah only through the mediation of tradition, as the community of Rabbis defines it. The sacred pre-text, that is, becomes a latticework around and through which are intertwined the ideas and perspectives of those who ascribe authority to it.

Y.'s commentary, in this view, is a thoroughly dialogical literary creation—a text which quite literally "speaks through" the more prestigious pre-text of the Mishnah. The statements of third and fourth century Rabbis recorded in the commentary claim a hearing not on their own merits, but rather on those of the text in reference to which their statements are to be correlated. The pretext in this lies in the fact that in speaking *through* the Mishnaic pre-text, Rabbinic exegetes speak *for* it as well. That is, they take control of the authoritative Mishnah through the very means by which they ascribe authority to it—through the pretext of interpretation. Talmudic editorial techniques link the Mishnah and its commentary into a seamless conversation in which the distinction between Torah and commentary, Mishnah and Talmud, loses significance. The commentary, through the posture of submissive interpretation, itself becomes part of that Oral Torah it claims to explain. In its turn, the Yerushalmi follows the Mishnah as the subject of intense exegetical study in the Rabbinic academy.[6]

Appropriation of the Pre-Text

In order to trace the procedures by which Y.'s commentary becomes part of the Mishnah's Torah, it is necessary to begin with a general account of those literary traits characteristic of the document as a whole. At least on the surface, this commentary is a chaotic work. Composed of diverse literary sources which themselves employ a wide selection of genres and formulaic conventions, the commentary is rich in discordant voices competing with both the Mishnah and each other for the reader's attention. This immediate appearance of literary chaos nevertheless masks a systematically applied conception of how the Mishnah is to be appropriated for interpretation. Nowhere spelled out in any editorial preface, this conception is nevertheless exemplified in the procedures by which every pericope of Mishnah Maaserot is mediated to the student and subjected to comment.

The immediate effect of Y.'s editorial presentation of M. is to prevent the reader of the commentary from construing the Mishnah as a text with its own independent literary and conceptual integrity. This is achieved by dismembering the Mishnaic pre-text into discrete propositions which reach the reader of Y. only through the filter of the commentary's supplementary discourse. Such meaning as the Mishnah now conveys is construed only when the gnomic utterances captured within its textual shards are merged with the quite independent text of Y.'s commentary. In this way the commentary supplants the Mishnah by incorporating it into a new text, that of the commentary itself.

In this new text the Mishnah now participates only as one voice among many in defining the content of the law of tithes. Its carefully crafted units of discourse, often extending to many pericopae of sustained theoretical exploration, must now be interpreted as a series of isolated dicta, organized under the rubric of tithing law, but linked necessarily to the exemplary models of interpretation supplied by the Talmud's framing discussions.

Y.'s refraction of M.'s rulings both preserves intact the authoritative pre-text and transforms it into a series of departure points for the construction of the new text of the Talmud. The result is a work of kaleidoscopic character which presents familiar Mishnaic rulings in interaction with novel units of literary tradition. Precisely because the Mishnah is at the center, as the pre-text, the reader fails to see that the Mishnah has been transformed into something other than itself.[7] It has become the Talmud. Mishnaic fragments, cited with the reverential formula, "it is taught," are nevertheless deprived of their elementary context of meaning and enjoy a relation to each other only insofar as the Talmud itself, for its own purposes, chooses to bring them into correlation.

In illustration, consider a representative discussion appearing in Y.'s commentary on the very first paragraph of Mishnah Maaserot (M. 1:1). The pre-text itself consists of two parts, a general definition of the kinds of produce which must be tithed (i.e., all edible produce sown in Israelite fields), and a definition of the stage in a crop's growth at which it becomes subjected to preliminary restrictions regarding secular use. (In this translation I italicize all quotations of Mishnaic passages or other non-Mishnaic sources believed by the Yerushalmi's editors to stem from the work of Mishnaic authorities.) This latter definition is in two parts:

A. *Anything which at its first [stage of development] is food, and which at its ultimate [stage of development] is food—even though [the farmer] maintains [its growth] in order to increase the food [it will yield]—is subject [to the law of tithes] whether it is small or large.*
B. *But anything which at its first [stage of development] is not food, yet which at its ultimate [stage of development] is food, is not subject to the law of tithes] until it becomes food.*

The point of the whole, obviously, is that produce need not be tithed if it is consumed before it has become useful as food. Part A points out that untithed produce is subject to restrictions upon its use as soon as it reaches a stage of growth at which it is edible— even if the farmer himself plans no harvest until the food is more profitable. Part B supplies an important extension of the thought. If produce remains inedible until a late stage of growth, it is not subject to the law until this late moment. Let us now see what the Talmud makes of this passage.

Y.'s interest in the ruling is confined to A, making no effort to read this portion of the Mishnah in light of B, its most immediate context of interpretation. Indeed, Y.'s only interest is in the clause of A which begins with "even though." After citing the Mishnaic pre-text, Y. continues (Y. 1:1, ed. Venice, 48d):

1. Consequently, if the farmer does not maintain the growth [of such a crop] in order to increase the food it will yield [but, rather, harvests the produce at an early point in its development], [should we then conclude that] it is not subject to the law of tithes when it is either small or large?
2. R. Immi in the name of R. Simeon, the son of Laqish: [Not at all!] The point [of the Mishnah] is to exclude from consideration a claim of Rabban Gamaliel, for we have learned elsewhere [at M. 4:6]: *Rabban*

Gamaliel says: Shoots of fenugreek, mustard plants and hyacinth plants are subject to [the law of] tithes. [The present Mishnaic ruling, therefore, undercuts that of Rabban Gamaliel by stipulating that the law applies only to plants, or parts thereof, which are actually eaten. This excludes the inedible portions described by Rabban Gamaliel.]

3. Said R. Yose: But is it indeed on account of the edible plant [of which the inedible shoot is a part] that Rabban Gamaliel declares the shoots subject to the law? On such grounds, [he would have stated that] even the leaves of such plants should be declared liable [even if they are not intended for consumption]! Rather, Rabban Gamaliel holds that the stalks are regarded as edible in their own right, while the Masters [cited in our Mishnah] hold that they are not regarded as edible.

4. And, furthermore, we are instructed by the following, which is taught [in the Tosefta]:[8] *Said R. Joshua: Never in my life did I presume to tell a man, 'Go pick yourself shoots of fenugreek, mustard and hyacinth', so as to declare them exempt from [the law of] tithes!*

Let us now focus on the basic interpretative strategy of the discourse before us.

The editor of this discussion points out, first of all, that the clause, "even though . . .," seems entirely superfluous. Whatever the farmer's intentions, we cannot imagine that edible produce will be totally free of tithing restrictions (stich 1). Why, then, does the Mishnah include the ruling? Stich 2 provides the answer. Our clause is not designed to address its immediate literary context, but rather finds its meaning in reference to an entirely different ruling, that of Gamaliel in the Mishnah's fourth chapter! True enough, Gamaliel discusses the tithing-status of shoots of fenugreek, etc., while M. 1:1A is concerned with the moment at which produce becomes edible. The point, however, is that the passages share a common thesis regarding the determination of what is edible and, accordingly, within the jurisdiction of the tithing law. The thesis is that general conventions of diet, rather than the whim of particular individuals, determine when produce is suitable for tithing. This is Yose's point (stich 3). In his view, both the anonymous clause of M. 1:1A and Gamaliel are at one in their conviction that personal whims do not alter the "natural laws" of appetite which tell us when the growth of the earth is indeed "food". The two sources differ only on the question of whether or not certain kinds of growth, e.g., the hard stalks of otherwise edible plants, are conventionally regarded as sharing their value as food.

Our interest here is not with the plausibility of Yose's argument. Rather, we ask, what is the true object of the discussion to which he contributes so decisively? The true object of exegesis, it should be clear, is *neither* M. 1:1, to which the passage is appended, *nor* M. 4:6, which is forced into the context of M. 1:1. Rather, of interest to the editor is the *relation* between apparent incomparables. Where two equally authoritative texts seem at odds, it is necessary to establish a relationship between them which, while retaining the apparent contradiction, synthesizes the texts at a higher level of theory. Thus, yet a third authoritative Rabbinic dictum (stich 4) is called upon as testimony to Yose's exegetical *tour de force*. The Toseftan citation confirms that the taxonomical status of fenugreek shoots—food or fodder?—was indeed under debate during the days of Gamaliel.

We have seen what Y. can do with a simple Mishnaic statement. Imagine, then, the result of such exegetical procedures multipled throughout the length of an entire Mishnaic tractate. The result is an exegetical text shot through with paradox. The more the Mishnah is inspected, with new dimensions of its meaning uncovered, the less likely is its meaning in the context of its original universe of discourse to become clear. This paradox reveals a fundamental assumption of Y.'s editors regarding the nature of the Mishnah as a literary work. For them, the Mishnaic tractate is not itself regarded as a complete text, a coherent linguistic composition conveying within its own limits a unified statement of meaning. Rather, it is viewed as a collection of utterances organized by topic, but mounting no cumulative argument or statement larger than the sum of its individual sentences. The true text of which any Mishnaic utterance is a part is not the Mishnaic tractate in which it finds its place, but rather the entire deposit of literary tradition regarded as Oral Torah. The task of Y. in so many cases, therefore, is to weave diverse dicta of Mishnaic Sages, within and across discrete tractates and collections, into new patterns of meaning. In this way, Y.'s commentary, the model for weaving these strands of Mishnaic law into a single text, appears inevitable and, indeed, indispensable. The Mishnah, deprived by its interpreters of the power to mount its own discourse, becomes inseparable from their commentary, and speaks through it alone.

Obscuring the Pretext

It is, of course, beyond doubt that the intentions of the Yerushalmi's editors are not to ignore the Mishnah, but rather to fulfill what they regard as its primary purpose as Oral Torah—the construction, in an age of Exile, of an Israelite society modeled after the will of Heaven. This explains why, despite Y.'s literary atomization of the Mishnah, its concrete exegetical interests are overwhelmingly in the application and extension of laws and principles explored in Mishnah Maaserot and other tractates concerned with agricultural matters. Nearly 90% of all exegetical pericopae found in Y., after all, are devoted to this concern. The apparent submission to the legal agendum of the Mishnah, however, is precisely the means by which Y.'s editors complete their domination of the Mishnah. In order to trace the nature of this domination, it is necessary to refine the previous observations with a more focused discussion of Y.'s primary unit of exegesis, the *sugya* (pl., *sugyot*), or exegetical paragraph.

For present purposes, Y.'s units of exegesis may be divided into two general literary types, the gloss and the *sugya*. The former, of which I find only sixteen unadorned examples in Y. (13% of 124 exegetical units), are brief, pointed explications of the Mishnah's text. On the whole,[9] they constitute clear evidence that Rabbinic exegetes of the Mishnah can indeed spell out the Mishnah's plain sense when they wish to. A most helpful gloss appears, for example, in Y.'s comment on the opening ruling of M. 2:2. The Mishnah is concerned with whether or not a person's place of business is regarded as offering him the personal privacy of his home. If so, he must remove tithes from produce which he brings into this specific area. The reason is grounded in the Mishnah's assumption that produce brought into the home must be tithed—a portion of it set aside for God's purpose—before it may be used for a person's private benefit. Thus, M. 2:2 rules:

A. *[If people] were sitting in a [shop's] doorway or [vending] stall, and [a passer-by with untithed fruit] said, "Take figs for yourselves"—they eat [the figs where they stand] and are exempt [from tithing].*
B. *But the owner of the doorway and the owner of the stall are required [to tithe].*

The Talmud's gloss is brief and to the point (Y. 2:2, ed. Venice, 49d):

This distinction [between the shop customers and the owners] demonstrates that a person's home renders his own produce forbidden for untithed use, but has no effect upon the produce of others [who might enter his home with produce of their own].

The gloss not only highlights what is implicit in the Mishnah's ruling, but draws an important inference as well. Namely, the privacy a person enjoys in his own home is not "transferable" even to those who enjoy his hospitality. Thus, he must tithe whatever of his own produce he feeds them, but they need not tithe what they bring into his home.

If the Yerushalmi were composed largely of such glosses, it would be impossible to mount the argument of this paper, that the project of Rabbinic exegesis of the Mishnah is, in a profound sense, to displace the latter's authority. As it happens, Y. is not composed of glosses, but rather, of some 108 *sugyot* of varying length and complexity. These are not only much longer and conceptually more ambitious than the gloss, but normally pursue an exegetical program of a far different order. Y.'s editors construct their commentary by arranging a sequence of such *sugyot* for study with selected Mishnaic pericopae to create a series of running comments on the latter. It is in the context of this sequence of *sugyot*—a sequence rarely displaying any literary or substantive continuity within the series—that the Mishnah is mediated to its audience.

The conceptual traits of the *sugyot* in particular, and the cumulative impact of their redaction in series extending to as many as eight for any given pericope, offer impressive evidence that the goal of the Yerushalmi's commentary is not textual explication in any conventional sense. Quite to the contrary, the primary impact of these exegetical units is to draw attention *from* the specificity of the Mishnaic pre-text to which they are joined and *toward* the complex internal discussions established within and among the *sugyot* themselves. Both the conceptual traits of the *sugya*, therefore, and the method of its arrangement with atomized statements of the Mishnah, suggest that the editors' prime interest is not to explain the Mishnah *per se*, but rather to absorb it into the discourse of the *sugya*.

Consider, for example, the fundamental distinction which can be drawn among Y.'s *sugyot* on the basis of their literary and substantive relation to the Mishnaic pericope they serve. In a legal commentary of an explicative sort, one might expect most discussions to exhibit a close dependence upon the text or to engage matters emerging plainly from the latter's language or principles. In Yerushalmi Maaserot, however, units of discourse displaying clear dependence upon Mishnah Maaserot comprise less than two thirds of the tractate (sixty-four of 108 *sugyot,* or 59%). That is, a full 41% of Y.'s exegetical paragraphs (forty-four in all) *seem not originally to have been produced as comments to the Mishnaic pericopae of their present redaction.* These commonly bear one of three quite independent stances toward the Mishnaic materials they now serve. A given *sugya* can be (1) fully intelligible without reference to any particular pericope of M., (2) concerned with issues or principles addressed in passing or not at all in the latter, or (3) thoroughly unconcerned with the Mishnah from start to finish. While such *sugyot* are usually of thematic relevance to Mishnah Maaserot— dealing with agricultural or other issues emerging from the tractate—they have clearly been formulated in some context other than the exegesis of the pericopae with which they are now linked by the redactor.

In order to appreciate the *sugya's* capacity to reorient the reader's attention from the Mishnaic pre-text to itself, it is necessary to confront a rather typical, if unusually brief and simple, example. The present *sugya* is redacted with M. 2:3, a pericope which continues M. 2:2's interest in the role of surrogate homes in imposing liability to tithing upon untithed produce brought within them. Of interest now is the problem of a farmer who transports untithed goods to a distant market. Need he tithe produce brought into the homes of those from whom he accepts lodging along the way? The Mishnah reads:

A. *One who transports produce from Galilee to Judea . . . eats of [his untithed produce] until he reaches his destination. . . .*
B. *R. Meir says: [He eats untithed produce] until he reaches the place [where he intends to] spend the Sabbath.*

A's point is familiar from M. 2:2. We may even apply to it the reasoning of Y.'s gloss on the latter: the host's home renders his own produce liable to tithing, but not that of his guest. B, however, adds a complication. Meir seems to assume that a person who accepts Sabbath hospitality is more than a mere guest. Rather, he has the run of the house, and is in this sense analogous to the householder himself. Accordingly, since his Sabbath residence is a genuine surrogate for his own home, the traveller must tithe produce which he brings into it, even if this occurs prior to reaching his destination.

Without further comment, I invite the reader to a study of Y. 2:3's contribution to this ruling (Y. 2:3, ed. Venice, 49d):

1. Produce which was not picked for Sabbath use, yet which the Sabbath consecrated—R. Yohanan said: The advent of the Sabbath renders it forbidden for untithed consumption. R. Simeon, the son of Laqish said: The advent of the Sabbath does not render it forbidden for untithed consumption.

2. R. Simeon, the son of Laqish retorted: Have you in mind to claim that the advent of the Sabbath [in and of itself] is sufficient to render produce forbidden for untithed use? But have we not learned the following [at M. 2:3]: *One who transports produce, etc.?* And concerning this it is taught [elsewhere,]:[10] *[A traveller's produce remains exempt during his journey] even if he spent the night [in a private home along the way], and even if he established a Sabbath residence [prior to the journey's end].* [This authoritative amplification of the Mishnah clearly holds that a person intending to complete a journey need not worry that the fall of the Sabbath will impose liability upon his produce. Thus it is the Mishnaic view that human intention activates the Sabbath's power of consecration.]

3. [R. Yohanan] said: [My position is immune to your challenge, for you take no account of the fact that] at issue [for R. Meir in M. 2:3] is a case in which the traveller desires to establish a Sabbath residence [at a predetermined location]. You may be sure that matters are thus, for concerning this it is taught [in the Tosefta]: *Even if he established a Sabbath residence on the second day [of the week, he is required to tithe whatever he eats in that residence henceforward].*

4. [R. Yohanan continued:] Now is there such a thing as a Sabbath residence on the second day of the week? Rather, [the point is that the obligation to tithe is incurred] when he desires to establish a Sabbath residence [at this particular place]. Here, too, [in our dispute, I have ruled as I would] when he desires to establish a Sabbath residence [for now the residence is regarded as his home, and imposes liability to tithing, regardless of whether or not the Sabbath has fallen].

The first and most obvious point we observe about this discussion is that we cannot possibly regard it as formulated with the intention of serving as a commentary on M. 2:3. This is clear primarily because it is the dispute between Simeon and Yohanan (stich 1), rather than M. 2:3, which is the primary subject of exegesis. M. 2:3 is only adduced at stich 2 as evidence in support of Simeon's view regarding the role of human intentions in activating the consecrating power of the Sabbath. It is precisely this issue which Simeon, at stich 2, proposes that we find in M. 2:3. Our redactor, in turn, sees Simeon's exploitation of the Mishnah as sufficient grounds for appending the *sugya* as a whole to the Mishnah as its commentary.

It should be clear, however, that if this *sugya* is a commentary on anything, it is in fact a commentary on itself. Without entering too deeply into the technicalities of the Talmud's theory of the Sabbath, it is still possible to follow the course of the *sugya*'s self-explication. The discussion unfolds in a tri-partite structure, with stich 1, the opening dispute, setting the theoretical problem. Stichs 2 and 3, as a unit, provide evidence for each disputant, in both cases linking the disputed position to an authoritative pericope of Mishnaic exegesis ascribed to the Mishnaic Rabbis themselves. The discussion concludes at stich 4, which completes Yohanan's defense against the criticism opened up by Simeon at stich 2, and explains as well the grounds of the position Yohanan has been defending.

Yohanan appears to have won his debate with Simeon, but closer examination reveals that this is not the case. Rather, he has redefined the context of his original position so that, in effect, he holds a view quite unrelated to the primary dispute. In stich 4, Yohanan ignores his original view that the Sabbath's consecrating power functions independently of human intention. He merely states the obvious—the traveller is required to tithe his produce simply because he has brought it into a place analogous to his own home.

Our experience with Y. 2:3 can help us to generalize in a productive way about the bulk of the Yerushalmi's units of Mishnaic exegesis.[11] The reader of such a discussion, a series of which may comprise Y.'s entire contribution to the elucidation of a given pericope of the Mishnah, is required to perform at least two procedures of abstraction. First, the reader must puzzle out the meaning of the *sugya* on its own terms. This entails, as we have seen, filling in assumptions of principle and fact left unstated by the *sugya*, as well as paying close attention to the way in which the *sugya*'s internal elements illumine each other. Secondly, the reader must define the relationship of the *sugya* to the context created for it by its redaction with the present Mishnaic pre-text. In what way, that is, does a given *sugya* open up the meaning implicit in the Mishnah itself? Thus Mishnah and *sugya*, original pre-text and imposed context, are placed in an exegetical tension which can only be resolved by the ingenuity of the student. The problem is to construct the implied series of inferences or corpora of facts by which the *sugya* can be interpreted as a forum for the development of the Mishnah's ideas.

That our tractate continually requires the student to engage in these operations testifies to the fundamental assumption of its editors regarding the kind of knowledge deemed appropriate in understanding the Mishnah. That is, significant knowledge of the Mishnah is *not* mastery of the text itself (although this is certainly taken for granted), but rather mastery in articulating the manner of its interaction with other units of Rabbinic tradition beyond the confines of that text. Within this framework of priorities the *sugya* serves a dual function, as both *means* and *subject* of interpretation. Under the pretext of interpretation, the *sugya* interposes itself between the Mishnah and the student, requiring that the Mishnah be understood in terms generated by a discussion which, to begin with, is often formulated with no thought to the exegesis of that pericope. Indeed, the successful student's skill at creating the conceptual bridge between Mishnah and *sugya* obscures the disjuncture of pre-text and commentary, implicating Y.'s reader as well in the pretext of interpretation arranged by the commentary's editors. Like them, the reader sees all discrete statements of Oral Torah as part of a uniform structure of revelation, beginning at Sinai, continuing through the Sages of the Mishnah, and unfolding here and now in the statements of the Talmudic Masters.

Oral Torah and the Pretext of Passivity

The force of these observations regarding the exegetical functions of Y.'s units of discourse can now be summarized. Insofar as given Mishnaic rulings receive extensive attention in Y., this occurs primarily in order to incorporate these authoritative utterances into the context of the *sugya*'s own discourse. When a given pericope of the Mishnah, therefore, is assigned a series of such exegetical paragraphs for study in conjunction with it, the effect is to swallow the Mishnah up into whatever range of issues the editors themselves define as pressing.

Here, of course, we face the fundamental pretext of Rabbinic exegesis as represented in the Yerushalmi. Exegetical discourse, precisely because it presents itself as dependent upon the pre-text of the Mishnah, is able to shift attention from that pre-text to the new work created by the conjunction of the Mishnah and its commentary. Thus, the exegetical act, which draws attention to the Mishnah as an authoritative text—a text of revelation—is at the same time a means of extending the charisma of that revelation to the exegetical act itself. By legitimating, through the act of interpretation, the canonical authority of the Mishnah, the Yerushalmi's editors legitimate *themselves* as its definitive expositors and *their work* as its authoritative meaning. To conclude: the posture of submission to revelation is the very condition by which its authority is conveyed to the community of exegetes.

This last observation returns us to the starting point of this essay, the mythic role of the Oral Torah in Rabbinic Judaism. Not only do the Rabbinic exegetes of the Mishnah *receive* Oral Torah, and so participate in the charisma of revelation; they also *make* Oral Torah, and so mediate that charisma to their own community. The pretext of interpretation, therefore, which permits the Rabbinic group to perceive itself as the passive deposit of unchanging revelation, at the same time grants license to transform what is received. The Rabbinic understanding of Torah becomes itself a part of that Torah the Rabbi seeks to understand. As our Talmud itself would have it, in the words of the third-century Sage, Joshua b. Levi: "Even that which a seasoned scholar shall declare before his Master, that too has already been spoken to Moses at Sinai" (Y. Peah 2:6, 17a).

NOTES

1. The most recent and inclusive discussion of the origins of the idea of Oral Torah is that of P. Schäfer, "Das 'Dogma' von der mündlichen Torah im Rabbinischen Judentum," in *idem, Studien Zur Geschichte und Theologie Des Rabbinischen Judentums*, 153–197. Here Shâfer builds upon the pioneering work of Jacob Neusner (see *Ibid.*, 154 n. 6). For Neusner's most recent discussions, see J. Neusner, *Formative Judaism. Third Series*, 7–82. Both Neusner and Schäfer depart from earlier views, which locate the origins of the Oral Torah myth in the Second Temple period (ca. 200 B.C.E.). For a recent argument on behalf of this view, see E. Rivkin, *A Hidden Revolution*.

2. The sources from which this characterization is constructed are available in E. Urbach, *The Sages: Their Concepts and Beliefs*, I:286ff. Urbach's discussion conforms for the most part to the views generally held prior to the work of Neusner.

3. The Talmud Yerushalmi may be viewed as a prototype of the larger and more well-known Babylonian Talmud (ca. 600 C.E.). For thorough discussions of the Talmud Yerushalmi from the perspective of literary criticism and the history of religions, see respectively, J. Neusner, *The Talmud of the Land of Israel: Taxonomy* and *idem, Judaism in Society: The Evidence of the Yerushalmi*.

4. For a preliminary exploration of these issues, see M. Jaffee, "The Mishnah in

Talmudic Exegesis," in W. Green, ed., *Approaches to Ancient Judaism* 4 (1983):137–157 (hereafter, "Exegesis").

5. All translations are adapted from M. Jaffee, *The Talmud of the Land of Israel: Maaserot*. Documentation for the literary observations made in this essay appears in the notes to the Introduction of that work.

6. The extent to which the Yerushalmi's exegesis of the Mishnah exhibits traits similar to the Biblical exegesis of the contemporary Palestinian schools has recently been discussed in J. Neusner, *Midrash in Context*, 53–110.

7. This description of matters benefits from the recent essay of W. Green, "Reading the Writing of Rabbinism," in *Journal of the American Academy of Religion* LI/2 (1983):203.

8. The Tosefta, probably redacted in the fourth century, is a companion text to the Mishnah, containing supplementary laws and other materials transmitted in the names of Mishnaic Sages and conforming to the canons of Mishnaic literary style. Normally, each tractate of the Mishnah will have a corresponding tractate of Tosefta. All Toseftan passages cited in this essay are from Tosefta Maaserot.

9. For notable exceptions, see Jaffee, "Exegesis," 143–146.

10. This tradition appears neither in the Mishnah nor the Tosefta. In talmudic terminology, it is a *baraita*, an "external tradition," believed to stem from the Mishnaic Sages, but redacted in none of their extant collections. As such, it is accorded the status of Oral Torah along with statements compiled in the Mishnah and the Tosefta.

11. *Sugyot* formulated independently of the Mishnaic pre-text naturally present the most obvious evidence in support of my characterization of the exegetical procedures of the *sugya* in general. As I have argued, however (Jaffee, "Exegesis," 149–152), the same traits of self-referential discourse characterize at least one-third of those *sugyot* which clearly have been formulated in response to the Mishnaic passage of their present redaction. Thus, despite the many *sugyot* which are directly concerned with intensive Mishnaic exegesis, the Yerushalmi *as a work* remains remarkably unconcerned with the explication of its pre-text.

BIBLIOGRAPHY

Green, William Scott. "Reading the Writing of Rabbinism: Toward an Interpretation of Rabbinic Literature." *Journal of the American Academy of Religion* LI/2 (1983).

Jaffee, Martin S. "The Mishnah in Talmudic Exegesis: Observations on Tractate Maaserot of the Talmud Yerushalmi." *Approaches to Ancient Judaism*. Vol. 4, *Studies in Liturgy, Exegesis and Talmudic Narrative*. Ed. W.S. Green. Chicago, 1983.

———. *The Talmud of the Land of Israel*. vol. 12, *Maaserot*. Chicago, forthcoming.

Rabbinic Oral Torah and the Charisma of Revelation

Neusner, Jacob. *Formative Judaism: Religious, Historical and Literary Studies. Third Series. Torah, Pharisees and Rabbis.* Chico, CA, 1983.

————. *Judaism in Society: The Evidence of the Yerushalmi. Toward the Natural History of a Religion.* Chicago, 1983.

————. *Midrash in Context: Exegesis in Formative Judaism.* Philadelphia, 1983.

————. *The Talmud of the Land of Israel.* vol. 35, *Taxonomy.* Chicago, 1983.

Rivkin, Ellis. *A Hidden Revolution: The Pharisees' Search for the Kingdom Within.* Nashville, 1978.

Schäfer, Peter. "Das 'Dogma' von der Mündlichen Torah im Rabbinischen Judentum" in *idem, Studien Zur Geschichte und Theologie Des Rabbinischen Judentums.* Leiden, 1978.

Urbach, Ephraim Elimelech. *The Sages: Their Concepts and Beliefs.* 2d ed., enl. Trans. I. Abrahams. Jerusalem, 1979.

Culture and Language in the God Talk

GILBERT E. M. OGUTU

> When we speak about God, we have to use words which apply in the first instance to finite things and people that exist in space and time. But God is not an object in space and time.[1]

The pre-Christian way of life of the Luo of Kenya was made manifest by such cultural norms as were regarded as requisites for the preservation of the cohesion of the society: the clans and the families which constituted it. The depth of their religious life was marked by a series of rites and ceremonies which remain deeply entrenched in their way of life, and which they also believe to be protected by their ancestors. Although the immediate orientation of their religious practices seems to center on the veneration of the ancestors, the Luo traditional social norms and values are believed to have been given to the ancestors by some supreme being whom they refer to as Nya-saye. An examination of their religious beliefs and practices should lead us to an understanding of their claim that to them Nya-saye is no fiction, and that any doubt of the existence of Nya-saye was absurd, notwithstanding such assertions as that Nya-saye was ultimately responsible for the entire universe, maker of all things, primary and initial condition of all things, and that Nya-saye is constantly involved in their continuation. Further claims are made that Nya-saye was not unconscious but knowing. Nothing that was knowable could remain outside of his divine awareness, nor was Nya-saye aimless but exercised will. His making and sustaining of the universe was not an automatic outpouring of his power of being but a considered act performed out of conscious preference. In brief, the Luo conception of Nya-saye was that of *Jachwech* (molder), *Nyakalaga* (the one found everywhere), and *Jarit* (protector or sustainer). In spite of these, their idea of Nya-saye still rests within the meaning they attached to the word *Nya-saye* itself.

In this paper we look at the familiar secular words that the Luo have employed to convey the theological message, and which words cannot, to our mind, be adequate when they are applied to God. We intend not only to find out what the descriptive terms bear when they are applied to God, but also to try to grasp the basic functions of the words and their symbolic meanings in the religious context. It is perhaps apt to begin by identifying the Luo and their neighbors and then proceed to analyzing the term Nya-saye which we have chosen to break into the prefix *Nya-* and the root verb *-saye.*

The Luo are a Nilotic-speaking people living in the western part of Kenya.[2] They are the second largest ethnic community in the country. In western Kenya their neighbors include the Bantu-speaking Luyia and the Kalenjin, the Gusii, the Maasai and the Kuria. They surround the Kenyan portion of Lake Victoria where they spill into Uganda and northern Tanzania. They were among the very first people to be introduced to Christianity by the European and American Christian missionaries at the wake of the present century. At the time of writing, they are reckoned to be 90 percent Christian.

As far as religious ideas are concerned, the Luo seem to have had more interaction with the Luyia than with their other neighbors. Both the Luo and Luyia believe in a Supreme Being whom they call Nya-saye and whose power is manifested in the sun. Both communities prayed to God by spitting at the rising and setting sun, asking the sun to rise well so that peace may abound in the day and that any misfortune should set with it in the west. To both communities, every notable feature of the world about them, every mountain or river, or big tree, every striking event or influences which affected their lives such as storms or disease, every difficulty or trouble that they encountered received some religious explanation centering on God. With that background let us go back to our term Nya-saye.

The Lyuia people, on the one hand, have a verb *okhusaya* which means to worship, to adore, to request kindly, to bow down to, to implore and so forth.[3] The Luo, on the other hand, have the verb *sayo* which means practically the same things as the Luyia verb. *Okhu-* is a common prefix to most Luyia verbs, hence we find such expressions as *okhukasia* (to prepare), *okhulima* (to till the land), and *okhusaya* (to worship) and so forth. The Luo do not have a prefix for *to,* and so we find *loso* (to prepare), *pur* (to till the land) and *sayo* (to worship) and so forth. If we were to leave out the Luyia prefix *okhu* we would remain with the verb *saya* for the Luyia and *sayo* for the Luo. However, when it comes to addressing oneself to the third person the Luyia will say *omusaye* (you adore him) where the Luo say *saye* (you adore him). Removing the prefix *omu* from the Luyia verb makes nonsense of the root word. Otherwise, were it possible to remove it we would remain with the clause *saye* for both the Luyia and the Luo.

A detachable prefix *nya-* does not exist in the Luyia language. In the Luo language the prefix *nya* gives special weight in meaning to the root word, with a strong sense of sacredness. Let us explain this with reference to the clan which is the hub of the interfamilial relationships in the Luo society where one clan is distinguished from the other by a sacred name known as *nono*.

Among the Luo, a family is referred to by the name of their grandmother; for example, Kapiyo, Kaduol, Kadongo which refer to the grandchildren of Apiyo, Aduol and Adongo respectively. But the clan, in most cases, takes the name of the grandfather who must have lived some generations back. They consequently have, for example, Kadimo, Kanyamuot, Kager and Karuoth, meaning grandchildren of Dimo, Muot, Ger and Ruoth. What then are the *nono* of these clans? This is where the Luo applied the prefix *nya-*; so that we find Nya-Dimo, Nya-Muot, Ny-Ger and Nya-Ruoth as the sacred names *(nono)* of the clans imbued with the strong feeling of blood relatedness. Could we get the same weight in meaning when the prefix is applied to a verb? Let us go back to the clause *saye,* and recall that the Luo had no proper name for the Supreme Being to whom they referred politely as Nya-saye (the adored one). How would they have come to that title?

Proper names are used very sparingly among the Luo. To call an elderly person or a person from whom one expected assistance by his proper name signified disregard and was a sign of rudeness. The moment one did that one's needs were never met. How then could the Luo address themselves to the being who protected and sustained them? This is where they could have drawn analogy from their familial relationships and therefore referred to him politely as Nya-saye (the adored one) as a more polite way of referring to him just as they refer to women married from *loka* (overseas) as *nya-loka*.[4] Because of his universal nature and having no known progenitor, the supreme being's *nono* could not have a proper noun as its root but a familiar secular verb indicating his relationship with the people and the world. The thesis I am postulating is that the term Nya-saye is more of *nono* to the supreme being denoting how he relates to man.

At another level the Luo speak of *Nyasache ber* (he is lucky); *Nyasach dhako* (the uterus of a woman); *ok in nyasacha* (you have no power over my success or failure). *Nyasach,* as used in these factual statements, further explain the Luo doctrine of Nya-saye whom they believe molds people in the wombs of their mothers, blesses them and takes care of their daily needs.[5]

There are many other terms which the Luo employ to describe Nya-saye. We shall put the terms or images into situations and then figure out what they portray of the Luo understanding of the nature of Nya-saye. We shall call each category a model, as follows:

Familial Model	*Wuonwa* (our father), *Wuon kwere* (father of the ancestors), *wuon ji* (father of all people) and *wuon ogendini* (father of all races).
Charismatic Model	*Ruodh ruodhi* (king of kings), *Janen* (seer), *Rahuma* (the famous one), *Hono* (the incomprehensible), *Ratego* (the powerful one), *Piny kinyal* (the unconquerable one), *Jalweny* (the great warrior).
Temperamental Model	*Were* (the blameless one), *Jahera* (the loving one), *Jang'wono* (the kind one), and *Jamrima* (the one with temper).
Spatial Model	*Hagawa* (all embracing one), *Nyakalaga* (the one found everywhere).
Pigmental Model	*Dibo* or *Rachar* (the white one), *Rapenda* (the brown and red one).[6]

Here then are words that are commonly used in the secular situations of family, charisma, temperament, space and color being employed theologically to refer to Nya-saye. What do the words tell us about the Luo understanding of Nya-saye?

First, the Luo society is a patrilineal society with inheritance passing from the father to the son, and, through the fathers, the related families were bound together by their *nono* which had its origins in the progenitor of the clan. This was the ancestor to be appealed to whenever everything else had failed. Beyond him there was only Nya-saye. But the Luo were fully aware that beyond their clans there were other people *(ji)* and other races *(ogendini)*. The fatherhood that embraced all these people was the fatherhood of Nya-saye, whom they analogously called *wuonwa, wuon kwere, wuon ji,* and *wuon ogendini.* Thus, Nya-saye was conceived as the great father and guardian of all people. But this was not a biological fatherhood, for the Luo never talked of Nya-saye having a wife.

Secondly, the Luo saw charismatic power in their leaders who include *okebe* (rich men), *jobilo* (profits and diviners), *thuond lweny* (great warriors), *ogaye* (war mediators), and *ruodh oganda* (clan head). These were people who commanded respect for what they were and whose words were taken very seriously by the whole community. They were dependable people to whom Nya-saye had given unique power and ability. By analogy therefore, the Luo referred to Nya-saye as *Ruodh ruodhi, Janen, Rahuma, Hono, Piny kinyal* and *Jalweny.*

Thirdly, for one to be considered a successful guardian or leader among the Luo, one had to be blameless *(were)*, loving *(jahera)*, kind *(jang'wono)*, and in the event of a violation of the traditional customs *(timbe)* or disregard for the social interdictions *(kweche)* that would lead to divine punishment *(chira)*,[7] such guardian or leader was prone to be angry *(jamrima)*. Such cosmic characteristics the Luo attributed to Nya-saye whom they called *Were, Jahera, Jang'wono,* and *Jamrima.*

Fourthly, the Luo claim to have been always in the presence of Nya-saye (although it is not clear when they started using the term) who embraced every aspect of life *(hagawa)*, and who was with them wherever they were *(Nyakalaga)*. And so the Luo conceived of Nya-saye in space *(Nyakalaga)* and in time *(wuon kwere)* implying existence from time immemorial.

Finally, although the Luo traditions are silent on what Nya-saye looks like they attributed certain colors to him. They called him *Rachar* or *Dibo* (the white one), a color that symbolized purity or peace. They also called him *Rapenda* which is indicative of productivity.

The Luo, it needs to be emphasized, came into contact with different peoples in the course of their history of migrations and settlement in western Kenya.[8] I would therefore wish to recall the old dictum that, when people who possess different cultures meet and live together for some time, it is unlikely that the cultures they possess, after their contact, shall ever be the same again. Experience has it that in such a situation there will be some borrowing going on all the time, the end product of which, though it might be dominated by one of the cultures, is certainly a sequence of the contribution of all of them. The same applies to the religious language of a people, more so, the deeper meaning of some theological assertions and claims they make.

From the foregoing illustrations, it is now clear that the Luo conception of Nya-saye is anthropomorphic. He is father. The father in the patrilineal Luo society is the head of the homestead and the family. All the problems are directed to him for solution. While the father is believed to protect and care for the family, he never leaves unpunished any misbehavior and disregard for the customs of the community. In the same way the Luo believed that Nya-saye molded them in their mother's wombs, protected them against the hazards of life, but also punished them whenever they violated the ethical norms and values. Thus the Luo believed that Nya-saye determined their fate in the present life by bringing them rain or drought, plenty or famine, health or disease, peace or war. He is both good and bad.

The Luo cannot comprehend Nya-saye. However, they maintained that Nya-saye was aware and knowledgeable. When a man in a position of power, either because he was rich or because he was a leader, despised those under him, the oppressed advanced such falsifiable hypotheses like *bende norum* (that will also come to an end), *Nya-saye nonene* (Nya-saye will attend to that), or *Piny kinyal* (the world cannot be conquered). By these assertions they meant that Nya-saye who blesses would not only withdraw the blessing if it is misused but would also punish those who misuse his blessing. In most cases such empirical hypotheses are rarely falsified, thus concretizing the efficacious nature of Nya-saye whose abode is vaguely defined as the sky and who is believed to be both near and far.

The Luo also associated Nya-saye with natural objects and phenomena and referred to Nya-saye by the language commonly applied to such objects and phenomena. The most common among these is the sun *(chieng')* as meaning brightness. In the sun the Luo saw great power beyond which there must exist a power generating being. Thus they called the sun *wang' chieng'* (the eye of brightness). Nya-saye is also called *chieng'*. It would not be out of place to refer to the sun as the eye of Nya-saye. To them the sun was the most powerful single object of awe. While to the desert dweller it symbolized death, to the Luo it symbolized life and protection, thus being the most fascinating image of Nya-saye. They believed that Nya-saye saw them through the sun. Because of its power and influence in everyday human activities, the rising sun did not only remind the Luo of a new day but also of the presence of Nya-saye. And so they directed their morning prayers to the sun saying "rise well that peace, health and good luck may abound this day." The heads of the families whose duty it was to offer such prayers woke up very early every morning, walked about their homesteads until the sun came above the horizon and then said their prayers which were accompanied by simple rituals like spitting at the rising sun. As the sun went down in the evening, they repeated the ritual, asking for blessing and peace in the night, and appealing that any possible misfortune should set with the sun in the west. That the sun set in the west and rose in the east, the following morning, was yet another puzzle to the Luo. Their conviction was that the sun flashed across the sky in the night and that only some very lucky individuals saw it flash past, and also that such lucky people would be blessed with dung, ropes, and seeds. What these mean is that the lucky individual would keep large herds of cattle, goats, sheep and have many children with enough food to feed them.

I would like to reiterate at this point that although the Luo addressed themselves to the sun in the morning and in the evening, they did not regard the sun as Nya-saye per se, nor, in the least, as a replica of Nya-saye.

If Nya-saye means the worshipped one, could the moon be Nya-saye? It is common to find the Luo offering prayers to the new moon at the first sight. The elderly men spat at the new moon and said *aneni maber mondo ayud ogogo moro* (let me see you with luck so that I may come across a divorcee). The young men said *aneni maber mondo apor gi nyako moro* (let me see you with luck so that I may find a woman to marry). The girls said *aneni maber mondo onyuoma* (let me see you well so that I may be married).[9] These prayers were spontaneous and involved the simple ritual of spitting at the new moon. The prayers, the Luo maintain, were not directed to the moon as such but to Nya-saye through the moon. In other words, the moon was not in itself Nya-saye. Stars, mountains and certain species of fauna and flora also featured very prominently in the Luo religious language. It is in the light of this that we consider the Luo attitude to the celestial objects and phenomena as being reflective of the Luo perception of awe in such objects. The wild animals were not out either. Whenever wild animals and snakes visited the homesteads, peacefully, they were never harrassed but left to leave at their pleasure. Often they were given food to eat, whatever they naturally eat. The belief being that such rare visitors could have been sent by Nya-saye to bring some luck. But are these celestial and terrestrial objects any less Nya-saye (the worshipped one) than the incomprehensible and remote divine being? What effect, then, does language as a medium have on our knowledge of God?

The language spoken by a people is closely tied to the people's culture and historical experience. The Luo of Kenya had been on the move for centuries before they finally settled in their present homeland. They are sometimes referred to as River-lake Nilotes because they are both fishermen and pastoralists. Their understanding of God is rooted in their culture and language as well as in their experience in history. What happened when the missionaries came to propagate Christian religious ideas?

The late Okot p'Bitek, in his book *African Religions in Western Scholarship*,[10] has blamed the missionaries for having imposed the Christian God on the Africans. Basing his claim on the religious language of the Luo who live in Uganda (also known as the Central Luo), he argued that the missionaries and African theologians "are busy introducing Greek metaphysical conceptions into African religious thought. Attributes of the Christian God are . . . beyond recognition to the ordinary African in the countryside."

When the missionaries arrived among the Luo of western Kenya, their primary task was to translate the Bible into the Luo language. In the process, the Luo term Nya-saye was employed as translation for the Anglo-Saxon term God. Do they mean the same thing? Let us see.

In the Luo Bible, John 1:1 reads as follows: "Kar chakruok wach ne nitie. Wach bende ne kod Nyasaye. Wach bende ne en Nyasaye Mano ne nitie kar chakruok ka Nyasaye." Literally translated, the reading goes like this: "At the beginning the word was there. The word was also Nyasaye. That was there at the beginning at the place (home?) of Nyasaye."

There are two key words in the verse above: word rendered as *wach* and God rendered as *Nyasaye*. In the Luo language *wach* means several things. It means, for example, speech, argument, debate, or discussion. The preliterate Luo society thought in terms of names and expressions, not the individual words. To them *wach* could not be a translation for word. It could only mean words.

Be that as it may, to claim that *wach bende ne en Nyasaye* is beyond anybody's comprehension if it is not absurd. I am a Luo, a Christian, and between 1970 and 1972, I participated in the revision of the Luo Bible. But I am still tempted to agree with the late Evans-Pritchard[11] when he lamented that, "Missionaries have battled hard and with great sincerity to overcome these difficulties, but, in my experience much of what they teach the natives is quite unintelligible to those among whom they labor." The missionaries are no longer in command as the church leadership has largely been Africanized in Kenya. Is the situation any different? What of the Bible as it is now?

We have already referred to the social norms and values that held the Luo society together. We have recalled the divine punishment *(chira)* which came as a result of the violation of the revered social interdictions. According to the Luo, the ancestors, who were the intermediaries between men and God, were happy when the norms and values were adhered to. Everything went bad when the contrary was the case. The helping hand of Nya-saye was sought when the relational arrangements had been violated. Whenever the rules were adhered to, to the letter, and everything was going well, libations were poured to the ancestors and Nya-saye was thanked. In other words, to understand the Luo concept Nya-saye, and how the people related to the supreme being, one has to understand their culture[12] and what certain expressions mean in the light of the people's experience in time and space. Otherwise the words do not convey much.

I would like to conclude by emphasizing the fact that the culture of a people and their language determine what the people conceive God to be, and that the words a people employ in their theological assertions about God are neither univocal nor are they equivocal. We have to diagnose the people's analogy and symbolic expressions to make sense of what they mean. Language outside of the cultural milieu can be deceptive, although it remains the only way we express our estimation of God.

NOTES

1. Colin Brown, *Philosophy and the Christian Faith* (Illinois: Inter Varsity Press, 1968), 176.

2. The Luo group of people have been grouped into Northern, Central, and Southern Luo. The northern group are found mostly in Sudan and Ethiopia. The central group are in Uganda; while the Southern Luo are found in Uganda, Kenya and northern Tanzania. Our paper is based on the southern group.

3. It is important to bring in the Luyia because they use the same term with the

Culture and Language in the God Talk

Luo. At the same time they share a lot of cultural traits because of the inter-marriage that has been going on between them for a long time.

4. *Nya-* also means daughter of, and is sometimes rendered as *nyar.*

5. B. A. Ogot, "Concept of Jok," *African Studies,* 20, 1961.

6. The models are discussed in detail by the author in his M.A. dissertation entitled "An historical analysis of the Luo idea of God."

7. T. Abe, "The concepts of Chira and Dhoch among the Luo—transition, deviation and misfortune" in *Themes in Socio-Cultural Ideas and Behavior Among Six Ethnic Groups in Kenya,* ed. N. Nobuhiro, (Tokyo: Hitotsubashi University Press, 1981).

8. B. A. Ogot, *History of the Southern Luo* (Nairobi: East African Publishing House, 1967).

9. The association of the moon with marriage and the family is beyond the scope of the present paper but it is noteworthy.

10. Okot p'Bitek, *African Religions in Western Scholarship* (Nairobi: East African Literature Bureau, 1970).

11. E. E. Evans-Pritchard, *Theories of Primitive Religion* (Oxford University Press, 1965), 14.

12. A. B. C. Ocholla-Ayayo, *The Luo Culture* (Wiesbaden: Franz Steiner Verlag, 1980).

7

God and Authority

SHLOMO BIDERMAN

I

One of the classical problems concerning God-talk is often formulated in terms of the connection existing between the will of God on the one hand and the existence of autonomous moral rules on the other hand. The problem is by no means new with us; it was lucidly introduced by Plato in *Euthyphro;* namely, are the moral rules dependent on the will of God or does God will only what is good?[1] In other words, if we take some actions to be obligatory, does God command them because they are morally obligatory, or is their obligatory status totally anchored in God as an unlimited supreme commander?

The problem in *Euthyphro* is usually taken to present the difficulty stemming from any attempt at reconciling religion and morality. Religion and morality seem to be diametrically opposed to each other. If you adopt the religious standpoint, you must view God as logically independent of his commands, thus seeing what God wills as right. But if you adopt the ethical standpoint, you naturally see the moral rules as independent of the will of God, thus accepting God's commands if and only if they strictly follow the autonomous moral rules. The problem in *Euthyphro* can thus be presented as a dilemma posed to the religious believer. To use Bernard Williams' formulation of the dilemma: "[E]ither one's motives for following the moral word of God are moral motives, or they are not. If they are, then one is already equipped with moral motivations, and the introduction of God adds nothing extra. But if they are not moral motives, then they will be motives of such a kind that they cannot appropriately motivate morality at all."[2]

The difficulty of the relation of religion and morality can be solved in several ways. It can be claimed that, since God is omniscient, his will cannot be limited or bound to rules that exist independently of God's will. Such a view was presented by Wittgenstein, who argued that the claim 'Good is what God orders' is deeper than the view claiming that 'God wills Good because it is Good' (characterized by him as a "superficial, rationalistic" view).[3] I shall not dwell on the question whether the term 'fideism' is appropriate for such a view; suffice it to say that at first glance this view can be regarded as presenting the standpoint of the naive believer of a monotheistic religion. Another way of dealing with the relation of morality and religion consists of attempting to reconcile the two, in one way or another. Swinburne, for example, tries to bridge the gap between moral rules and divine commands by offering a distinction between actions which are contingently obligatory (which should be regarded as good and obligatory just because God wills them) and actions which are necessarily obligatory (which God wills because they are good).[4] It can, however, be argued that any attempt to reconcile religion and morality is doomed to failure; either you accept divine laws as obligatory, thus rejecting the claim for an autonomous moral law, or you choose to act according to the moral code, hence refusing to see any divine command as obligatory. This consideration leads us to a third way of solving the problem in *Euthyphro*. It can be claimed that man is an autonomous moral agent and as such cannot worship God or blindly obey his commands without abandoning his role as an autonomous moral agent. Hence belief in God is morally harmful and as such should be abandoned. Rachels, one of the advocates of such a view, maintains that the acceptance of moral rules as autonomous is sufficient not only for rejecting divine commands but also for disproving God's existence. According to him, "(a) If any being is God, he must be a fitting object of worship; (b) No being could possibly be a fitting object of worship, since worship requires the abandonment of one's role as an autonomous moral agent; (c) therefore, there cannot be any being who is God."[5]

These standpoints offer three different solutions to the problem of the relation between religion and morality, but they nevertheless share a more or less definite picture of monotheistic religion and can be presented as based on two tacit assumptions concerning the status of God within religion. First, God is assumed to exist. His existence is not contingent but rather necessary, and as such he is regarded as omnipotent, omniscient, and perfectly benevolent. Secondly, God's existence entails, in monotheistic religions, the existence of his will. The will of God can be, and often is, manifested in history. Believers are required to follow the will of God and strictly obey his commands.

If we view the *Euthyphro* problem in light of these two assumptions, we can easily see that the problem is raised only when we are committed to accept these assumptions together. That is, the apparent conflict between religion and morality will be present only if religion is based on the conjunction of the two assumptions and sees God's will and commands as dominant factors in the life of every member of the community of believers. The 'word' of God is seen as possessing absolute authority. It seems therefore that 'authority' is one of the necessary constituents of the very existence of a meaningful religious language (at least in monotheistic religions). Consequently, it will be appropriate to look for some clarification of the nature of a religious system of divine commands and to offer an analysis of the role played by the concept of authority within the language of such a system. My aim at this analysis is to take a few initial steps towards an analysis of the notion of religious authority. The notion of authority is often covered by thick theological clouds. My approach however will be 'minimalistic'. I shall not review the development of the notion of authority in monotheistic religions, nor shall I dwell upon any theological claim regarding the authority of God. Instead I shall concentrate mainly on the uses of authority-claims in religious language. I shall argue that seeing God as the authority of a monotheistic religion does not necessarily involve the acceptance of specific ontological statements concerning his existence or specific theological doctrines concerning God's nature.

II

Divine commands can have different fields of application. In several religions (such as Judaism or the ancient Hindu Mimamsa school) religious imperatives are meant to direct daily and continuously each facet of the believer's behavior on earth; religious precepts impose social and ritualistic duties as well as they prohibit different kinds of activity. Other religions regard religious imperatives as meant to regulate human spirit, and are thus related to the mental sphere of life rather than to the practical one, and to the future dimension of possible salvation rather than to the present dimension of activity on earth. In any case, the notion of religious duty plays an essential key role in monotheistic religions.

The status of God as the absolute authority behind the religious commands seems necessary not only from the religious viewpoint but also from that of the logic of commands. It has been claimed that a command has to be grounded on some authority on the part of its source.[6] Moreover, the existence of an authoritative source of a command is an essential component in attributing to verbal utterances the status of a command. As Searle points out, the difference between "request" on the one hand and "order" and "command" on the other hand is that in the latter cases there is a preparatory rule that the commander must be in a position of authority over the commandee.[7] The grammatical criterion of the imperativeness of an expression has indeed been abandoned thereby. That is to say, if you determine the illocutionary force of a sentence or utterance according to its source, you must take into account not only grammatical or semantical properties of the sentence or utterance, but also certain features of its context of utterance. Within the monotheistic context, then, a sentence will be regarded as expressed in order to issue a command only when it is ascribed to God or said on his authority. Similarly, recognition of God as authority entails the belief in the right of God to issue commands. As Carter rightly points out, "the notion of entitlement to authority is built into our everyday usage of the term."[8] To summarize, God is the source of religious commands as well as being the chief guarantor of the validity of the commands.

At first glance it may seem that submission to authority is irrational, thus standing in contradistinction with any genuine moral choice. The acceptance of a system of rules which has a divine Being as its supreme authority looks incompatible with the notion of the autonomy of morality. Or is it? It seems to me that the apparent contrast between religion and morality is, at least partly, due to some misunderstandings of the meaning and uses of the term "authority." I shall therefore offer a short conceptual clarification of the term "authority" and its uses, and then suggest a possible way of reducing the apparent tension between "authority" and "autonomy."

III

"Authority," says Peters, "is a word that has an aura about it, a mystique. And there are some who like to keep it that way."[9] Surely, Hobbes is not among them, since he provides a clear definition of authority: "the right of doing any action is called authority, so that by authority is always understood a right of doing any act: and *done by authority,* done by commission, or licence from him whose right it is."[10]

Following Hobbes we can immediately reject any attempt at defining authority in naturalistic terms. Authority is one of the characteristics of social institutions; only within such a framework we can meaningfully talk of the right of X to command Y to do something, and the duty of Y to obey X's command by doing what he is required to do or by refraining from doing what is forbidden. In some social institutions the right to command and the duty to obey will be explicitly conferred by the rules governing the institution. In other social circumstances authority might be determined much less clearly and much more implicitly. In any case, however, authority must be regarded as a social, or, to use Hobbes' terminology, an artificial phenomenon.

In his well-known analysis of the concept of authority Max Weber states three different sorts of authority, marked by their different sources of legitimacy:

1. Authority based on rational grounds, "resting on a belief in the 'legality' of patterns of normative rules and the right of those elevated to authority under such rules to issue commands (legal authority)."

2. Authority based on traditional grounds, "resting on an established belief in the sanctity of immemorial traditions and the legitimacy of the status of those exercising authority under them (traditional authority)."

3. Authority based on psychological grounds, "resting on the devotion to the specific and exceptional sanctity, heroism or exemplary character of an individual person, and of the normative patterns or order revealed or ordained by him (charismatic authority)."[11]

I shall not dwell upon the differences suggested by Weber between authority based on laws and authority based on tradition,[12] but if we adopt the characterization of authority which I have offered above, seeing it as presupposing social institution which is governed by rules and norms (whether explicitly or implicitly), it is clear that the relation between a commander and a commandee based on purely psychological factors must be precluded from any analysis of the concept of authority. If the notion of authority involves the existence of social institution, it is a misunderstanding to use the term "authority" as an explanatory term of personal relations between members of a given community. Moreover, if "charismatic authority" is to be taken as explaining human behavior, seeing it as stemming from some inner need to command and obey, then the use of the term, "authority," becomes practically vacuous, since it can explain any and every pattern of behavior. Psychological factors may indeed serve as *causes* of some pattern of behavior but they cannot be seen as *grounds* of legitimacy of authority, and the notion of charisma cannot stand apart from the rules governing ways of behavior which are obligatory, forbidden, or permitted within a certain social institution. As Carter rightly argues, "charisma is much more akin to the hypnotic influence of a magician than it is to the ability to evoke a sober and reasoned acceptance of the authoritativeness of a command."[13] More generally, authority cannot be described in terms of some kind of influence, physical or mental, of one will upon another. To quote Winch, authority "is not a kind of *causal* relation between individual wills but an *internal* relation." By calling the relation internal, Winch rightly emphasizes the conceptual (rather than contingent) connection between rule-governed activities and authority.[14]

Since authority operates within a social context, it cannot be defined in terms of power or use of force, even though the power of authority is, as a matter of fact, sometimes exercised by imposing force on the members of the community. This point was well stressed by Arendt's account of political authority. The fact that authority is connected with obedience, so she argues, led to the commonly mistaken view according to which authority is some sort of power or violence, "yet authority precludes the use of external means of coercion; while force is used, authority itself has failed."[15] Prior to any use of force, there must be some free and voluntary decision, taken by the majority of members of the social institution, to accept authority. The existence of authority is thus dependent on the co-operation of the members of the community. As Hart puts it, "the coercive power of law presupposes its accepted authority."[16] Or, to quote Winch again, "to follow an authority is a voluntary act. Authority ends where voluntary assent ends."[17]

Notice that the characterization of authority as involving a voluntary act of assent does not preclude the existence of a system of rules which will issue sanctions in order to exhibit its authority.[18] The relationship between authority and sanction is intricate and for reasons of space will not be discussed here. Suffice it to say that even if the existence of sanctions is seen as directly connected with the existence of authority, it does not necessarily follow that authority must be based on coercion. Sanctions in general, and religious sanctions in particular, involve the performance of an act, A, (or an omission) that the authority regards as a violation of prevailing laws or norms. The authority thus performs an act, B, that it regards as harmful to the person who carried out act A. Act B is presented as sanction or punishment. Issuing a sanction by an authority is thus tantamount to manifesting its will to harm the offender. The interpretation of "harm" depends, in turn, on the point of view of the authority, in our case religion. What religious laws may consider harmful to the offender does not have to be a natural harm, that is to say, need not be something (such as using force against the offender) that most people would regard as harmful.

So far I have drawn several characteristics of the concept of authority and its use in social contexts, which can be briefly stated as follows:

1. Authority is an internal concept of society. That is, the existence of social institutions governed by rules is presupposed by it.

2. Authority cannot be reduced to the psychological level of charisma, influence, and the like.

3. Authority cannot be understood in terms of coercion or force.

Turning now to religious authority, or, to put it more specifically, to God as a divine commander, we can see that the analysis of authority offered above can be easily applied to religion. To start with, the notion of religious authority is meaningful only within the social context of institutional religion. It does not stem from some personal relation between an individual and some divine entity. That is to say, religious authority cannot be conceived of as issuing personal commands. As I have argued elsewhere, the command given to Abraham to sacrifice his son Isaac cannot serve as a model of the institutional system of religious commands. For the system of religious commands to keep its vitality, its authority has to put forward general regulations which are impersonal in nature. In this respect the system of divine commands is on a par with legal systems. For this reason, religious authority cannot be reduced to the needs, feelings, and other psychological traits of the individual. Furthermore, religious authority cannot be explained as enforcing itself on the believer by means of exercising power, threats, and the like. If we were right in assuming that authority in general must be based on a voluntary assent of the majority of members of the community, it is all the more true as far as religious authority is concerned. In contradistinction with systems of legal injunctions, most religions include not only commands that refer to the public domain of behavior, but also commands that may refer to the most private areas of human life, even ones which have no outward manifestations. Thoughts and acts whose existence is known only to the agent can be, and often are, included within the realm of religious commandments. Since religion deals with the inward as well as with the outward realms, it would be meaningless to base its authority on the possibility of exercising external force.

IV

How can the analysis of the notion of authority help us in discoloring the apparent contrast between autonomous moral rules and divine commands which seem to rest on divine, absolute authority? The contrast, let us recall, is presented in terms of a possible contradiction between the statement that 'God wills what is morally good' and the statement that 'what God wills is morally good'. Hence the dilemma: either you accept the first horn, thus reducing God's status as a supreme being, or you accept the second horn, thus presenting religious commands as, in principle, inconsistent with moral rules. It seems to me that this dilemma evolves out of a prevailing conception which sees religious authority as identical with a specific *content*, thus adopting a mistaken view concerning the nature and character of religious authority.

It is customary among some theologians and philosophers to view monotheistic religious authority, and the scriptures as its main manifestation, as having a specific content, often referred to in terms such as 'revelation', 'the Word of God', and the like. Thus theologians often hold that the authoritative element of the scriptures lies in their content. Moreover, in trying to justify man's submission to divine authority they point to some facts that are taken as granting the status of authority to the holy writ. Presenting the notion of 'authority' as content may sound evasive to the philosopher's ear. Take, for example, the view according to which authority of God (as manifested in the scriptures) is absolute and infallible because of some *intrinsic* properties it possesses. Such a view tries to secure by all means the infallibility of the content of God's will, even by ascribing to his word the mysterious, not to say magical, quality of self-validation. In an effort to avoid the logical pitfall of self-reference it has been claimed that religious authority can be factually justified without ascribing some intrinsic property to the scriptures. The holy writ can be seen as serving as a witness to some past events in which the will of God was most significantly, and sometimes even dramatically, manifested.[19] I shall not indulge here on this theological viewpoint. Suffice it to say that such a view takes the notion of religious authority to be dependent on the truth of its content. In other words, to utter an authority-claim is tantamount to making a statement of fact. Hence a sentence in the form of 'God's will was proclaimed on Mount Sinai' is to be interpreted as establishing religious authority by pointing at it in a rather factual and direct manner, even though it cannot be validated or refuted in the standard ways by which we normally treat factual statements.

In the same vein there are some philosophers who vehemently oppose any theory of religious language which claims religious expressions are not meant to be strictly assertoric. They attack mainly the attempt, made by Wittgensteinian philosophers of religion, to present religious expressions as embedded within a particular language game which is played according to its own rules and for its own purposes. Against the Wittgensteinian approach they argue that the language-game theory does not take religion at its face value, thus committing the all-too-common philosophical sin, that of disregarding the obvious. As Walsh claims, religious belief presupposes certain facts, the falsity of which would render it invalid: "unless God really exists religious language does not make proper sense."[20] According to Walsh and others, it seems that religious claims should be understood as having a specific cognitive content. Consequently, the study of religious language seems hardly relevant to the study of religion, and the attempts at grounding the understanding of religion mainly on the study of the meaning of religious discourse results in a distorted presentation of the religious phenomenon.

Regarding authority-claims to be peculiar kind of assertoric statements may seem a possible answer to the need to justify any submission to religious authority. It seems to me, however, that the problem of the meaning of religious language is still with us, in spite of the attempts mentioned at rendering it obsolete. In fact, the factual attitude towards authority encounters a cluster of problems in regard to the meaning and uses of cognitive statements in religion. These problems are well-known and need not be elaborated here. As far as the clarification of the notion of authority is concerned, suffice it to say that according to the analysis of authority offered above, any view according to which religious authority is to be based on straightforwardly factual claims should be abandoned; authority-claims need not, and in fact cannot, possess a primary factual meaning. In fact, the use of authority-claims is at its core functional rather than descriptive.

What do I mean by "functional"? Consider the following example. If I say to my friend: "Jones is a clever man; therefore you should follow his advice," do I use the sentence in order to convey to my friend some information regarding the intelligence of Jones? In a certain way, that is exactly what can be deduced from my utterance. But if we consider the illocutionary force of my speech act, it is clear that by uttering it my intention is, first and foremost, to ascribe some authority to Jones over my friend. By performing the speech act I am offering my friend an answer to a question that may bother him, which takes the form of "What shall I do?" My answer points to Jones' advice as a solution to my friend's problem, and by ascribing authority to Jones I am suggesting the reason why a certain act should be taken. My factual reference to Jones' intelligence may help my friend to make up his mind and submit to Jones' authority. Thus the factual element of my statement can perhaps be connected with the perlocutionary aspect of my speech act, that is to say, with the desired consequential effects of my authority-claim. As such, the factual element of my sentence does not in itself constitute the illocutionary force of ascribing authority to Jones. Put differently, by uttering the sentence mentioned I have performed a speech act of urging my friend to submit himself to Jones' authority. The same holds, of course, for authority-claims by means of which I refer to myself, that is, expressing *my* commitment to some authority.

To generalize, authority-claims must be understood as performative utterances by which the speaker expresses his commitment to certain rules and norms governing the social institution in which he is a member, or to a certain practice in which he participates. To utter a religious authority-claim is to perform an illocutionary act of commitment to a certain set of obligations, or, if I may misuse

Wittgenstein's terminology, commitment to a certain form of life. Needless to say, as all illocutionary acts involve, in one way or another, conventions, so the performance of any authority-claim too must be seen within the framework of the conventions present in the situation. Furthermore, it will make little sense to see the performance of an authority-claim either as manifesting some inner mental disposition or as being dependent on some sort of external, coercive power. Speaking of an illocutionary act of commitment that has resulted from some use of force or threat actually amounts to denying the very performance of such an act, or at least to assuming some insincerity on the part of the speaker. Pointing to the inner state of mind or to other personal considerations as grounds of authority may or may not be significant within a psychological theory that offers explanation of human behavior, but it is nonetheless totally irrelevant as far as the performance of a speech act of submission to authority is concerned. Thus the presentation of authority-claim as a performative act of commitment fits well the three characteristics of authority mentioned earlier, namely regarding authority as an internal concept of society and denying both external power and psychological factors as possible grounds of its establishment.

The primary use of the notion of religious authority can thus be seen as the performance of a speech act of submission to divine authority. The factual recognition of the existence of God as supreme Being is far from being presupposed by the performance of an authority-claim. On the contrary, any factual statement concerning an authority presupposes, in its turn, the performance of a speech act of submission to that authority. Consider, for example, the texts of prayer in monotheistic religions. Usually prayers are described as talking to God or as encounters with the divine. At first glance it may seem that the texts of prayer are used to convey information on God and his relations with man. Such a view is, according to my analysis, mistaken since it does not take into account the most important feature of prayers—the role they play in the life of the religious community. Prayers must be understood as involving illocutionary acts, expressing the submission of the believer to divine authority. In praying, the believer actually performs an act of commitment to his religion. The function of factual statements in prayers is to serve as declarations of the believer's will to accept religious authority and to act according to its precepts.

Much more can be said with respect to the role the notion of authority plays in monotheistic religions. This notion still awaits its proper philosophical analysis. I should remind the reader that my approach in the present paper has been strictly "minimalistic." The analysis of the notion of religious authority offered concerns only what might be called the "hard core" of the term, without presupposing any specific assumption as to the nature of God and the qualities usually attributed to him. It is my hope, however, that even though I have taken only some preliminary steps towards that analysis, we can nevertheless conclude that the notion of religious authority cannot be reduced to its factual element.

If we return now to the conflict between religion and morality mentioned in Plato's *Euthyphro*, we can conclude that the analysis of religious authority offered above can contribute towards reducing the apparent conflict between "autonomy" and "authority." If religious authority-claims are taken as illocutionary acts of commitment, it follows that it will be pointless to describe the conflict in terms of the different *contents* of religion and morality. Nor would it be plausible to present the contrast between morality and religion by pointing to the arbitrary nature of religious commands. It has indeed been argued[21] that either God's commands are subject to some justifying reason, losing their divine character thereby, or God's commands are regarded as independent of any justification, thus rendering them arbitrary. The alleged arbitrariness of the divine commands is, however, theologically problematic, since "the concept of God is such that it seems inconceivable that God would issue arbitrary commands."[22] However, such a presentation seems to me unsatisfactory since it disregards the fact that the notion of justification is context-bound; what can or cannot be regarded as justification depends on the basic presuppositions and rules of the specific system within which a justification is required. As far as religion is concerned, it is evident that the believer's illocutionary act of submission to authority serves as a final justification for obeying the divine commands. And one should resist the philosophical temptation to push the quest for justification beyond its limits. We need not adhere to Wittgenstein's conception of philosophy in order to accept his claim that any procedure of giving justifications must come to an end.

If a conflict between religion and morality occurs at all, it is a *structural* rather than a factual one. Although there are surely many resemblances between these two, nevertheless religion and morality cannot be seen as two conflicting contents since they do not share the same basic concepts. Thus religion and morality are to be seen as two different frameworks governed by two different systems of rules. Put metaphorically, the conflict between them may resemble the one between two different games that take place on two different courts, rather than the conflict that may result from the existence of two different teams of players that play on the same court.

NOTES

1. *Euthyphro* 9e.
2. Bernard Williams, "God, Morality and Prudence," in *Divine Commands and Morality*, ed. P. Helm (Oxford University Press, 1981) 136.
3. F. Waismann, "Notes on Talks with Wittgenstein," *The Philosophical Review*, 74, (1965):12–16.
4. G. G. Swinburne, "Duty and the Will of God," in *Divine Commands and Morality*, ed. P. Helm (Oxford University Press, 1981) 120–134.
5. James Rachels, "God and Human Attitudes," in *Divine Commands and Morality*, ed. P. Helm, 45.
6. See, for example, N. Rescher, *The Logic of Commands*, New York, 1966. See also Alf Ross, *Directives and Norms*, London, 1968.
7. John R. Searle, *Speech Acts: An essay in the Philosophy of Language*, Cambridge University Press, 1969, chap. 3.
   David R. Bell ("Authority," *Royal Institute of Philosophy Lectures, Volume 4: The Proper Study*, London, 1971, 199) rejects Searle's demand that the person ordering will be in authority over the person ordered. He argues that there are cases in which "the person giving the order has the ordered persons in his power in a sense which implies that the ordered person believes it right to obey because if he does not he will thereby suffer some bad consequences to himself threatened by the other." According to Bell there is no contradiction in saying that a man may reject all authority and yet still obey orders. As I shall argue later, Bell's account seems to me mistaken since he confuses the causes of obeying orders with the reasons for yielding to authority. The use of power can be seen as a possible *cause* for obeying orders but it cannot serve as sufficient condition for establishing the *reasons* for seeing a command as obligatory.
8. April Carter, *Authority and Democracy* (London, Routledge & Kegan Paul, 1979) 14.
9. R. Peters, *Authority, Responsibility and Education*, London, 1959, 13.
10. T. Hobbes, *Leviathan*, ed. C. B. MacPherson, chap. 16.
11. Max Weber, *The Theory of Social and Economic Organization*, tr. A. M. Henderson & T. Parsons, London, 1964, 328.

12. Winch, for example, argues that legal authority presupposes the idea of tradition. See: Peter Winch, "Authority," *Political Philosophy*, ed. A. Quinton, Oxford University Press, 1967.

13. A. Carter, *Authority and Democracy* (cf. note 8), 23.

14. P. Winch, "Authority," 98–99.

15. Hannah Arendt, *Between Past and Present*, New York, The Viking Press, 1961, 92–93. See also Timo Airaksinen, "Coercion, Deterrence, and Authority," *Theory and Decision*, 17 (1984): 105–117.

16. H. L. A. Hart, *The Concept of Law*, Oxford University Press, 1961, 209.

17. P. Winch, "Authority," (cf. note 12), 102.

18. For a discussion of the religious concept of punishment, see S. Biderman & A. Kasher, "Religious Concepts of Punishment and Reward," *Philosophy and Phenomenological Research*, 44 (1984): 433–451.

19. See G. W. Stroup, *The Promise of Narrative Theology*, London, 1984, 248–253.

20. W. H. Walsh, *Metaphysics*, London, 1963, 127f.

21. See, for example, Thomas C. Mayberry, "God and Moral Authority," *The Monist*, 54 (1970): 106–123.

22. *Ibid.*, 110.

8

Does Saying Make It So?
The Language of Instantiation
in Buber's *I and Thou*

ROBERT P. SCHARLEMANN

In the history of theological thought, it is a fairly common notion that what is meant by the word or name 'God' is finally ineffable. There is a kinship, in this respect, between the words 'God' and 'nothing'—both of them have a meaning that is contradicted by the existence of a word for it, and both of them are, for that reason, a source of the dialectical power of active thought. The chief difference between them is that the meaning of God contains, as it were, an additional negative, since God is not only not this or that or any other thing but is also not nothing either. But, as treatises on the divine names always tried to show, one cannot draw from this only a negative conclusion, because the other side of the picture is that language is also the medium in which anything real is what it is. This function of language is dependent upon its capacity to show the reality it means through its names. But among these names, in turn, a distinction must be made between those which have "intentionality" and those which have—not merely intentionality but also—"instantaneity," or instantiating capacity.

In this paper I use Martin Buber's treatise of 1923, *I and Thou*, for some reflections on the way in which language and reality coincide in the event of instantiation.[1] This treatise is widely known for its having worked out the category of the 'thou' in contrast to that of the 'it' and is certainly one of the more influential documents in the history of philosophical and theological thought in the twentieth century. But it is usually regarded from the point of view of the category defined rather than from the point of view of the power of language that is contained in such *Grundworte* as I-thou and I-it—that is to say, the power by which language brings about, rather than reflects or clarifies, reality, especially, in Buber's case, the reality of a relation between the self and its other. Hence, I should like here to direct attention to just this aspect of the treatise and, at the end, to raise a question about the role of the word 'God' in the context of instantiating language.

The Language of Instantiation in Buber's *I and Thou*

Instantiation here refers to a relation between language and reality different from intentionality. Words that are names of physical objects have intentionality in the sense that when we hear or read the words, we are directed toward that of which they are the name while, at the same time, we recognize that the word is not the same as the thing. The word 'dog' is a name *of* the animal to which it refers; but the word is not the same as the animal. That we recognize both aspects—it is of the thing but not the thing—is our understanding of the intentionality of language. Other words, however, have more than intentionality because their meaning is such that we cannot think it without simultaneously bringing about the reality they name. The word 'I', for example, is one whose meaning we cannot think without becoming the very one meant by the word. This kind of word has not only intentionality but also instantiating capacity. Buber's term for such instantiating words was "basic word *(Grundwort)*"; and in his treatise on I and thou he developed the instantiation of I in two directions, as correlative with thou and as correlative with it. Buber did not claim to be the first to have discovered the category of thou. Indeed, in the epilogue to *Schriften über das dialogische Prinzip,* he showed how his own work fit into a considerably longer history including such names as Ferdinand Ebner, Søren Kierkegaard, and even Ludwig Feuerbach. It is safe to say, however, that more than the work of the others whom Buber mentions, the treatise *I and Thou* is the one to which most people owe their recognition of the fundamental distinction between the two categories. The linguistic, rather than the categorial, aspect of it is, similarly, not unique to Buber but can be found, among other places, in the work of the Patmos group, which counted among its contributors not only Buber but such other figures as Franz Rosenzweig, Eugen Rosenstock-Huessy, and Karl Barth.

Here I shall offer some reflections on the treatise under three headings: its importance for the theory of language; its importance for epistemology; and its importance for philosophical theology. The reflections are guided by the question of linguistic instantiation, or of how saying can make it so.

Importance for the Theory of Language

The importance of Buber's treatise for theory of language lies doubtless in the understanding of the relation between language (either as spoken or as written, though, in Buber's case, the emphasis is clearly on the spoken) and reality. What is important in the I-thou and the I-it relation is not only that a different category is involved in each case but also that the very words bring about a relation at all. Without saying or thinking the words there is no relation; and where the words are spoken, the relation comes about through the speaking.

According to Buber, the world is twofold, and one dwells in it in a twofold way, with a twofold attitude *(Haltung)* depending upon whether one speaks the basic words I-it or I-thou. That the basic words effect what they name means one cannot say 'I' without thereby being an I, and one cannot say 'thou' or 'it' without thereby making the other into a you or an it and without, at the same time, speaking and being I as well. The relation that is meant by each basic word "enters into the word and stands in it (tritt in das Wort ein and steht darin)" (p. 79). This entering and standing in the word, as Buber calls it, is what we can designate as "instantiation." It is, then, the instantiating capacity of language to which Buber refers with the term *Grundwort.* The instantiating of language is the power of language to bring about the reality it names or to actualize the relation it means. It would correspond to what Hegel in his *Logic* spoke of as the "existing concept (daseiender Begriff)"—a concept that does not serve only to grasp the being that is given but that, as a concept, is not only thought but also something present. Thus, the concept 'I' is, by contrast to object-related concepts like "tree" and "dog," one that is realized as soon as it is thought or said. It is possible to think of a tree and to say the word, tree, without making something into a tree actually, or without realizing a tree. But one cannot say or think 'I' without becoming a thinking subject; I become such by that thinking or saying. This is something that may be more obvious in vigorous controversy when a person feels obliged to say to another: "That's what *you* say; but *I* say . . ." For at such times it becomes clear how one becomes a self-conscious subject through the saying of the word. In contrast to Buber's account, one would have to add that this takes place not only in the speaking but already in the thinking of the content of the word. To think 'I' and to be a self-conscious subject are, in this sense, the same. It is only in relation to others that speaking, in contrast to thinking, comes into play; the relation between I and thou is established though the speaking. Only in speaking, as actually done, and only in the power of language, as a possibility, does this relation of the one to the other become actual. A basic word that, in this way, brings about, or establishes, a relation differs from other words and concepts because meaning and reality converge in such a word.

From these remarks it is clear that the I-you relation, as Buber set it forth, is not identical with the relation of person to person. In that sense, Buber is not classifiable simply as a philosophical personalist. This is evident even in the example that he uses to illustrate the I-you relation. For one example that serves for both the I-you and the I-it relation is a tree. In other words, what is involved is not the question of whether the other is a person or an object but how, in respect to the other, one enters the relation that is made actual by the basic words. A spiritual entity, as in a work of art, another human being, and even a natural object can all be encountered as 'you'. Thus, Buber initially adduces the example of a tree and explains that one can take up several different stances toward it. One can perceive it as a picture or image; one can sense a movement in it; one can assign it to a genus and view it as an example; or one can, finally, "volatilize and eternalize" it as an expression of a law or a mathematical formula. In all these cases, the tree is an it. But it can happen "out of will and grace together" that, while viewing the tree, I am taken into relation to it, as its "power of exclusiveness" grasps me. Then it is no longer an it, but a you. When that happens, one does not suddenly give up all observation of one's own; rather, it happens in the very midst of one's scrutiny of the object (p. 81). The same thing can happen when dealing with other persons: "if I am over against someone as my thou, if I speak the basic word I-thou to him, he is no thing among things and does not consist of things" (p. 83). Finally, the same can happen with respect to a work of art: "It is the eternal origin of art that a figure emerges over against oneself and desires through oneself to become a work. . . . If with one's whole essence one speaks the basic word to the appearing figure, then the effective power streams in, the work arises. . . . Objectively the figure is not 'there' at all; yet what is more present than it is? And it is a real relation in which I stand toward it: it affects me as I affect it" (pp. 83–84).

Buber calls this an "immediate" relation because it is not mediated through any concepts. Hence, it is not possible to say *what* the other is as you; for the you meets one as a whole, not as a divisible unity. A tree as a thing can be divided into its perceptible and cognizable elements, its singular and general aspects. A tree as a you cannot be so divided; for it is not there as an object but as a presence. This is not, however, the same as saying that the encounter with you is wordless or silent. Rather, it is language that actualizes the relation to the you. The sphere of immediacy is, for Buber—as it was also for Hegel in his *Logic*—the sphere of language. To exist immediately means to exist in the word that names the thing or presence. If a tree is immediately there, it is there in such a manner that the name, tree, is not reflectively separated from the object-tree. There is, to be sure, a difference between a tree and a person in the I-you relation; but it is not a categorial difference between things and persons. It is, rather, a distinction derived from the three spheres in which the I-you relation is actualized: the spheres of nature, of human being, and of spiritual entities. In life with nature, the I-you relation "hovers in the dark and is sublinguistic"; in life with other human beings, it is "manifest and in the form of language"; in life with spiritual entities, it "reveals itself, is without speech but gives birth to speech" (p. 81). This contrast in the three spheres, as Buber drew it, is thus a contrast with respect to language—the difference depends on whether, in a given case, life is carried on with the sublinguistic, the linguistic, or, finally, the speechless-but-speech-bearing aspect.

From the point of view of the philosophy of language, this is probably Buber's most important principle. Language as a power that effects a real relation, language as the realm of immediacy that can be reflectively mediated—that is how one might formulate the content of the phenomenon of Buber's conception of *Grundworte* or of what here is being called "instantiation." One might see in this an effect of his work with the Patmos group in the period after the First World War; for the notion that language was the sphere of the immediate and also of the creative was one of that group's basic insights. It is true that the insight was not formulated in just those terms; but one can recognize it in the way that Buber treats the basic word I-you as a word through which an immediate relation is brought about. The principle also makes clear how it is possible to enter an I-you relation with a thing—such as a tree— despite there being no consciousness or soul or selfhood to such objects. Buber himself puts the question: "Does this mean that the tree has a consciousness like ours?" And he answers: "I have no experience of such a thing. . . . What I encounter is no soul of the tree, no dryad, but the tree itself" (p. 82). It is the tree itself that we meet when saying "you" to it.

Importance for Epistemology

To this basic insight one can add some observations concerning the epistemological significance of this way of approaching the dualism in the self-world relation. Buber was one of those who, in the first decades of the century, sought to overcome what has been called the Cartesian split between subject and object. He does so both through his understanding of the relation that is actualized through the basic word of I-you and also through his understanding of the way in which knowledge is achieved in the relation. An indication of this is given by the formulation that one has to speak the I-you with one's whole essence.

Since about the beginning of the century, Descartes has more or less been the scapegoat for what is wrong in modern epistemology, if not in human self-understanding. The subject-object split attributed to his philosophy divides reality into two different kinds of things—thinking things, or subjects, and extended things, or objects. With that division, it is always problematic how a bridge is to be built from one side to the other. Built from one side alone, it implies either idealism or realism (criticism or dogmatism). Built from two sides, it implies an unsolved dualism. Not only that, even by giving attention to such questions, by trying to find a theory to explain how there can be a bridge between subjects and objects, epistemological theory has become increasingly removed from everyday thinking, which is always, from the start, a thinking involved with the world in its very existence (as Heidegger set forth in his *Being and Time*). To exist is to be in the world; it is, from the start, to be involved already with so-called objects. Over and against this kind of everyday understanding of the self and its world, epistemological theories seem abstract and inconsequential. They have no importance both because they seem to contradict, in an artificial way, what everyone always already knows and have nothing to do with what are real concerns of existence, and also because the validity of the one or the other theory seems undecidable. The consequent isolation of theory from actual life and from a concern for truth can then be viewed as a result of the Cartesian epistemology.

One cannot, of course, simply undo the whole philosophical development from Descartes on, and Buber did not attempt to do so. Rather, one must understand what Descartes's concern was, why he was misled, as it were, into separating subjects and objects, and how one might better bring out the element of truth that lay in this separation. Buber declares in the first sentence of his essay: "The world is twofold, depending upon the twofold attitude toward it" (p. 79). That is to say, it is not two metaphysically distinct realities with which we have to do but rather two different kinds of attitude, or relation, to the actual world. The attitude is twofold, moreover, "according to the twofoldness of the basic words that one can speak" (p. 79). With this description, Buber retains something that Descartes had not held—the immediacy of language. What, in Descartes, is two different spheres of reality is, in Buber, two possible relationships to the one reality of the world. And what Descartes understood as two separately existing kinds of things, the *res cogitans* and the *res extensa*, Buber understood as two attitudes (*Haltungen*: attitudes, bearings, postures, positions), which are established by the basic word pairs. That the attitude has, from the start, two possible explications brings with it the consequence that the instantiating word is not a single one but a word pair—either the pair "I-it" or the pair "I-you." There is no I as such without a reference to either you or it; and no you or it without I.

The second thing that distinguishes Buber from Descartes in their epistemology lies in Buber's assertion that the basic words must be spoken with one's "whole essence." This assertion does raise a difficulty as soon as one tries to explain what it means to speak a word with one's whole essence. Negatively, such a speaking is set off against the kind of neutralized subject that is characteristic of scientific statements. That much is clear. For a scientist who discovers or ascertains something about an object of investigation does not need to make his or her discovery or ascertainment with his whole essence. What is discovered may be important or unimportant; but, in either case, it does not demand that a scientist set it forth with his whole essence. In this sense, it is not difficult to say what speaking with one's whole essence means: it means speaking in such a way that the speaker's understanding, will, feeling, and sensibility are activated together. But in another sense, it is difficult to determine what this possibility is. More than once, Buber emphasizes that he is not speaking of something supranatural or extraordinary but of everyday actuality. But one does at least wonder whether it is ever possible to speak in such a way that one's whole essence is brought to bear in the speaking itself.

Perhaps it is never possible to do so while being conscious of it. If that is so, it points to something to which Buber alludes but does not explicate here: such "essential" speaking may be apprehensible only retrospectively, after it has passed. In such a case, we are aware of those realities always in the past tense, as moments that we can remember but not be conscious of as such when they occur. Even so, this would not alter the phenomenon; for whether or not something is real does not depend on whether one can be conscious of it in the present tense. That is illustrated by an example that Buber uses in the English translation of his essay "What is Man?" (The illustration does not appear in the German text in the three-volume *Schriften*.) In that essay, he uses a kind of phenomenological observation for which the actuality of human activity can be made an object of thought only through a reflective recollection of the occurrence. The example used is that of anger. Anger as a movement of the whole self cannot be ascertained through external observation of another's behavior nor through introspection of one's own states of mind; rather, it can be made an object of reflection only through being able to recall the moment in which, with one's whole being, one did respond to something angrily. Having-been-in-anger is the mode in which the phenomenon as a whole can come into view, without its being reduced to an externally observable pattern of behavior or to an introspected state of mind. Indeed, Buber maintained that only through this kind of holistic method could one set forth a philosophical anthropology differing from that of the particular sciences by its holistic character. Such a method does not abstract from the totality of actual life; but it does acknowledge that this totality, this life as a whole and each of its acts as a whole, is accessible to reflection only retrospectively, when one self-consciously recalls the act in its very unself-conscious vitality. This example might be, then, a clue to what Buber means by a speaking that is done with one's whole being. Such a speaking is one in which, in formal terms, understanding, will, feeling, and sensibility are all involved in the actual performance. What that means existentially or really can be known only through recalling an instance in which such speaking actually, prereflectively, took place. Language is the medium that makes the recollection possible.

Importance for Philosophical Theology

A third question connected with these epistemological concerns leads to the matter that is of most importance from the point of view of philosophical theology. If the word 'you' is what instantiates, then how, on the one hand, are the many you's distinguishable from the one you, and, on the other hand, how is the eternal you, who is God, related to the presence of you as such?

God is the one you that encounters us in all particular presences. This implies that one cannot abstract from the human you in order to encounter the divine; for one encounters God not in an independent relation but in the midst of other relations. But asserting this raises the question of how the divine and human are differentiated in the encounter with you at all. If, in the end, one has to do only with a single thou, the thou that meets us in all particular you's, does this impugn the real presence of the other you's? Are they mere ciphers, through which we are to meet the one but which have no standing of their own? Buber himself raised this question, and it is easy to see how it occupied his thinking. His reply seems to me to be, despite his efforts, insufficient; and the reason for the insufficiency appears to lie in his not taking account of the way in which the word God, too, has instantiating power.[2] That leads to the thesis that I would propose concerning the distinction between the many presences of you and the one you in all of them; namely, it is possible to distinguish between them only if both the word you and the word God, like the word I, have instantiating capacity. Before developing this thesis, we may take a look at how Buber himself endeavored to make the distinction.

Buber saw four marks by which, in principle, one could distinguish the eternal from the temporal you. With every other you, one cannot avoid also making it into an it; by contrast, God is the you that can never become an it. That is the first mark. The second is that God is the eternal you implied in every you; every relation to you is, on that account, of itself a relation to God. Seeking for God is thus as impossible as it is unnecessary, because God is always already there in the encounter. Third, the relation to the eternal you is distinguished by its being not only exclusive, as is every you-relation, but also inclusive. It is to be noted here, parenthetically, that Buber does not say the eternal relation is inclusive *instead of* exclusive, but inclusive *as well as* exclusive. Conceptually, that is a much more difficult thought. It leads to the fourth mark: the eternal relation is purely paradoxical, including in itself a contradiction that cannot be resolved but can only be lived.

In all of the marks, no reference is made to a particular role played by the word God. Rather, this word is referred to the basic word you. As Buber put it in the third part of his *I and Thou*: "People have addressed their eternal you with many names. When they sang of the one so named, they always meant you: the first myths were songs of praise." Then Buber put the question: "Of what importance is all the senseless or raving talk *(Irr-rede)* about God's essence and works . . . compared to the one truth that all people who have addressed God have meant him? For anyone who speaks the word, God and really has 'you' in mind, whatever be his illusions otherwise, addresses the true you of his life which cannot be restricted by any other one and to which he stands in a relation that excludes all others" (p. 128). From these quotations it is easy to see that Buber here regards the word God as a designation that can differ among peoples and that serves, as it were, as a representative of the basic word you: "whoever speaks the word 'God' *and really has 'you' in mind,* addresses . . . the true you of his life." That is to say, one can use the word God as well as other words in order to address the eternal you. But what counts is whether the speaker has you in mind while doing so; for if he does so, then he or she enters a relation to the eternal you. This same point could be documented by other passages in Buber's writings. What they make clear is that Buber considered the word God to be dependent on the word you. It does not set up a relation, as do the basic words, by the very instantiating that takes place through the figure and meaning of the word; rather, it gets its meaning from its connection to, and from its being a bearer of, the word you.

In a certain way, then, the name God is related to the word you much as each you is related to the eternal you. The many have a certain transparency to the one, which Buber formulated by reference to a geometric figure: "The extended lines of the relations intersect in the eternal you. Each you is a window *(Durchblick)* to it. It is from this mediating role of the you of all beings that the satisfaction *(Erfülltheit)* of relations to them comes, and also their dissatisfaction. The inborn you is actualized in every relation and is completed in none of them. It is completed only in the immediate relation to the you that, by its essence, cannot become an it" (p. 128). In thus identifying God with the eternal you, always in real relation to the I, Buber consciously took a position against every notion, mystical or other, in which the I is ultimately absorbed in or identical with God. "The Father and the Son—the two who are essentially alike—or, we can say, God and man, are the irreducibly real two, the two bearers of the original relation," he said of Jesus' words "I and the Father are one" in the Gospel of John, "which, from God to man, has the form of mission and command and, from man to God, that of seeing and perceiving and, between both, that of knowledge and love. . . . All modern attempts to reinterpret this original reality of dialog into a relation of the I to itself, or such things, that is, into a process enclosed in the self-sufficiency of human interiority, are in vain" (p. 135). But Buber does not seem to have been quite so clear on the relation between one you and another you.

The third mark of the relation to the eternal you is that this relation is both exclusive and inclusive. "Every actual relation to a being (Wesen) or to a presence (Wesenheit) in the world is exclusive" (p. 130) because everything else lives in the light of that being. Not that there is nothing but you there. Rather, everything that is there is seen as having its life in the light of the you. The light lasts as long as the presence of the relation lasts. "As soon as a you becomes an it, the cosmic reach of the relation appears to be in the wrong in the world, its exclusiveness appears as an exclusion of the totality" (p. 130). That is true of every actual you. However, in the relation to the eternal you who God is, the "unconditional exclusiveness and unconditional inclusiveness" are one and the same. Though the nature of this paradox would need some further exploration, we can leave it with Buber's statement, in order to move to the last mark of this relation, its antinomy.

This antinomy lies in the religious situation of human beings (p. 142). Human existence in the presence of the eternal is marked by "its essential and insoluble antinomy." It is a different antinomy from the philosophical one that Kant explicated in his critique of reason, for the two sides of the contradiction cannot be ascribed to two different spheres, as can the Kantian freedom and necessity. "If I have in mind necessity and freedom not in the world of thought but in the actual reality of standing in the presence of God; if I know, 'I am in the hands of another,' and simultaneously know, 'It all depends on me,' then I cannot try to evade the paradox, which I have to live out, by ascribing the incompatible propositions to two separate spheres of validity, and I cannot make a conceptual resolution by an artificial, theological concept; rather, I must take it upon myself to live out both sides in one, and when lived they are one" (p. 143).

Distinguishing the Thou

What Buber intended with this kind of phrasing is clear. In distinction from an accent that he found not only in Kierkegaard but also in Ferdinand Ebner, two predecessors in the same concern, he wanted to insist that the human you in its temporal concreteness is a real other for the I; it is not an indifferent and ultimately inessential cipher for the divine you as the only real other of the I. So he had a double opposition in mind: first, against a mystical identification of I and God, and, second, against a Docetic view of the temporal thou. To see the extent to which Buber may or may not have succeeded in distinguishing you and you, it will be helpful initially just to make a list of the ways in which anything is distinguishable from something else at all. Thereafter, it will be clearer how one might maintain, conceptually or otherwise, the distinction between the eternal and temporal you (and with that also the distinction between I and you).

The first possible way of making a distinction is the formal one. For example, we can distinguish between a tree's being a tree and its being a giver of shade; or we can distinguish between the tree as it is actually there before us and the tree as it might be made into furniture. What is materially one and the same thing can be viewed from a number of different formal possibilities. Second, we can distinguish things materially. We can thus make a distinction between one tree and another tree. Formally, they are both the same, as a tree; but materially they are different trees. Third, there is a personal distinction, which is neither formal nor material but historical (or "spiritual," if the word is rightly understood). What distinguishes one person as a personality from another is not the material difference (although there is a material difference present) nor a formal difference (as there may also be) but the historicality of the person (the particular set of memories, occurrences, encounters, and the like that have made the person an individual personality or a unique subject).

Fourth, one can distinguish one thing from another thing temporally. With respect to the appearances of the you, this is the kind of distinction that initially is employed. Thus, the difference between the you that is actualized in a tree and the you that is actualized in another person is neither material nor formal nor personal but temporal. The time of the one and the time of the other are distinct. Since the you essentially lets everything appear in its light, when it is encountered, the you of one encounter can be distinguished from that of another only in this temporal way. If there were no difference in time, there would also be no possibility of distinguishing the one you from the other. "Who" the you is of a given encounter can be recognized and named only by reference to the time of the appearance; the material and formal differences, which are, of course, also there, are not essential. Materially we can distinguish between several examples of one genus or species; formally we can distinguish between different possibilities of development or formation of a given material content. But neither the one nor the other of these two distinctions is the same as the distinction between the one and the other you. What becomes named as a you is time.

In the fifth place is the distinction between the two basic words. The I of the I-it relation is not the I of the I-you relation just because the relations that are established by the words are different. Finally, there is the difference of the infinite from the finite, which can be grasped only dialectically, not in linear concepts, because the infinite is not the simple opposite of the finite (otherwise it would be limited by the finite and would not be infinite) but is rather the opposite of the opposition that constitutes the finite—what limits something finite is something else that is finite. This distinction is neither formal nor material but speculative; it is not a distinction that is given but one that arises and shows the emergence of any given thing; it does not distinguish some things from other things but represents the coming-to-be of any thing at all.

This brief and rather unsystematic enumeration of the possibilities makes clear how difficult it can be to make a distinction between a temporal you and the eternal you. For, according to the distinctiveness of the basic words, we can distinguish between you and it but not between you and you or between a temporal and an eternal you. If, moreover, the distinction is speculative, so that every you and every it bear the eternal you in themselves as their origin or their coming-to-be at all, then the eternal you is not a genuine you whom we encounter but, as it were, the framework in which the relation to you or it takes place at all. That, clearly, would not fit Buber's intention, precisely because he was concerned to maintain the genuine dialogical relation between the human I and the divine you. It is a concern that, he reported, had occupied him from early youth (p. 297) and that made the dialogical principle so important for him. Still, it is not clear how that dialogical principle can be maintained if one cannot show how, conceptually or otherwise, the difference between the many and the one of the encountered you is to be understood.

It appears to me that the one recourse which Buber did not take, but which seems to suggest itself, is that of the instantiation brought about by the word God. For if this very word instantiates what it means, then the difference between the temporal and the eternal you hinges upon the difference between these two words, and the problem of the distinction is solved. If one wanted to take a biblical verse as a guideline, it might be the words with which the Doubting Thomas acknowledged the risen Jesus: "My lord and my God" (John 20:28). For this expression indicates that what came about was not only the relation of I-you ("my lord") but also that of I-God ("my God"), the temporal and the eternal presence. I-you and I-God together maintain both the identity and difference in the presence. It is a real difference only if the instantiating capacity of the one word is equal to that of the other; it is a real identity, because it is one and the same physical figure, and one and the same time, that evokes the two words. If that is the case, then one can say that the saying of "it" (with which there always goes a corresponding "I") is what establishes the world of objectivity; the saying of "you" (with its corresponding "I") is what establishes the world of exclusive relation; and the saying of "God" (which can accompany either or both the saying of "it" and of "you") establishes the world of the eternal. Through the saying of the word "God," what is shown is the "not" of every it and every you, as well as of I—God is not this or that or any other one, and not I either. But, at the same time, God is not nothing either, so that the presence of the eternal is not only the negative that is shown upon any it, you, or I but also the negative of that negation in turn.

NOTES

1. The text used here is that published in Buber's *Werke*, 1, *Schriften zur Philosophie* (Munich: Kösel-Verlag, 1962).

2. This may need correction. Paul Tillich reported, for example, that he had once asked Buber whether "God" was not a *Grundwort* and that Buber had replied in the affirmative. This reference is contained in a transcript of a lecture Tillich gave in 1954 before the Cooper Union Forum in New York. The transcript is in the Harvard Tillich archives.

Words of Silence:
The Context for God

FREDERICK SONTAG

> But I should answer him: I know what a word means
> *in certain contexts.*
>
> Ludwig Wittgenstein, *The Blue and Brown Books*

A Time and a Place for God

We live in a time when few people claim to hear God speak to them directly, as some have in the past. If we have been passing through an era of God's silence, one thing stands out by contrast: on every page of the biblical documents, everyone who writes about God has a forceful and a compelling sense of his presence. However, a reading of the biblical record produces another striking impression: the context within which God appears, and the means by which his presence is made, vary considerably for each group of people and for each time and each place.

What every person discovers, if he or she relates successfully to God, is a context within which God is able to appear and become real. If we have failed to hear God's voice in our own time, it may not be because God is unavailable to us but because we have not learned the context within which, for our time and our age, God might become concrete for us, too. If we practice a religious discipline, read scripture, study church history, and learn theology, we have light shed on how and when God made the impact he did on each group of seekers. Still, to hear interpretations of God's former words is not the same as to discover in our time the context within which God may be heard in new ways, in fresh words and with contemporary power.

God in the Old Testament

For the early Hebrews the events recorded in the Pentateuch combined to make God real for them. Genesis began with an account of creation, so that God's standing at the origin of time made him a force to be reckoned with. Adam and Eve dealt directly with God. Even when they left paradise they felt the immediate presence of God in the form of anger. Cain complained to God that the punishment imposed on him for killing his brother Abel was too severe. Thus, Cain came to know God because he was pressed by a divine judgment.

Noah followed God's direct command and survived a liquid devastation. Abraham heard God's call to lead a people and was tested directly by him in the sacrifice of his promised son, Isaac. How many today feel such immediate contact with the Divine? In spite of its incredible aspects, it might be a relief if God would make himself known directly to us rather than leaving us with the lack of direction so many enjoy today.

All through the pages of the Old Testament, as the wars rage and righteous ways are forsaken, "the people of God" are either aware of his presence or are called back to be made aware of it. As reported there, some of God's actions are horrifying—such as his command to the Jews to slaughter their enemies. Nevertheless, at least God was made so real that they could not escape him. Instead, for us he is so absent that we cannot find him when we need him.

The children of Israel were sure about their context for God because the strict code of behavior set down for living and eating made God's commandments inescapable. Yahweh brought Israel out of slavery in Egypt, and no one was allowed to forget the debt due him for that release. Moses was summoned into God's presence and returned with laws written on stone. His contact with the Divine was real and immediate and concrete, right up to the threat of his destruction.

The writer of each *Psalm* was aware of the divine presence in the midst of trouble, although God was equally real for him in times of gladness. The Prophets spoke fiery words in God's name and pronounced devastating judgments on anyone who offended him. Whether or not you accept the words they announced, there is no doubt that God was real to the Prophets because they spoke so boldly in his name.

God in the New Testament

God's presence was no less vivid for the writers of the New Testament documents, but the circumstances in which God appeared were different. The contexts were not the same and the experiences of God were not identical, nor were the Gods disclosed of one nature. In spite of their variances, God in the four Gospels became real for those who sensed his presence in those accounts through the life, actions, and words of Jesus. Actually, most of those who came into contact with Jesus were slow to realize the way God had become present at that time.

In the *Acts* and in the letters of Paul, God became present in what happened to the disciples as they preached, although not all of this was pleasant. Paul's churches are involved in trouble from their inception, but God was felt in the turmoil of the spread of the Gospel. In *The Revelation to John* we discover God drastically judging and changing the world. In expecting these catastrophic events, God's power becomes real. All early Christians lived on in the hope of things promised and still to come. Nevertheless, God was present to them in their hope.

These contexts vary, yet God became real in each one. There must be no one context within which God's appearance can be guaranteed, not even in churches dedicated to his name or in services which praise him. He is too unpredictable. We can study past appearances and learn how men saw God in previous times. But we are still left with the question: "In what context and in what events might God become powerful again and his voice be heard in the land?"

Divine Contexts for Today

The apostasy of millions and the influx of new religions indicate that many old forms of religious ritual and practice have lost their forcefulness. What new context, then, might be a source of divine presence? The trouble, of course, is that we feel the power of intrusive forces today. Yet we need to distinguish those which are destructive and demonic from those which might become a vehicle for a divine return.

Two prominent features of our present age suggest themselves as possible context for the divine: (1) The deafening silence of God, and (2) the roar of the whirlwind which increasingly threatens to destroy us and our culture and every tradition we have known. Whereas some people in other ages were certain of God's existence and his words, the absence of God combined with his awesome silence often are our most pronounced religious experiences today.

This difference becomes more startling when contrasted with the hesitancy and reticence of both philosophers and theologians to speak for God today. Yet, in spite of all that can be said to account for his absence and our uncertainty, it might be that we should seek God in that characteristic phenomenon of our time: his absence and his silence.

If we agree to use this as our context for God, what kind of God will we discover? If we start from silence and absence, can we find a God who is sufficiently concrete because he fits the most prominent feature of our times—"threatened destruction"? What can a God be like who would be silent in his relationship to us in times such as these? Like Job we may find our answer in the midst of the whirlwind.

> He will wipe all tears from their eyes; there will be no more mourning or sadness. The world of the past has gone. (*Revelation* 21:4)

As indicated in the above passage from *Revelation*, a new world can be discerned only when the old is about to be destroyed. In this case, today's most significant contrast is between God's silence toward us and the roar of the earthly tempest whose fury seems to increase daily. If God has been lost, it may be because the religious age which is just past was too peaceful and too prosperous to allow God to appear. He can hide his face more easily in a time of calm. Now we are in trouble. We reject and destroy our own success. What we have achieved our children often spurn. We are no longer certain we can control the forces loose in the land. Now, not in peace but in turmoil, God may be heard to speak again. When we are proud of our own national and individual powers and certain of our success, no voice can be discerned above man's. As destructive as violent storms are, perhaps God has no other way to get our undivided attention. We are shaken loose from self-absorption and made ready to listen only when the noise level becomes threatening.

If the presence of God becomes real in the midst of anticipated destruction, how is this related to that other significant experience of the time: our sense of God's silence and absence? Silence, however, is not necessarily the absence of all noise. It may involve calling attention to natural sounds not of our own structuring and production. God's silence may be an attempt to force us to listen to something other than ourselves. Job was so busy arguing with those who came to console him in his troubles that he did not have time to listen. It took God's coming at Job with the force of a whirlwind to stop the flow of his words. Finally, in silence, he heard God speak out of the tempest. Only then could Job respond to God's words. What does it take to stop each of us dead in our tracks so that, exhausted at last, we listen to voices other than our own?

God does not speak at all times and in all places but only in some. We cannot complain if God does not address us openly. If God is silent, there must be a reason. If he is heard when destruction threatens, it may indicate that not even oblivion is outside of God's control. The threat of death may be one way into his presence. Destruction can be the prelude to a new heaven and a new earth, once the world of the past has been taken from us.

Can Words Make Elusive Objects Concrete

Usually we think of words as referring to objects and as being less substantial than that to which they refer. Certainly this is Augustine's view about the status of words in his dialogue, *Concerning the Teacher*. Since God is seldom an immediate object, and since he becomes concrete only within a specific context, we ask: Are words capable of making an elusive object become real for us? Perhaps we ought to discuss God only in some arena of actual discourse, one within which the terms we use take on specific meaning (cf. Wittgenstein). If so, most abstract discussion of God is doomed to failure. Unless God is approached in a context where discourse has concrete rootage, both in its particular reference and in its immediate imagery, no concept of God can become real.

This, at least, is the way God is discussed in the biblical literature. The settings are often mundane and everyday and immediate. Yet the terms drawn out of these contexts give solidity to the idea of God. There are many areas of discourse; there is not just one. Therefore, the context from which we speak must be understood before our meaning can be appraised. In each instance we can discover what gives God concrete meaning. For example: rescue from slavery, success in battle, unity as a nation, sacrifice to save others, etc. We must learn how each particular context functions. Of course, we can seldom adopt a past context for our own, but at least we may learn how language about God accomplished its goal in virtue of that past setting. Then we can ask: What areas of actual discourse around us might perform the same function today? Should our words be set in divine silence?

The same contextualism is true for every philosopher and theologian. Each does not speak like all the rest. They neither use the same terms nor refer to the same frame of reference. Rather, each philosopher and theologian builds a framework of interpretation within which his doctrines take on solidity. He creates a context within which we who read him can think clearly. By way of contrast, the everyday contexts given to us do not allow thought about God to become so clear. Unlike certain natural settings, such as those in which we find God located in the biblical accounts, it is the philosopher's business to construct verbal contexts. Theologians must use a little of both types. They ask: Within what natural context might God be concrete today? At the same time, they have to blend these with artificial technical languages, because these have greater clarity and precision than immediate experience and so allow us to put experience into words.

The Meaning of Religious Symbols

If we learn how words operate to make God concrete, we will understand what is peculiar about the power of specifically religious symbols. Of all the forms power can take, how can there be such a thing as "symbolic power?" We must begin by asking this question, since in the case of God we never deal directly with an object but encounter him only in terms of symbols. If such indirect discourse is to be meaningful, we must learn how symbols appropriate power in religious discourse. Through their mediation an otherwise inaccessible object becomes real for us. Like all symbols, religious symbols can lose their effectiveness, but they are still the most potent human symbols we have—both for good and for evil.

What, then, does this situation tell us about God? If symbols properly used can make him real for us, and if language provides a context within which he may be apprehended, God must neither care to appear directly nor to have his nature read directly off the facts of the world or the historical process. Words and symbols serve as intermediaries to God, and yet both are human instruments. Thus, if they represent God, he must share the same characteristics which require man's use of word and symbol. He must have an abstract nature capable of becoming concrete within a particular process such that his nature cannot be grasped directly.

It must first be reflected in a medium. It is beyond direct grasp but not beyond all grasp.

Religious symbols at times contain power, but it is always an indirect power that is involved in the meaning of a symbol. God's power is seldom expressed directly or made unavoidably evident, although it probably was on the momentous but unwitnessable day of creation. His power can be felt even when it appears in non-obvious forms, and its effectiveness depends upon its recognition. Furthermore, when we observe how symbols, religious or otherwise, gain and lose their power, we know that God is not always able to operate through the same medium. A once powerful symbol can be revived, but its power is never sustained without effort. Evidently, a God like this does not commit the expression of his power to one form irrevocably or without change.

In his famous essay, *Archetypes of the Collective Unconscious,* C. G. Jung gave his analysis of how symbols are formed and how they function. In particular, he offers us a brilliant illustration of how and why most religious symbols have lost their power in the present age. Modern men have been iconoclastic and blatantly empirical in denying any power which transcends the observable. We have rejected traditional symbols, part of whose function it was to protect our fragile psyches against internal and external destructive forces. With this wall broken, the psyche is left prey to powers that can be devastating. When this occurs, it indicates that we are dealing with a God of great powers who uses symbols to shield us from his full face; at the same time he provides the means whereby he may be understood.

Interestingly enough, a symbol may be a form of silent communication. That is, we can convey meaning by symbols without the use of words so that the symbols communicate nonaudibly. Direct verbal communication may indeed limit us because it tells us explicitly what it wants to say, whereas a certain indirectness, distance, and flexibility should exist between speaker and hearer. If I tell you directly in so many words what I want to say, you are limited in the ways you can interpret and respond to such an openly displayed intent. If God is discernible only via symbols, he retains a certain flexibility that allows him to keep his distance from humans and yet communicate with them directly.

If the means which reveal God are not compelling, he is free in his own nature to adopt various forms. He must intend to leave man free in relation to him, and he does this by adopting only a symbolic or indirect form of disclosure. The divine-human relationship allows flexibility even to the point of rejection. No writer more clearly asserts the necessity for, and the power of, symbols as an approach to God than Dionysius the Areopagite. His *Divine Names*[1] discusses the way in which verbal terms can be applied to, and are descriptive of, God. He begins by discussing how the "names" (or attributes) we use are appropriate to describe God. Because the object is never symbolized directly, Dionysius knows that such a project can never be completed once and for all (p. 51). If God's dichotomous attributes transcend speech and knowledge, we reach one decision about the Divine nature: Ultimately it cannot be contained within our form of language without distortion.

If God lies "beyond thought," thought must either use indirect means or adopt silence. Silence, then, indicates an awareness of the unsuitability of language to capture God fully, that is, unless speech is used in a way that corrects its own inadequacies. For instance, after making his point about the transcendence of God, Dionysius makes numerous direct statements about God's nature. Thus, the context Dionysius creates makes God real but only with the use of an initial caution. He advises us that man must make his mind "passionless and spiritual" (p. 58) in order to approach God. The language Dionysius uses demands that we correct a state of affairs that otherwise blocks apprehension. Language, fortunately, can correct its own initial deficiencies and then structure a correct approach. When you stop and think about it, that is an amazing capacity of the mind.

What is an Appropriate Symbol?

Dionysius uses the phrase "appropriate symbols" (p. 58), thus raising an important issue: If only certain symbols are appropriate for certain objects and others are misleading, is this so because the mind is able to select and to recognize a symbol which is, in fact, "appropriate"? If a symbol can enable the mind to grasp an object otherwise inaccessible, its success in guiding our apprehension indicates its usefulness for any mind which can follow this lead. When our thinking is blocked and led only to the term in front of it, we cannot be certain about the symbol's "appropriateness." Unfortunately, no symbol is likely to affect everyone in the same way at all times, and religious symbols are especially subject to variation. Still, some indications of appropriateness can be obtained.

The Medium of Language: Text, Talk, and Silence

Our main question concerning language about God is: How can any discussion of this subject be completed successfully? We know that a controlled use of words opens enlightenment to some, but we also know that this process can never be brought to an end once and for all. God remains "nameless" (p. 61) in the last analysis, since no single symbol can be fixed as applicable to him always or without revision. Words cannot define God's nature so rigidly that they capture divinity completely or become the only avenue to that accomplishment. By the use of words we merely begin to distinguish various attributes and functions of God. Yet we know that certain godly aspects (e.g., compassion) do not exist in him exactly as the distinctness of the terms might indicate.

As we ordinarily use words, one term is distinct from another, for example, "difference" and "undifferentiated." Where God is concerned, a term may apply and yet not do so, so as to exclude the application of its opposite. This difficult theological fact bothers any logician wedded to the ways of nature. Of course, this apparently contradictory application is at times true of human nature too. But by structuring words and symbols God can be grasped, even if his nature is not identical with a rigid structure described by definite terms.

Dionysius warns us that, by using words to characterize God, we do not draw God down to us. Instead, the primary function of language is to lift the mind up. It must become structured until it is in a position to see beyond itself and the world's immediate objects. Words properly used are props to hold up the mind. Of course, even by this use of symbols and by the discovery of contexts within which God can become real to us, we do not gain a complete knowledge of God. That is not possible (p. 85). To think that it is indicates a misunderstanding about the lack of finality and the absence of rigidity present in the divine nature, plus the flexibility possible within the various forms of human knowledge. Nevertheless, these means provide some information. We must use it for all it is worth, but not for more than that.

Since words sometimes function to deny as well as to affirm or to describe positively, we have to contend with "negative theology." The structuring of a concrete context often proceeds by denying what is inapplicable to God. The mind may grasp the inappropriateness of some symbols before it recognizes the appropriate aspects of others. If these conditions are a prerequisite to acquiring an understanding of God, simply by pointing out this fact language enables God to be real. For instance, Dionysius says that we must be transported "wholly out of ourselves" (p. 147). In this case, we cannot know God unless we make an effort to escape our natural attachment. Even if we cannot translate God's nature directly into words, we can formulate the conditions for such intelligence. Furthermore, if we cannot state directly all that is in God's power, we can more easily state "what God cannot do" (p. 157). As the impossibilities are discovered, more is revealed about the divine nature than a direct attempt to describe God could disclose.

The problem presented by any use of symbols is the danger of confusing the symbol, which is visible, with the object which may be beyond sense (p. 165). Yet the fact that God can be symbolized (this might not be possible for all divinities) indicates that he is not completely detached from sensible nature. When, for example, movement is attributed to God, motion as it is ordinarily perceived may not be a perfect example. Our problem is to alter the normal meaning of the symbol to make it appropriate to God. As Dionysius did, our problem is to find the right way to explain the names of God. Since God transcends our nature, we move in that direction to correct the inadequacies of our symbols. If the imagery becomes concrete in this context, it yields a view of God that can, when necessary, correct its own expressions.

As mentioned above, Jung's famous essay on the archetypes[2] indicates that the concept of God is itself connected with the idea of a divine image in man. In Jung's explanation, however, an archetype is essentially an unconscious content in the mind that is altered by becoming conscious (p. 5). According to Jung, in earlier centuries we had religious formulae for everything psychic and therefore did not need modern psychology. However, as a result of our rejection of everything transcendent, these "lovely symbols" lost their richness and their power. To our sorrow, we discovered only too late that they had protected man from a direct confrontation with God, as well as offering some indication of the divine. When traditional symbols broke down or were weakened, other forces swept in to inundate the mind, and we lost sight of God. The era in which the power of symbols is transferred from one set to another is not an easy time, and the psyche is left vulnerable in the transition. We see the result in the disoriented persons all around us.

Dogmatic symbols formulate a tremendous and a dangerous psychic experience in a manageable way, fittingly called "an experience of the divine," Jung reports. They do this in a manner tolerable to human understanding (p. 11) without limiting its scope or doing damage to its divine significance. Religious iconoclasm, then, releases destructive forces which no individual can cope with, whether this happens in the Protestant Reformation or in Roman Catholic renewal. The poverty of symbolism usually follows an age destructive of orthodoxy, such as the Protestant Reformation or Vatican II, and it is dangerous to the psyche of the individual. God disappears when the symbols related to him lose their power to lead the mind. Where God is closest, the danger is the greatest, especially if man has lost the protection provided by the symbols formed from accumulated experience.

But descent into the depths always seems to precede ascent (p. 19). Thus, the forces which a reform movement unleash within the soul can be turned to good purposes, but only if new symbols begin to rise to the surface. If our symbols remained powerful constantly, we would never turn inward to discover the ground for new symbolism, which happens when the psyche struggles not to drown in its own internal chaos. Traditional symbols support us. As long as their power is not challenged, they keep us from unleashing a devastating inner conflict. Today, for better or for worse, many are locked in a sometimes destructive inner psychological struggle. We are unsure which symbols we should use for God, because we are not clear which ones can deal effectively with the destructive powers we face.

We have learned that words can provide a context to make difficult subjects concrete, in this case God. Yet when old symbols are lost or rejected, when stored-up psychic terrors are unleashed, we lose sight of God. As Jung argues, however, an inner disturbance may also indicate our nearness to God. But such closeness often leaves us without adequate protection against the overwhelming forces. Pushed around psychologically, with no symbols strong enough to stabilize the religious conditions, post-modern man asks: How can we deal with the potential destructiveness of an unrecognized divine presence? God can become real for us again if we control threatened destruction by the use of symbols made equally powerful.

God's Silence as Our Context

If we accept an awesome divine silence as our starting point, we learn something about God by asking: What could a God be like who would be silent toward us? The issue concerns God's contemporary speaking and the fact that we often face an extended silence. Yet we know we have not been left without all words, since so much divine advice has been recorded by various authors. Perhaps all divine discourse is set down "after the fact" rather than in the immediate moment. We recognize this as true in the New Testament records, for example. Is this what we should conclude from the present divine silence we feel? Will we be able to discover only later what God has been saying to us now? If so, this restricts us less than if we were confronted by God's direct statements. But we still have less guidance in the present. Whatever the similarities, our situation now is slightly different from any previously recorded divine past words. Thus, whenever we alter the application of words previously attributed to God to fit a present situation, a process of reinterpretation is involved for which we are responsible. We have divine words recorded, but we must take the initiative in adapting them to the current situation. It is always possible to go astray in this process.

Whenever anyone whom we would expect to speak to us is silent, we are not without some idea of what this might mean, even if we do not know for certain whether our inferences are correct. Often a lack of response from others will answer our question more eloquently than a thousand words. We are at least sure that anyone who is unresponsive in the face of a direct question does not intend to give us specific advice, or that such advice is not going to come in an explicit form. Silence does not preclude a direct answer's being given from time to time, but this never comes as a normal routine or as our rightful expectation. We are never in a position to determine what God's response might be. In spite of the inequality of power that exists between him and us, more often than not we must answer our questions in his place.

Questioning often indicates a need. That is, the petitioner hopes to enlist support. Since God does not plead with us openly, his power must be sufficient to sustain itself without external aid. Only the very strong can afford to be silent for long. Uncontrolled words are a sure sign of weakness. God's frequent unresponsiveness indicates his natural independence and self-sufficiency—those central divine perfections. Unfortunately, this does not tell us much one way or another about his concern or his seeming lack of concern for those who listen and hope for his reply. Because immediate assistance and answers are seldom forthcoming, we are thrown forward to the future for our resolution.

In the midst of silence we are better able to hear ourselves think and to talk to ourselves. God's lack of direct speech encourages our solitude. If his voice is cut off, we have a model of how to avoid noise from others. In this way God's silence provides the best context for our own silent meditation, although we cannot block out every intrusion. In fact, we might ask whether we would ever be left alone to think if God did not provide us with the context for our deepest silence. Noise would have no end and our own inner understanding thwarted if God constantly interrupted us with his powerful voice. The best service God can render us is to wrap us in his silence, since otherwise we might never know what this means for our spiritual health. When God appears to have abandoned us, we may learn to use our solitude productively.

Since a few divine words uttered could save men much anguish and even death, God must be able to stand the sight of men wasting themselves for lack of direction and certainty. He risks a lot for a little. Either he does not care about human waste or else he is capable, in some incredible way, of picking up the broken pieces and of restoring them as he wills and in his own time. If God is as sensitive to the needs of others as the best men are at times, we know that he does not evidence this concern immediately. We do have recorded divine words of consolation, and we have some of promise, e.g., Jesus' ministry. Yet such words are seldom spoken directly to us at the time of our direst need, and the assistance needed to back up the words is either not apparent or postponed until an indeterminate future. God's silence can be rough on us. We can only assume that his attention is more on the future than on any immediate moment.

Solitude to Appreciate Silence

Thomas Merton gained a reputation based on making the contemplative life clear to a generation not very inclined, at least overtly, to be contemplative. He once recorded his own impressions of a period spent in complete solitude. This might be helpful to us in understanding how God can "speak" through silence.[3] Merton talks of man's dialogue with God in silence (p. 12), by which he means that some people find both question and response in solitude. Man has a right to such solitude, Merton thinks. It is the source of his interior freedom. Even society benefits when the individual discovers this to be true. For only those who have a center of solitude can unite freely in social relations (p. 13). Material things do not become "unreal." They only appear so in contrast to the growing spiritual reality which silence brings.

The desert is the logical dwelling place for those who want to find themselves in solitude. God's silence drives us to consider the desert as one context for discovering him. The first thing to note about existence on the desert, whether this is a physical or a spiritual desert, is that it is a country which drives some to madness. God did not pale at the thought of creating conditions which drive us out of our minds. Barren places are also spots where devils hide. A desert offers us beneficial solitude, it also opens us to hostile attack. Everywhere there is a desert and solitude (p. 22), so that internally we must learn to exist under spiritually rigorous conditions always open to attack. The desert is lonely and dangerous, but it can be purifying.

A God of silence does not often put a stop to our trials. Thomas Merton's main conclusion was that life under desert conditions is a gamble which involves a risk of all that we can see and taste and feel (p. 35). Inner upheaval is a necessary part of this gamble (p. 48), and hope is the secret of such a life (p. 39). Thus, silence forces us to depend on hope, although God's lack of direct presence does not make it easy to hold on to hope. Life becomes a listening. To hear and to respond correctly demands that life be lived silently, at least in part. Silence either does or should detach us from other considerations. In this circumstance we are prepared to hear God. The arrogant and the self-centered do not want to be silent, so that cultivating an inner silence is impossible without humility and mercy. Unfortunately, the sly and the deceitful are often outwardly silent so that exterior silence is in itself no test. We must discover an inner state of silence which exists and unfolds beneath the outer surface of activity.

Solitude is not only a matter of location or external state; it involves an inner disposition. Words sometimes get in our way. Often we have spoken so much that it becomes hard to see the objects we talk about in themselves. Silence can clear the air and let existence stand out as it is. Words stand between silence and silence (p. 74). To achieve inner silence is not easy; it is like repeatedly bending over an abyss (p. 86). "It is not speaking that breaks our silence but only the anxiety to be heard. The words of the proud man impose silence on all others so that he alone may be heard. The humble man speaks only in order to be spoken to"

(p. 87). If Thomas Merton is right about this, God's self-imposed silence could be an attempt to teach humility. When our words include an effort to listen to others rather than indicating our anxiety to be heard, God's silence becomes revelatory of him as the road blocks are removed.

"If our life is simply poured out in useless words, we will never hear anything . . ." (p. 88). Silence can be liberating. It frees us from imposed self-concern. Of course, no guaranteed techniques exist for finding God. God speaks when he pleases, and his predominant lack of direct response should convey that message. If we have no assured formula for divine capture, we must face up to uncertainty in divine manifestations or else miss God as he slips by. Silence could of course indicate God's non-existence, or a lack of concern, but it may tell us other things as well. Everlasting silence would impose a humiliating uncertainty on us, for then no single choice we make would ever be approved or disapproved to our satisfaction. Yet, it can also indicate God's direction that human decisions should be made in this neutral but disturbing atmosphere, rather than indicate God's total disinterest. We must gamble on our interpretation of silence and base our decision on what we conclude.

Combatting Evil Forces

The existence of evil causes perhaps the greatest strain on our credulity when God maintains silence. Religiously, we are offended if someone, be he man or Pope, does not speak out against obvious evil. To live quietly in solitude while accepting God's silence is possible only if it is based on an invincible faith or on a belief that the goodness of God is evident. If you feel the presence of evil strongly, you will break silence and speak out and act to oppose it. At least, that is what we expect an uncorrupted man to do. Thus, if God remains silent in the face of brutalizing and destructive evil, we must either deny his existence or reevaluate his nature in reaction to what seems to us to be shocking behavior.

If we deny God because of evil's destructive presence, coupled with his silence, this may be too quick a judgment. In the first place, God has not been totally silent, since we have been given so many words attributed to him. It is just that the ancient utterances do not seem very specific nor are they directed to the details of our particular pleas. Still, we know that God does not speak out continually and immediately in the face of all evil, and such behavior stands in opposition to his asserted good intentions. He plays a waiting game. Thus, his challenge to man in silence must be to join him in the waiting. Clearly God is capable of hard action and of pressing us with awful burdens. But we can search his announced words for an indication of what he has done in the past, and what he may intend to do in the future, to protect us against destruction.

In the midst of the roar of a technological civilization, we are not used to the idea of living in silence. Thus, it is hard to learn to interpret God along these lines. The Swiss philosopher Max Picard moved against his time and wrote about *The World of Silence*.[4] What he discovered is that the noise of machines has not done away with silence. It is just more difficult, but all the more necessary, to locate. Faith depends upon our success, since religious trust does not grow in noise but is founded on what we discover in silence. However, silence is more than simply what happens when we stop talking. It has a structure of its own which we must discover. If we can uncover silence, our language gains greater significance.

Is there a complete world of silence itself? If so, to live there would amount to the ultimate test of man. And this test is a divine test, since divinity is discovered in our connection to silence (p. 4). Silence is also a way back to the experience of ultimate origins. In noise and motion we face the other objects in the world around us; in silence we can find ourselves confronted by the original beginnings of all things (p. 6). Silence allows us to think back to origins. Silence is like the world prior to creation before speaking emerged (p. 13). It would not be necessary to experience silence in this way if words were capable of expressing the whole truth for man. Since they cannot, since they are only symbols which give direction, words need to be placed against silence so that their nature as symbols is not distorted by pretending that they offer a literal truth.

How Words Relate to Silence

Words set limits. That is their function as we construct definitions. But since our definitions cannot be wholly accurate, we need to locate a silence underneath thought in order to help the mind move freely. If words in themselves have an affinity with finitude, then the mind has a natural disposition to move in infinity, and silence enhances this capacity. It frees the mind from a slavish dependence on words and opens us to experience the larger realms out of which words came to be fixed in their meaning. Without words no precision in expression would be possible; without silence words might attain a false solidity. When the mind knows that it cannot utter all it would like to by using words, it discovers its unrecognized home in the world of silence (p. 23).

"When a man is silent he is like man waiting on the creation of language for the first time" (p. 25). When speech comes and stands in contrast to silence, it has power and novelty as a mode of expression. If we are aware that something is more powerful than language itself, we are not tempted to attribute more value to verbal discourse than we should. Silence teaches us that, because it arises from something else, language is not ultimate. It is formed in order to express something other than itself. Silence properly understood releases us from dependence on language, so that we are not shut up within the circle of our own words. Silence is the only "place" where we can stand outside of language to gain perspective on it. Often we understand words only when we stop using them.

Silence should not be confused with inwardness. Certain forms of solitude simply isolate the individual and turn him inward to consume himself. Properly understood, silence is expansive and should direct the person outside of himself. Silence should liberate us from all confines, because it does not mean quietly listening to oneself talk. Silence puts a stop to talk and diminishes self-concern by encouraging listening. Thus, knowledge, whether of the self or of other matters, no longer becomes a burden. What we know in silence seems to come to us and not to be manufactured by us. Therefore, we do not constantly have to hold on to our understanding and defend it as if our life were at stake in forcing the final acceptance of our words. What we learn in silence does not have our ego tied to its continuance, because it has not been constructed by us but has come to us. We constantly fight to preserve and to justify our own words, that is, we do until silence teaches us to stop verbalizing in self-defense.

How we treat silence depends upon the theory we hold about how words are related to objects. If the reality of the world and of ourselves could be exhausted by description in words or formulae, silence is not important. But if every fact and person has a reality of a deeper sort, a word which designates this hidden fund of reality is encountered only by the use of silence. Silence breaks the hold language has on the mind and allows it to experience reality, both inner and outer, as something more than words and concepts and symbols and formulae. This is the lesson of Zen meditation. And images are more closely related to silence than words are, since images are silent and yet speak to us. They are a silent language (p. 80). In this sense, poetry and art are closer to the world of silence than the average philosopher is when surrounded by his own words and constantly multiplying thoughts. Thus, some recent metaphysicians have rightly turned to poetry as a source of inspiration and Zen meditation encourages art forms.

The noise of words will level everything down if we allow it to. It makes everything seem the same (p. 183). The trivial and the crucial exist on the same level of importance if speech is not discriminating. Turning thoughts into verbal or written words does nothing in itself to assure us that what is crucial will be given the attention it is due. If we are careful, we can detect what is important in what is spoken of, but doing so depends on our ability to listen. And listening is possible only where there is a silence in man (p. 174). If our age of instant communication has conspired to banish silence from the world, all sense of the crucial *vs.* the trivial goes with it. That may be the central agony of our time. If we are constantly assailed by noise and attacked with words, our sensitivities grow dull. In such a situation words may be distinguished only by what is loud and shrill, unless we take great care to speak some important words softly. Silence can restore a sense of balance and importance to language. This is why obscenities, and so much else that is harsh but real, traditionally were left unspoken. To say too much overtly actually limits our freedom of expression, a fact that the "free speech" movement of the '60s did not understand. They confused freedom by trying to say too much.

If God dwells in silence, he will be missed if we live in noise and violence, like today's teenagers each with a stereo radio. Action is often necessary to relieve suffering, but the life which dissolves into nothing but a frantic series of efforts will stumble onto God only by accident, if at all. If silence should be the context we use for God today (that is, his silence), we miss the opportunity for divine disclosure unless we match our silence with his. If God's silence toward us is intended to carry a message, we cannot grasp it if we do not leave room for our own silence or learn how to deal with it. Our rediscovery of God requires, as a precondition for reaching a new understanding, our developed silence in the face of his.

NOTES

1. Dionysius the Areopagite, *The Divine Names,* trans. C. E. Rolt (London: S.P.C.K., 1940). All page references are to this edition.

2. C. G. Jung, *Archetypes of the Collective Unconscious,* trans. R. C. R. Hull (London: Routledge & Kegan Paul, 1959). All page references are to this volume.

3. Thomas Merton, *Thoughts in Solitude* (Garden City, N.Y.: Doubleday Image Books, 1958). All page references are to this volume.

4. Max Picard, *The World of Silence,* trans. Stanly Godman (Chicago: Henry Regnery, 1952). All page numbers in this section are of that edition.

Part Three
PROBLEMS IN RELIGIOUS LANGUAGE

Wittgenstein, Language, and Religious Belief
MICHAEL J. COUGHLAN

Wittgenstein had a great deal to say about language, but comparatively little about religious belief. The mature Wittgenstein's views on this subject are conveyed to us largely by the notes of some of his students, published under the title *Lectures on Religious Belief*.[1] We also have, of course, the well-known remarks near the end of his early work, the *Tractatus Logico-Philosophicus*.[2] The general thrust of these earlier remarks is that *nothing* can be said about God. Yet it does not follow from this contention that language bears no relation to our concept of the divine, for some things which cannot be said, according to Wittgenstein, are *shown* by our language. From this point of view, one thing that our language shows clearly is that God is transcendental. In the only explicit reference Wittgenstein makes to God in this context, he says, "God does not reveal himself *in* the world" (6.432). At one fell swoop this claim wipes aside all of the time-honoured attempts to demonstrate the existence of God from our experience of the world, that is, by way of causal, teleological, miracle, and suchlike arguments. Although Wittgenstein later came to reject the theory of language from which this claim followed in the *Tractatus*, it seems, nonetheless, that he continued to hold that those who purport to prove the existence or attributes of God in the manner of this theistic tradition are involved in some kind of deep confusion.

Critics of Wittgenstein, and of those Wittgensteinian philosophers who have developed his ideas in this sphere, have objected that this view is indefensible, or, at least, that it clashes with the general spirit of Wittgenstein's own later work. The central aim of this paper is to show to what extent the Wittgensteinian approach to religion is not only not opposed to the general trend of Wittgenstein's philosophy, but rather that it follows logically therefrom. A by-product of this exercise, it is hoped, will be to earn for the Wittgensteinian view a more sympathetic hearing than that which it is frequently accorded.

Problems in Religious Language

* * *

Essentially the Wittgensteinian position under discussion is that central religious beliefs, such as belief in the existence of God, or in the immortality of the soul, or, to use one of his own examples from the *Lectures on Religious Belief,* belief in the Last Judgment, are not to be construed as beliefs in facts, not even very special kinds of facts, for which one might seek and adduce evidence, and which we might discover to be true or false at some future date. To treat religious beliefs in this way is to treat them as, if not empirical beliefs, at least quasi-empirical beliefs; beliefs, that is, with a logical form (or grammar) which is significantly comparable to the logical form of routine empirical beliefs such as: 'I believe that it will rain tomorrow'. But there are too many important differences between the ways in which we operate with these beliefs: evidence, expectations, certitude and doubt, acceptance and rejection, all function in fundamentally different ways in the two spheres.

No doubt the latter observations will appear unobjectionable to most theologians, perhaps even as trivially obvious. But many find the conclusion which is drawn from them, that is, that central beliefs of the kind mentioned are not beliefs in facts which may be true, rather less acceptable. Why does Wittgenstein draw this conclusion, and why is it thought to be discordant with the general spirit of his later work? What is at issue here can best be seen by contrast with the philosophy of language of the *Tractatus.* In that earlier work we are told the form which language *must* take if it is to make sense, and all statements must share one general form (roughly: 'This is how things are', where 'This' is a picture of a state of affairs). The requirement that all statements must share this logical form is, apparently, a logical one; a requirement that holds in all situations, in any world, for any kind of language-user. The later philosophy is utterly opposed to this stipulative account of language. Language is now portrayed as having scope for countless forms. Furthermore, to understand the form of a linguistic utterance one has to have a grasp of the particulars of the situation in which it is uttered, and of the general context, both historical and contemporary. In short, linguistic form is no longer predetermined by logic, but is a function of the particular historical community in which it is employed. This appears to give communities licence to generate linguistic forms, or language-games as they are now called, without reservation. But, more significantly for our purposes, if we ask for the *justification* for a particular language-game, the answer ultimately will not consist in observations on the requirements of logic, but in the conversation-stopping: 'That's just what we do'. Wittgenstein holds that even that apparently most logical of language-games, mathematics, has in the end no more sound a justification than physical theories or religious beliefs. Why do we produce the series: 2, 4, 6, 8, 10, etc., when asked to consecutively add 2? There is no non-question-begging proof; ultimately all we can say is: "That's the way we do it!"

But, given this view of linguistic practices, how can we consistently go on to claim that particular "language-games," such as those in which individuals argue theistically for the existence of God, or claim to be evaluating scientific evidence for immortality, are objectionably confused? In fact, the little we know of what Wittgenstein had to say, and the volumes written by his followers, suggest the view that it is only exceptionally that this kind of confusion arises, or, to put it more precisely, it is unlikely to arise in our ordinary, everyday lives, but only when we somehow abstract ourselves from our everyday dealings and begin to theorize—when our language is not in use, but "on holiday." For the paradigmatic religious believer, his "beliefs" are not so much truths which he sees as more or less supported by independent evidence to be found in the world, but rather regulative principles for his life, or rules of perspective which govern *how* he sees the world. A genuine belief in the Last Judgment, according to Wittgenstein, is not a belief about an event to come, to which his current conduct is relevant, but the embracing of a particular way of looking at his current conduct; a picture, regulating his way of life. It is with this aspect of the Wittgensteinian view that Patrick Sherry, for example, has taken issue:

[Wittgenstein] distorts the particular examples he discusses. Many people *would* regard the Last Judgement as a future "event" albeit of a highly unusual kind, and would regard their conduct in this life as having a determining influence on their fate after death. Wittgenstein does not do justice to Christian eschatological beliefs, nor does he explain the real fear which such beliefs can arouse, fear which would not be caused by a mere picture.[3]

It has been suggested that what may have "misled" Wittgenstein into "reducing" belief in the Last Judgment to commitment to a picture was the frequent use of mythological language in this connection. But myths are not just pictures, and "the fact that we use mythological language when describing a future happening does not mean that we do not believe that it will, in some way, take place."[4] But, one may ask, in what way might it take place? As an empirical event in the history of the natural world? Surely not, for the Last Judgment is said to be a *supernatural* affair. But what kind of events are supernatural events? Are they like natural events, except that they involve supernatural objects rather than natural objects? This appears to be the view of Stephen Satris, who takes Dewi Z. Phillips, a leading exponent of Wittgensteinian philosophy of religion, to task for denying that 'God' is the name of an object. Phillips writes:

Coming to see that there is a God is not like coming to see that an additional being exists. If it were, there would be an extension of one's knowledge of facts, but no extension of one's understanding. Coming to see that there is a God involves seeing a new meaning in one's life, and being given a new understanding.

Satris comments:

One problem with this and similar arguments of Phillips is that it is unclear how such terms as 'object', 'being' and 'fact' are to be understood. According to how these terms are interpreted the conclusion becomes either too weak or too strong. If, on the one hand, the conclusion is that God is not a physical object or finite being, then the argument becomes superfluous. For the God whose nature is in question is the God of the Judaeo-Christian tradition, and according to this tradition God is spiritual, not physical, and infinite, not finite. . . . If, on the other hand, the argument is that God is not an object of any kind, then if this is not an expression of atheism (which would in fact be a quite natural interpretation of it), Phillips is failing to do justice to the tradition with which he is concerned. He himself says: 'The criteria of what can sensibly be said of God are to be found *within* the religious tradition.' Yet, according to the tradition, God is indeed an object, that is, a spiritual object (as also are angels and souls), and his existence is a matter of supernatural fact. In addition to the world of space and time, it is said, there are spiritual and supernatural beings, and God is one of these.[5]

Sherry and Satris typify a pattern of anti-Wittgensteinian criticism which seeks to show that, although the Wittgensteinian conception of religious belief might be one which approximates to some religious traditions, it does not have the universal applicability which

Wittgenstein and some of his followers seem to claim for it. In particular (and paradoxically, perhaps) it does not seem appropriate for the religious traditions with which Wittgenstein was most frequently in contact, viz., Judaism and Christianity.

*   *   *

Later in this paper I shall take a brief look at whether the Wittgensteinian account is as inappropriate as its critics portray it. For the present let us assume, with Satris, that there is a clash with the traditional, Judaeo-Christian understanding of religious belief. One might be inclined to wonder whether there is anything objectionable in that, in itself. Why should Wittgenstein and his followers not formulate and promulgate their own theories about how religion ought to be construed, in opposition to how it is construed? Is that not precisely what prophets and reformers have done repeatedly, with greater or lesser success? Without innovation in moral ideas, for example, we would still have widespread slavery, feudal laws, and so on. If moral reform is to be welcomed, why not religious reform?

We do not need to concern ourselves here with the controversial issue of whether moral reform has, in history, been brought about by changes in moral theory. This issue does not even arise because no authentic Wittgensteinian is going to entertain a defense of the kind that has been suggested. Such a defense is inadmissible for two related reasons. In the first place, it is implied that Wittgenstein is advancing a theory, that he is making a claim about how religious beliefs must, or ought, to be taken. This would be emphatically and vigorously denied by a Wittgensteinian such as Phillips. However, it might not be obvious (and it is clear from his critics that it is not to them) how he can deny this interpretation. To see how Phillips can deny it we have to turn to the second reason for repudiating the reformer analogy.

The early Wittgenstein sought to tell us how language has to be structured in order to make sense. Bertrand Russell took Wittgenstein to be proposing an ideal language which would be a great advance, in logic at least, over our ordinary language, with all its ambiguities and indefiniteness. But Wittgenstein seemed unhappy with this interpretation of his views and, in fact, wrote in the *Tractatus:* "All the sentences of our everyday language, just as they are, are logically in perfect order" (5.5563).[6] Even at this stage, then, Wittgenstein was not proposing reforms of the way we speak.

It is not the aim of Wittgensteinian philosophy to remold our language or our ideas, but rather to uncover for us the ideas, the logic of the language which we already have. Wittgenstein makes it clear that he does not regard it as appropriate for philosophy to interfere with the actual use of language. On the contrary, his view is that philosophy should only describe how language is used. "It leaves everything as it is," he writes, such that in the end, "Philosophy only states what everyone admits."[7]

These observations on the nature of philosophy from Wittgenstein's point of view may serve to make it clear why a Wittgensteinian would be horrified to find himself being portrayed as someone who proposes to reform the way in which we use religious language, but they also bring to the fore the charge of inconsistency. The principle that philosophy should be descriptive and non-reforming is surely one which Wittgenstein blatantly violates? And even if we can manage to clear Wittgenstein himself of this charge, surely his followers, particularly in the field of philosophy of religion, cannot be cleared? It is my contention that, despite appearances, both Wittgenstein and followers of his, such as Phillips, are, for the most part if not entirely, not guilty of inconsistency here. To see this we must get quite clear about the sense of such claims as that philosophy leaves everything as it is and merely states what everyone admits. Taken literally and without qualification, it has to be admitted that these claims conflict with much of Wittgenstein's own work, for one thing that he certainly does not do is to state what everyone admits, and this does not apply solely to the *Lectures on Religious Belief. Philosophical Investigations,* the central work of his later philosophy, for example, is composed almost entirely of a series of arguments and observations which are expressly aimed at persuading us *not* to say certain things which have often been said. We are cautioned against saying the kinds of thing Augustine said about language, what Descartes said about sensations and mental activities, the theories of essentialists and behaviorists, and, indeed, Wittgenstein's own Tractarian theories, among many other contentions of a philosophical nature, past and present. It is evident that at least part of what Wittgenstein intended by the claim that philosophy does not conflict with what everyone admits is that philosophical reasoning ought not to issue in conflict with *ordinary* everyday beliefs. It is even more evident that he cannot have meant that it will not lead us into conflict with philosophical or metaphysical theory.

But, one might wonder, is it possible to draw a distinction of this kind? Without recourse to stipulative theory, which is excluded for the Wittgensteinian, it does not seem possible to draw a clear line between our "ordinary everyday" beliefs, such as that 'It is now raining', and a metaphysical thesis such as that mind and brain are identical; how should we classify, for example, "scientific creationism" or the claim that only human beings smile? But Wittgenstein would have been unperturbed by these difficulties; one of the key themes of his later philosophy was that precise dividing lines were unnecessary for clear distinctions. If a single streetlight is illuminated at one end of a very long street, then, although there will be no sharp boundary between the illuminated and the unilluminated portions of that street, it is, nonetheless, clearly the case that one end is illuminated and the other is not. Similarly, despite the ambiguity of some cases, the mind-brain identity thesis is clearly a philosophical or metaphysical "claim," whereas the belief that it is now raining, held in normal circumstances, is clearly not a metaphysical belief, but an empirical one.

We can, therefore, identify some of the things people say as unambiguously metaphysical, or philosophical, and it is with these that the philosopher may take issue. This is not to challenge the ordinary use of language, but rather some of the extraordinary things people have been inclined to say when they have taken that language out of its role in everyday commerce and begun to indulge in speculative theorizing. It is not the part of philosophy to engage in controversy concerning empirical claims of a standard type, or to question particular judgments of value, or to query the appropriateness of traditional religious practices. Wittgenstein conceived of philosophy as therapeutic, of its having a role like that of a healing agent; that is, by itself it does nothing, it leaves everything as it is, but once there is an appropriate ailment it can swing into action and try to effect a cure. It advances no theories of its own, but is parasitic on those of others, drawing out the implications of their theories in order to show how they inevitably lead to claims which conflict with what ordinary people actually do and say.

The only sense in which the Wittgensteinian might be characterized as a reformer, then, would be as a reformer of metaphysical theory, but, perhaps, a better description would be that of a *dismantler* of such theory; he has no reformulated theory to offer. In what would, we may presume, pass for a Wittgensteinian Utopia, viz., a world free of metaphysical theory, it would be literally true that philosophers would state only what everyone admits. Lest any professional philosophers should become excessively concerned about the possible personal consequences of the advent of such a state of affairs, I should hasten to add that Wittgenstein, in common with, for instance, G. K. Chesterton and R. G. Collingwood, held that metaphysical theories arise from the most basic general propensities of mankind, such that it is extremely improbable that we shall ever escape their allure.

*   *   *

Let us return to the specific issue of religious language. What relevance, if any, does the role of the philosopher as dismantler of metaphysical theory have for religion? Once the question is posed in this way, we can immediately see an answer suggesting itself. The philosopher's concern will not be with "ordinary everyday" expression of religious belief such as: 'God will reward the good and punish the wicked' or 'Mohammed is Allah's prophet', but with the more formal expressions we find in doctrinal theory, for example, formal statements of the nature of the Trinity, or the doctrine of transubstantiation. In the Western tradition, at least, theological doctrine has been formulated in terms and concepts borrowed from philosophical doctrine. The most fundamental theological divide in Western Christianity is that between Augustinianism and Thomism, and the difference of emphasis between Augustine and Thomas is explained, in great part, by the fact that one

was essentially a Neo-Platonist, the other much more of an Aristotelian. Their theological doctrines were built around their differing metaphysical and epistemological presuppositions. The intrusion of metaphysics into theology can be seen in our earlier quotation from Satris: ". . . according to the tradition, God is indeed an object, that is a spiritual object (as also are angels and souls), and his existence is a matter of supernatural fact." Claims of this kind, if they are not to be taken metaphorically, bear the distinctive marks of having been molded by a Platonic-Cartesian philosophy, with its theory of the soul as a separate substance, essentially intelligence or thought, or whatever. If such metaphysical doctrines are untenable (as Wittgenstein argues at great length), then the value of notions such as "spiritual objects" and "supernatural facts" needs to be re-examined. If Cartesianism leads us to the superstition of the mind of man as "the ghost in the machine," as Gilbert Ryle argued,[8] is it not likely also to lead us to a superstitious conception of God? Whether it does so might be a matter of controversy, but it is unquestionable that it affords us a notion of God which is heavily laden with metaphysical theory. Indeed, traditional Western theological doctrine is nothing less than *replete* with the theories of metaphysicians. Insofar as this is the case, Wittgenstein's stricture on philosophical enterprise, to leave ordinary language undisturbed, does not apply.

One might admit the legitimacy of Wittgensteinian philosophers' taking issue with metaphysical doctrines which have been imbibed by theology and yet feel that this does not excuse the whole of the Wittgensteinian approach. It might not seem to cover, for example, Patrick Sherry's example of the repudiation of the understanding of the Last Judgment as "a future 'event' albeit of a highly unusual kind." Surely this is a paradigm of an ordinary everyday belief of religious people? But a lot must depend here on what precisely is to be understood by such an event. In what sense is it "highly unusual," and what is the significance of the quotation marks encompassing "event"? Clearly such an event *cannot* be an ordinary everyday belief of the kind we have concerning empirical matters. If it were to be so taken, then it would be very difficult to account for the characteristic unshakability of the belief, given that unavailability of a shred of convincing empirical evidence to support it. One of the foremost themes of the *Lectures on Religious Belief* is the marked incongruity between religious convictions and beliefs about empirical matters. Certitude on an empirical matter is prudently proportioned to the degree and the quality of the evidence available to support it, but in religion we seem to find the firmest certitude in the absence of any relevant evidence. It is obviously mistaken, therefore, to treat belief in the Last Judgment as on a par with ordinary beliefs in a coming empirical event.

Sherry is in partial agreement, at least, with this. But if the religious belief is to be taken in some different sense, can anything be said about the nature of this sense? What other content can be given to the notion of a future event? Satris, as we have seen, portrays the realm of supernatural beings and events as *outside* of space and time. On this view it makes no sense whatever to speak of such events as "future." We are, it seems, forced back to the more common notion that the Last Judgment is something that occurs *in time*; sometime after our deaths. But, then, who or what is subjected to this judgment? A popular traditional answer is that it will be ourselves, living on as disembodied souls or possibly with resurrected bodies. But how can such a conception of the Last Judgment be entertained without embracing wholesale some metaphysical framework, such as those offered by Platonism or Cartesianism, in which the "real man" or "essential me" is separable from the body which I currently happen to inhabit? Thus, an apparently innocuous "everyday" belief *can* turn out on closer scrutiny to be embedded in, and an expression of, a particular metaphysical system. The philosopher's task is not to dissuade people from expressing belief in the Last Judgment, but to wrest that belief from the clutches of the metaphysicians, or of the pseudoscientists, who threaten to reduce it to a superstition.

What, then, we may ask, does unadulterated belief in the Last Judgment come to? Wittgenstein's response to this, as to so many other questions, is to enjoin us to refrain from flights of speculative fancy and simply look and see what function it has in the lives of believers. It will color the believer's whole view of his world; it will "regulate" for all in his life. "Take two people, one of whom talks of his behavior and of what happens to him in terms of retribution, the other one does not. These people think entirely differently," Wittgenstein remarks. "Yet, so far, you can't say they believe different things."[9] If it did turn out that they believed different things, for example, about whether there will be a Judgment Day in two thousand years' time, Wittgenstein's view is that the difference between them would not constitute a difference of a *religious* nature. The logic, or grammar, of religious beliefs and of beliefs about future events is quite distinct. It would be reasonable to demand evidence for the claim that there will be a Judgment Day in two thousand years' time, but seeking the evidence to support the religious belief would betray a misunderstanding. Again, denying the claim about the future makes sense; denying the religious claim does not. At most, one can say: "I do not see life in this way."

* * *

Religious belief, as construed by Wittgenstein, therefore, is about *how* we see life, *how* we see the world, rather than about *what* we see in life or in the world. It bears upon the *framework* within which we perceive, such that, for the believer, God will permeate his entire universe. Transferring this point to the linguistic sphere, it might seem that I am expressing agreement with Frank Harrison, who argues in his contribution to this volume[10] that existential claims might be embodied in the grammatical structures of a particular language or language-game. However, I wish to dissent from this view, at least insofar as it is the question of the existence of God which is at issue. If we take it that God is not *a* being, which clearly seems to have been Wittgenstein's view, then, despite appearances, 'God exists' is not an existential proposition. In order to see how commitment to God can be construed as something not involving existential commitment, I should like to make use of the Venn diagram introduced into one of our conference discussions by James Green. On this diagram the cosmos was represented as contained within a circle inscribed on a sheet of paper, the edges of which are to be seen, not as boundaries but, as representing the infinite within which the finite exists.

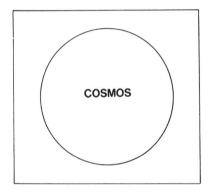

On such a diagram, the only way in which God can be represented, Green remarked, is by changing color. This claim struck me as remarkably reminiscent of Wittgenstein's ideas in his *Tractatus* period. The sole point of dissent would have been that Wittgenstein would not have wished to portray the cosmos as a bounded whole within the diagram; it, too, fills the diagram, but monochromatically, so to speak. It takes God, or value, to get us from black and white to color.

This imagery, I believe, can be carried over into the later philosophy. We have had a number of remarks in the discussions of this conference about the language-game concept. Most of these, although not all, have been expressions of reservations about applying the concept to religious discourse. The essence of these reservations seems to be that, if religious-language (God-talk) comprises a discrete language-game, it is not clear how it can tie-in with the rest of our language-games, or with life in general. In one sense,

these reservations are justified because of what many Wittgenstein-
ians have done with the language-game notion. But in another
sense, they are not, because Wittgenstein's notion has been too
often misrepresented by those who claim to follow him. Language-
games in general do not comprise discrete spheres of discourse for
Wittgenstein; rather, they overlap and crisscross each other in innumerable ways. For certain purposes it may be useful to distinguish particular linguistic patterns as language-games, but this is
always a dangerous exercise, for taking them out of the context of
life in which they belong is to mis-portray them; one loses at once
their binding role in the lives of those who share their use. Wittgenstein's best analogy here is that of the spun thread (*Philosophical
Investigations* I § 67). A spun thread is composed of innumerable
strands, overlapping, crisscrossing, and binding each other together.
One can separate individual strands to inspect them more closely,
but, however closely one inspects a particular strand, separated
from the thread itself, one will never discover how it meshes with
the rest, its role in life as a whole.

So much for the general notion of a language-game. When we
come to religious discourse, we have, I think, a special case; not an
entirely unique one, for ethics and aesthetics appear to be quite
similar. This is where, in my view, some Wittgensteinian language-
game theorists have gone astray, but here, I must add, I am, as
Nona Bolin remarked, "hearing the unspoken prescription of Wittgenstein's thought." If we are to speak of a religious language-
game at all, I suggest, we are to think of it, not as an individual
strand of the thread, but as a quality of the thread as a whole—its
color, or its texture, perhaps. In the only place where Wittgenstein
does say something more than enigmatic about how a religious
belief might bear on one's life, i.e., in the passages in *Lectures on
Religious Belief,* to which we have already alluded, note that he
conceives of the belief, not as a rule which governs one particular
language-game among others, but as regulating for *everything* in a
man's life. We might say that it gives color or texture to the whole
thread, or, in terms of the Venn diagram again, it is not a belief
about a particular state of affairs within the cosmos, or even a rule
about how we see a particular aspect of the cosmos; it colors the
whole diagram—it permeates everything.

Satris appears to want to say something akin to this: "To come
to believe [that God exists] is not to paint a new object into one's
picture of the world, but to paint an altogether new object which

bears a special relation to that picture" (p. 508). But why portray God as an *object* at all, when that term is likely to be so misleading, given its customary connotation of a spatio-temporal entity? Indeed, what content can the notion of object have outside of the spatio-temporal continuum? One is tempted to suspect that the motivation for its retention must be a fear that, without it, God would lose reality. The objectivity of the reality of God might seem to depend upon retaining the vocabulary of "objects," "events," "facts," and so on, in a supernatural or metaphysical realm. In his Plenary Address to this conference, Huston Smith voiced a general concern about antimetaphysical philosophies:

Existentialism and phenomenology . . . [a]ssuming that metaphysical objectivity is of a piece with scientific, . . . turned their backs on both varieties and launched the "post-Nietzschean deconstruction of metaphysics." A surprising variety of schools joined this project: Anglo-American philosophy with Wittgenstein, Continental philosophy with Heidegger, Deconstruction with Derrida, the advocates of narrative over formal discourse, and theologians as well. "The Bible does not give us a world view," we now read. The disclaimer goes back to Schleiermacher who broke with metaphysics to found religion on experience.

Smith has no doubts about the consequences:

The movement has left us sloshing in the historicism, relativism, and subjectivity of a single-storied universe where time reigns supreme. In Walker Percy's current title, we are *Lost in the Cosmos*.

I find this view unnecessarily pessimistic, and I shall briefly endeavor to show why.

It is now a relatively uncontroversial point that the meaning of a word is only exceptionally given by a hard and fast definition. Rather, it is determined by the *use* that word has, which is something dynamic, not static. So its meaning never has firm boundaries, around which clear lines can be drawn. This notion, perhaps not originally Wittgenstein's, but most influentially advanced by Wittgenstein this century, has now become virtually philosophical common property. But this notion is *all of a piece* with Wittgenstein's notion that it is a mistake to think that religious belief has to be based upon metaphysical theory.

Let me try to expand on this. Again, the antidote to the idea that words have definable meanings is to "look and see." Wittgenstein's prime example was that of "game" (which example he then exploited by extending it into the "language-game"). What is the definition of a game? Well, let's look and see what are called games. There are board-games, card-games, ball games, Olympic games, and so on. Some games involve teams, others do not; some involve winning and losing, others do not; and so on. Games, Wittgenstein says, have no one thing in common (*Philosophical Investigations* I § 66). Strictly this was wrong, for all games are, e.g., activities, but this does not affect his point which was that they have no characteristic, or set of characteristics, which mark them off as games: if all games are activities, nonetheless not all activities are games. The fear of abandoning definitions for words is the fear that we could no longer use words unambiguously; the fear of linguistic relativism, subjectivity, anarchy. But we *do* manage to use words which have no definitions all of the time, and we are not continually misunderstood; our language does not, as a matter of fact, degenerate into anarchy.

My suggestion is that worries concerning antimetaphysical philosophy are parallel to those of the one who fears that abandoning definitions for words will lead to linguistic anarchy. It is the fear that abandoning metaphysics leaves us open to "historicism, relativism, and subjectivity." The linguistic fear is that, if words have no definitions, I can mean whatever I wish by my words. But I *cannot*—not if I am going to communicate. I cannot give my words any use I wish; they already have a use in my culture and, if I fail to take account of that, I shall fail to communicate. Similarly, abandoning theological metaphysics is not going to lead to a situation in which I can mean whatever I wish by 'God'. 'God' can no longer be given a theistic-type definition, but do we seriously think that, without that, worship would become meaningless or without recognizable form; or that anything could count as worship?

* * *

Much more could be said on the latter issue, but it should be clear that neither relativism nor "subjectivity" follows from the dismantling of metaphysics. Furthermore, it should now be evident that Wittgenstein's remarks on religious belief, and Wittgensteinian philosophy of religion of the kind embraced by Phillips, are not as un-Wittgensteinian as they might initially appear. Rather they are a natural outcome of not only his general conception of philosophy, but also of the anti-dualism and anti-essentialism which follow from that conception. But is Wittgenstein's account one which, nonetheless, clashes with the understanding of the "orthodox" believer? The difficulty in answering this question is that what may count as the orthodox understanding of belief is not at all clear. Indeed, the thrust of anti-essentialism is a warning against such ideas as that there is something which might be called *the* orthodox understanding of belief. Despite this, I think that it is still possible to say that the Wittgensteinian account does not do as much violence to traditional understandings of belief as has been suggested. I shall, finally, try to illustrate this with reference to the issue of petitionary prayer.

From the Wittgensteinian point of view, it is clear that petitionary prayer cannot be construed after the manner of ordinary petitionary appeals. Ordinary petitionary appeals are directed to a specific agent, and the hope is that the agent will respond positively to the appeal, by acting so as to bring about the desired state of affairs. But if God is not a specific being, then it would be inappropriate to construe petitionary prayer in this sense. Dewi Phillips, in *The Concept of Prayer*, suggests that the appropriate understanding of petitionary prayer is as an act of consent to the Divine Will: such prayer "reduces" to: "Thy will be done."[11] He has been taken to task for this "reductionsim," again on the grounds that he misrepresents the believer's understanding of his prayer. The line of objection is clearly presented by Peter Geach in the following passage, although he is not here directing himself expressly to Phillips:

I remember a philosopher affirming in discussion that the Lord's Prayer was an example not of the 'lower' sort of prayer in which one prays for something to happen but only of the 'higher' sort in which one expresses acceptance of the Divine Will. He was, however, clearly wrong, even if we forget the petition for daily bread. For 'Thy will be done' in the context of the Lord's Prayer is not expressing resignation; it is a petition that God's will may be willingly obeyed by the inhabitants of Earth as it is already by the blessed in Heaven . . .[12]

Geach finds nothing amiss with praying for something to happen in the sense of asking for, and hoping to receive, even concrete realities such as our daily bread, in the manner in which children might hope that their parents will answer their pleas for more pudding. Indeed he takes it further, portraying even apparently submissive prayer elements, such as "Thy will be done," as also unambiguously petitionary in the same sense.

Geach is a Catholic philosopher, so it might seem that he can lay more claim than Phillips to authority on at least the Catholic understanding of petitionary prayer. But contrast his view now with that of Karl Rahner, who could well be acclaimed the leading Catholic *theologian* of this century:

A truly Christian prayer of petition is a prayer which is essentially human. . . . Such a prayer is the cry of elementary self-preservation, a naked expression of our instinctive clinging to life, arising from the very depths of human life and anguish. Yet, such prayer is also essentially divine. In the very act of, as it were, defending our earthly life against God, we adopt an attitude of complete submission to Him and to his inscrutable designs for us. . . . Thus, our prayer of petition is, in the ultimate analysis, not a plea for life and the things of this life, but a submission to the Will of God even when that Will points to deprivation and perhaps to death.[13]

It would appear, then, that the Wittgensteinian conception of religious belief and practice may not be as far removed from the religious traditions as it is sometimes thought to be. Nevertheless, I feel that, ultimately, we cannot wholly endorse Wittgenstein. There *are* people who understand and practice petitionary prayer in the sense in which Geach presents it. There *are* people who believe in the Last Judgment in the sense of an event which is to come in a certain, but unspecifiable, number of years. There are those who conceive of God as *a* being, and so on. All of these beliefs, and others of a similar kind, are generally labelled 'religious beliefs'; they form part of what is generally understood to fall under the description 'religious belief'. It is, therefore, mere stipulation, and uncharacteristic stipulation, on the part of Wittgenstein to deny that such beliefs may be called "religious." Phillips is more cautious than his master on this. Noting that not all believers have a Wittgensteinian understanding of their belief, but that some take a Geach-type view, he comments:

We can mark the distinction either as one between . . . religion and superstition, or say that not all beliefs which are called . . . religious are of the same kind. The important point is simply that we do draw a distinction.[14]

If Wittgenstein had put it like that in the *Lectures on Religious Belief,* and perhaps if Phillips had written it in bold type, we might have had far less controversy about the validity of the Wittgensteinian analysis.[15]

═══════════════NOTES═══════════════

1. C. Barret, *Lectures and Conversations on Aesthetics: Psychology and Religious Belief* (Oxford: Blackwell, 1966), 53 ff.

2. Ludwig Wittgenstein, *Tractatus Logico-Philosophicus* (London: Routledge and Kegan Paul, 1961).

3. Patrick Sherry, *Religion, Truth and Language-Games* (London: Macmillan Press, 1977), 15.

4. *Ibid.*, 199, n.10. The view is that expressed by Ninian Smart, *Philosophers and Religious Truth* (London: SCM Press, 1969), 181.

5. Stephen Satris, "Wittgenstein and the Philosophy of Religion," *Proceedings of the 2nd International Wittgenstein Symposium* (Vienna, 1978), 507–509.

6. See G. E. M. Anscombe, *An Introduction to Wittgenstein's Tractatus* (London: Hutchinson, 1971), 71 ff.

7. Ludwig Wittgenstein, *Philosophical Investigations*, trans. G. E. M. Anscombe (Oxford: Blackwell, 1971), 124, 599.

8. Gilbert Ryle, *The Concept of Mind* (Middlesex: Penguin, 1963), ch. I.

9. Ludwig Wittgenstein, *Lectures on Religious Belief*, 54 f.

10. "Language, Knowledge, and God," chap. 2 in this volume.

11. Dewi Phillips, *The Concept of Prayer* (Oxford: Blackwell, 1965).

12. Peter Geach, *God and the Soul* (London: Routledge and Kegan Paul, 1969), 86.

13. Karl Rahner, *Happiness through Prayer* (London, 1959), 86.

14. Dewi Phillips, *Religion without Explanation* (Oxford: Blackwell, 1976), 110.

15. I am particularly indebted to Nona Bolin for her stimulating response to the original version of this paper.

Act and Expression
in Henry Duméry's
Philosophy of Religion
CHARLES COURTNEY

I

I am seizing the occasion of this gathering of specialists in philosophy of religion to explore a topic that has both interested and perplexed me for a long time. I think it is an important topic in philosophy of religion and in the thought of Henry Duméry, but it is one about which I am not at all sure that I am clear. Thus, I welcome the opportunity to share my probings and reflections and, no doubt, my confusions with you.

Henry Duméry, a Frenchman, was born in 1920 and since the late 40s has been a major contributor to the philosophy of religion. For many years he has been an administrator of the International Institute of Philosophy. He taught at the University of Caen and is presently Professor of Philosophy at the University of Paris (Nanterre).

In the Introduction to my translation of *Le problème de dieu* (1964) and in my Northwestern University dissertation on Duméry (1965), I was concerned with his conception of philosophy and with his thinking on God or the One. I did not deal with his philosophy of religion as such. Recently, I wrote a paper on the religious intentionality as a transcending toward God. Now, as a contribution to our discussions of language as a medium of knowledge of God, I would like to look more closely at the principal elements of that intentionality. This has led me to study act, expression, and their interrelation. The topic interests me because it is basic to Duméry's philosophy. It perplexes me because, as was the case in my study of his treatment of the problem of God, I question whether Duméry has presented a single, coherent position.

II

Duméry claims to have shown that the transcendence of God is preserved only if God is transdeterminate, that is, if we refrain from locating ideas, essences, and values "in" God. All determinations, all determinateness, are to be found this side of God. They are freely posed, says Duméry, by the human subject. And with this we have introduced the key terms for our discussion; for the free human subject is *act* and the outcome of the act is language, idea, meaning, determination, and artifact, that is, expression.

The technical term that Duméry invented to characterize the human subject is "act–law." It points to a multiplicity or duality, not to a dualism. It is not as if there were two parts to human beings or two natures that are brought together. In order to be real, humans must act; what they create in acting are expressive determinations. So law or expression should be seen as modifying the free human act. Act–law is the structure that applies to all human projects and intentions, from perception to science to art to religion.

Humans, who must originate determinations in order to be, generate objects. Duméry does not develop the point, but he seems to be suggesting that the dynamic of act–law would enable us to understand all of the objectivities of our natural, social, and cultural world. How does the act–law structure apply to religion? It does apply but in a complicated way. Religion, as a human intentionality, takes shape through objectifying consciousness. Religious objects are constituted; God is among them. But if God is transdeterminate, if determinations arise this side of God, then God cannot be an object in the sense that worldly things and institutions are.

Duméry makes a place for both God's transcendence and religious objects by saying that the process of revelation consists not in acquiring an objective representation of God, but in seeing certain objects as revelatory of God. That is, the basic objectifying character of human consciousness is preserved, even though certain qualifications are introduced because of the peculiar goals of the religious intentionality. God is this goal and since God cannot be objectified, religious expressions are seen as indirect aids to the religious intentionality. Whereas the expressions which serve worldly intentionalities constitute objects, religious expressions always merely point to the "object" of religion.

To this point our exposition has brought out two sets of relations, one between act and expression and another between act–expression and the goal of religion. Let us examine them in turn.

III

Duméry insists not only on the indissolubility of act and expression but also on the primacy of act. The primacy, however, is not obvious for they are always together. In order to be, the human subject must act, and its mode of acting is to generate expressions. The act is not primary in the sense that expressions could be eliminated, leaving the acting subject remaining. Wherein lies the primacy?

It may help to consider expressions independently of act. Duméry says that when this is done, and it has been done by more than one philosopher, we end up with what he calls a notional formalism. We have an ordered system of ideas, but no sense of what intentions they are linked with. To take the expressions with no reference to the human subject and human intentions is to mistake them. This is a tricky point, for the mistake is not to have missed some objective evidence that is there. It is not a matter of observing and describing the expressions and then observing and describing the act. The act is not available in that way. It is only manifest to us as expressive. Yet an immediate awareness of ourselves as acting accompanies our acting. It is this nonobjective awareness that Duméry, along with Blondel and Sartre, appeals to when he says that we do not understand expressions for what they are when we dissociate them from the acting subject. The same criticism that is made of notionalism is also made of materialism and behaviorism. To take a much discussed example, there is no objective perceptual difference between the cases of having one's arm raised and raising one's arm. But there is a difference. In the one case I am acted upon and my arm moves. In the other I am the agent, and I can know the difference between the two cases not by looking ever so carefully at my arm, but by noting when the immediate awareness of acting is present or absent. Consider another example, that of the house and the builder. If the builder never builds a house, he or she is never a builder, strictly speaking. But it would be wrong to take the house as an autonomous entity and leave the builder out of account. The house and the builder require each other, but not in the same way. The relation is not symmetrical. A subject capable of action can produce a house and in the process "make" a builder, but a house can produce neither itself nor a builder. The act, then, is primary not because it is temporally prior to expression but because it is of a different and originating order.

Several important things for Duméry's philosophy of religion follow from his understanding of the act–expression relation. First, from the unobservability of act it follows that philosophical reflection has as its sole subject matter the body of expressions. Even though Duméry is critical of notional formalism, it must be admitted that only expressions are directly available to reflection. Whatever is said about acts, beyond the judgment that they are, must be the result of the hermeneutics of expressions.

Second, although Duméry says (*Critique et religion,* 201) that the philosopher must grasp religious expressions in relation to the religious intentionality (act) that they seek to mediate, this is not a relation about which much can be said. It is not a relation to be observed and described, for the reason that there are not two objects to be studied. Grasping religious expression in relation to religious act is knowing that the expressions are related to an act. Refraining from regarding the expressions as autonomous does not mean that you can then see more. It is not like refraining from looking only north and turning around to look south. If you do that you will see more. Recognizing that expressions are related to act does not allow you to see more; it allows you to see what you are seeing for what it is.

Third, Duméry uses his understanding of the act–expression relation to make a case to theologians and ecclesiastical authorities in behalf of his conception of philosophy of religion. Even though expressions must be related to concrete intentionality, they may be described, ordered, and judged by critical reason without reference to the act, that is, the religious life, of any particular individual. Practical judgments are to be made by the person or by religious authorities, not by the philosopher. Philosophers judge critically, but not in such a way as to be in competition with religious authorities. The philosopher knows that expressions are without efficacy until they are made operative by an individual or community. The philosopher also knows that the actions of religious persons are not to be judged. The philosopher takes the body of expressions generated by religious persons and sorts them out according to the various levels of consciousness. This kind of limited, reflective judgment permits a hierarchical ordering of expressions and it allows the interrelation of the different levels of expression to be seen. But it does not intrude on the religious life itself. And it does not import into religion substantive criteria from outside.

IV

Let us now turn to our second task and speak of the relation between the act–expression pair and the goal of religion. This is where the mediatorial role of language will show itself most clearly. It seems to me that Duméry's position makes it possible to distinguish eight kinds of religious act vis-à-vis God.

1. Direct mystical union with the divine. The human subject proceeds from the divine, and its goal is to return to the divine. Humans must make their way to God through the mediation of signs and expressions. If these are completely successful, an immediate union should be attained. The expressions function as a ladder and are left behind once the summit has been reached. In a note on page 208 of *Critique et religion*, Duméry remarks that there are two sorts of mystical ascent. One, a mysticism of feeling and imagination, uses expressions drawn from the psychological and sensible levels of consciousness. The other, a mysticism of intellect, is elevated to union by the mediation of concepts and principles. We will need to come back to direct mystical union, but for the moment let us present it as the rarest of religious acts, the one in which expressions are used and finally abandoned.

2. Intellectual contemplation of God. Mystical union is an ecstasy in which all difference is eliminated. Intellectual contemplation is the next highest. The difference between subject and object is maintained, but the instruments of mediation are the most pure and transparent. If God can be called the One, the conceptual principles used here are the most comprehensive, the most expressive of the unity of being.

3. Participation in cult and dogma aware of all the different levels of signification involved. This person, as well as the contemplative just described, probably has the benefit of philosophical discrimination and judgment. He or she says the creeds, sings the hymns, takes the sacrament, goes on retreat and pilgrimage, all with an awareness of how these various mediations move one toward the divine and how the different levels of expressions are interrelated. It could be said that (2) and (3) represent the preparatory paths taken by the two types of mystic described in (1). That is, (2) and (3) may be transformed into mysticism, but they need not be in order to be valid kinds of religious action.

4. Theologically and religiously informed religious action. This kind would have elements of (2) and (3) but without the dimension

of critical reflection. This person would know the history of the religious community and would know the religious reasons for "doing the things we do." This person would be aware of the gap between the religious goal and the expressive means. Thus, there would be little likelihood of idolatry and great likelihood of growth in religious maturity and understanding.

5. A simple faith and life of piety. This person would follow the customary forms with devotion and obedience. There would perhaps be a tendency to equate the revelatory objects with the goal of religion. This person's range of appreciation would be rather narrow and there would be little ability to cope with critical questions by self or others. Nonetheless, the spiritual cup of such a person is likely to be filled to overflowing. Within the bounds of its affirmations, this kind of religious action is fully valid.

6. A confused kind of action in which the different levels of expression are mixed together. Here the intention may be sincere, but things which are to be taken symbolically are taken historically. Duméry notes that some of the finest theological minds of the past made claims about the geographical location of the Garden of Eden. Such confusion is very possible among religious people since religion utilizes the full range of expressive possibility in service of its intention.

7. An ignorant or idolatrous kind of action. In this case the mediating expressions are taken literally, with the result that they do not mediate the religious intention to its goal. It is stopped short and the revelatory objects are taken to be divine objects. This kind of ignorance or idolatry can be found in connection with all the levels of expression—sensible, psychological, rational, and intellectual.

8. A knowing and willful subversion of religious expressions for other than religious ends. Here the person knows that religious expressions are constituted to serve the religious intention, but uses them for other reasons. Perhaps participation in religious activities is one way of achieving social respectability; the subverter will go through the religious motions without sincerity or conviction. Perhaps orthodox statement and practice is required for attaining ecclesiastical power; the subverter will say and do all the right things in order to advance in the religious institution.

I have contended that Duméry's position allows for this typification of the kinds of religious action. Now I would like to raise a series of questions which can serve to test both my contention and the adequacy of Duméry's account.

V

If Duméry's philosophy of the Absolute and the human subject teaches that humans must generate expressions in order to move toward God, it also teaches that in order to enjoy communion with God we must go beyond all the levels of expression. This teaching is illustrated most clearly by the mystics who are able to make the flight from the alone to the Alone. What can be shown to be a philosophic necessity is also an actual possibility. But it is not only the mystics who show the way. In the title essay of his book, *La tentation de faire du bien (The Temptation to Do Good)*, Duméry says that even in an intimate and sincere adherence to religious expression such as dogma and cult there is a certain inner disconnecting from their finitude and intermediary character (*La tentation de faire du bien*, 71). We need both attachment and detachment; the former because expressions are the means of an intention, the latter because they are merely the means to attain a goal. It is clear that his point about a fissure in the religious act itself would apply to the first three kinds of act in the list above and it may apply to a lesser degree for kinds (4) and (5). In any case, it would apply to anyone who participates in religion after even a modest encounter with modernity. For better or worse, most of us are seeking, as Ricoeur puts it, a second naïveté, having lost our innocence.

Theory and history conspire to make another point. If the expressive order must be transcended, if it is relative to its goal, then a multiplicity of valid expressive means must be allowed. An Absolute or a God that could be approached by only one scheme of expression would not be sufficiently transcendent, transdeterminate. History shows that in many religions several different expressive schemes have, across time, been admitted as valid servants of the religious intentionality. Perhaps the different schools of thought and forms of piety in Christianity and Hinduism are the best examples of this.

If, as we said earlier, the fabric of piety is torn a bit in the very act of devotion, does learning that many expressive schemes are valid not rip it into shreds? Isn't being surrounded by such a cloud of witnesses, all speaking in a different way, fatally distracting? Not necessarily at all. Of course, you will foul up your prayer life if you insist on philosophizing while on your knees. But the reflective recognition that expressive schemes other than your own are valid should not alienate you from your own. It should help you to keep your own in perspective and not absolutize it. It should open you to the possibility that today's expressive scheme may well be replaced by another in the future. And it should give you a clue which will help you enter sympathetically into the expressions of those in other times and other places. The question to be put to all forms of expression is, Do they serve the religious intentionality, and if so, how?

But now we must ask as to the standard for expressions. Duméry says that a representation is invalid if it directs the spirit back on the mediating object when the intention becomes stuck at any one of the expressive levels (*Critique et religion*, 197). A representation is valid if the spirit is led by it beyond the realm of determinations. We are talking here about the expressions themselves and asking if there is a standard that can be generated for use by formal philosophical reflection. Later we will take up the question of making judgments on the *use* of expressions. Is it possible that an expression can give an incorrect transcription of the impulse behind it? John Meagher, in an article in the *Journal of the American Academy of Religion* (Sept. 1975, 459–72), elaborates what he calls the principle of clumsiness in the gospel of Mark. He shows, for example, that the story of Jesus cursing the fig tree makes good sense in Matthew's version but is hopelessly botched by Mark. This, then, would be an example of a representation that would not lead the pious spirit toward the divine. Muslims yearn for Paradise where they will be in blessed communion with Allah; the Qur'ān contains some marvelous representations of Paradise. But some of the faithful, in uncritical enthusiasm, added to these images and described Paradise in all of its sensuous detail. Muslim authorities saw the danger in this and criticized those expressions which missed the spiritual truth in the doctrine of Paradise. Another example is the Zen Buddhist ko'an which forcefully resists a straightforward cognitive solution. The expression itself, by its paradoxical construction, helps to impel the spirit on to transdeterminate insight. Some have noted the spareness of biblical narrative; this would seem to be a way in which an expression could help prevent the religious person from fastening onto the expression itself.

In *Critique et religion* (218), Duméry asks whether structures (expressions) considered in isolation are finally indifferent. He answers Yes and No. Yes, because expressions without a subject have no meaning and efficacy. No, because a given intention will not be served by just any expression. He goes on to say that a meager or confused body of expression is paired with a poor and confused subjectivity. In *Le problème de dieu* he said that each person gets the God he or she deserves and here he says that each consciousness has the categories that it merits. A strong religious intention will tend both to purify and to enrich the expressions it uses. Exceptions to this can be found, but they serve to prove the rule. That is, pure forms can be linked up with a spirituality of mediocre quality, and very crude forms can be the carrier of an exceptional religious drive. The same verbal expression or cultic act can change meaning, positively or negatively, according to the quality of the spirit that uses it. In conclusion, we can say that there is *prima facie* evidence in favor of preferring pure and well-developed religious expressions, but judgment must be reserved for the examination of each case.

This leads to another way of articulating the sort of primacy that holds between act and expression. The religious person is not bound to any one form of expression, and the expression chosen is to be transcended. Yet some form of expression must always be chosen. The ongoing, temporal character of human life implies that we are never bound to, or liberated by, any single act that we have performed. The spiritual intention is one that is always to be continued. So we could say that the primacy is not simply located on the side of act as opposed to expression. Act considered statically is no better than act considered formally. The basic distinction cuts across both terms, so that the matter could be put this way: expressing (the capacity and possibility of acting anew) is primary to expression (the act accomplished).

This emphasis on the dynamic character of religion can be associated with a bit of Duméry's terminology which might appear strange to us. In *Philosophie de la religion* (I, 39), he insists on a functional interpretation of consciousness. Is he advocating the theory of functionalism? No. He links functional with intentional and contrasts them with a substantialist and naturalist interpretation of consciousness. He uses the term "functional" because he wants to put the accent on acting and thus to see the human being as *functioning*. His utilitarian language can also be understood along these lines. He says that the acting spirit submits to the law of expression (*Critique et religion,* 214, n.1), but he also says over and over again that the subject *uses* religious expressions. The paradox of being at once the submitter and the master disappears when it is seen (a) that the submission is not to a ready-made code but rather to the necessity of creating some expression or another and (b) that mastery over expressions is not for some sort of *self*-enhancement but, rather, to transcend the self *and* the expressions in the direction of union with the divine.

We must now ask about the possibility of judging not only expressions, but acts as well. Earlier, Duméry was quoted as saying that on principle and as a matter of practice the philosopher should not make judgments on the religious acts of individual persons. But we must ask whether, since Duméry says that only expressions and not acts are available for descriptions, it is possible to judge acts. If we can examine only expressions and the same expression can "carry" acts of different value, how can we judge acts at all?

First, we must note that the preceding statement indicates that we can know something about acts, namely, that they differ in quality. What is the basis for this claim? Duméry does not answer this question directly, so we must attempt to put together a response. A first point can be made without going beyond expressions, if we acknowledge that expressions originate with an actor. That is, we can take the ensemble of acts of a given person and see whether the expressions cohere. If expressions from different levels are mixed indiscriminately, there is reason to say that they are being used without understanding. If a person randomly took ideas and symbols from here and there one would have reason to suspect that the religious intentionality was weak and superficial or to suspect that a strong intentionality was coupled with limited understanding. Another approach would be to consider the ensemble of the behavior of a person. Duméry contends that all values and determinations are to be transcended. If a person professes religious convictions but then proceeds to absolutize a particular religious expression or make idols in other realms of life, there is reason to suspect that the quality of the religious intentionality is inferior. For example, the person who holds orthodox religious positions but who holds on to life and possessions at any cost is probably only superficially and perhaps deceptively religious.

Obviously, we have not yet set forth a firm basis for judging religious acts. Is there anything more to be said? I think that the philosopher as outside observer can go no further. But an advance can be made if we take into consideration the testimony of the acting religious person. We have additional, though not decisive, evidence if a religious person will talk about his or her intention. Of course, there is still the possibility that a person will try to deceive or will be self-deceived. But there is something more to consider if the actor tells what is meant, intended, by the expressions enacted. Such a statement might show that the person is taking religious expressions literally. A statement by the actor could be the starting point for a series of questions posed by the philosopher to determine what the expressions mean for the person making them.

We move even closer to the religious act if we take into account the religious person's own awareness, that is, understanding, of his or her religious acts. Duméry holds, along with other reflexive philosophers and phenomenologists, that there is an immediate awareness of one's act as one performs it. This immediate awareness is the basis for all subsequent philosophical reflection. So judgments can be made, but they are to be made by the religious person. Have we simply come back to our starting point, having made no advance? No. Although the philosopher cannot and must not make judgments about the quality of religious acts, philosophical criteria of clarity and coherence and order can be worked out and then handed to the acting persons for their use. The person equipped with reflectively generated criteria of judgment will be able to discern gaps between what is meant and what is expressed in his or her religious life. The philosopher has not imported an external substantive standard. Rather, the materials of concrete religion have been examined by critical reason and have been ordered rationally and connected with a theory of the human subject. It seems to me that this is a mutually beneficial interrelation. The philosopher receives the material to reflect on and then proceeds to discover its rational order and to make general judgments. The religious person generates the religious data and then, using the rational standards furnished by the philosopher, may make judgments about his or her religious acts.

VI

Up to this point I have worked out this discussion of act and expression while assuming Duméry's basic distinction between action and reflection, a distinction which makes it possible to mark off the philosophy of religion as a distinct enterprise. That is to say, concrete religion in all of its modalities is on the side of action and is the object of reflection. I would like now to call attention to some passages in which Duméry seems to violate this distinction.

In *Critique et religion,* he insists, as we have already said, that God, the religious object, is not God as such but rather a representation taken to be revelatory. God is transcendent to the God-representations; the expressed transcends the expression. So far so good. But, beginning on page 194 of *Critique et religion,* he develops this point in a way that is at least confusing. On that page he distinguishes between the orders of knowledge *(la connaissance)* and life or action *(la vie, l'agir).* It would seem that this is a restatement of the distinction mentioned above between action and reflection. But that is not the case. On page 195 he follows the claim that a God-object is a mere cogitatum correlative to the cogito with a distinction between the two orders: the order of action in which God can be directly intended and the order of knowledge in which God is intended indirectly by way of mediating expressions. What is emerging is a distinction within the realm of religion. We must pursue it and see whether it is consistent with the view of religion that has been presented so far.

On page 198 we are told that there is an intention *(visée)* in the order of action and another in the order of knowledge. Two pages later it is said that the Absolute, the apex of the spirit, and their point of contact are beyond determination and reflection. The act of faith is a suprareflexive principle revealed only by its effects in consciousness. It now seems that we must make a distinction in religion between the prereflective act and the manner in which it is reflected on the structures of consciousness. It is this religious reflection which is reflected upon by the philosopher. Whereas up to now we have been told that humans must obey the principle of act–law, that is, always to act by way of expressive structures, it seems that there may be another possibility. On page 202 Duméry distinguishes the religious intentionality, by which at the lived (prereflective) level we intend God without intermediary, from religious representation, by which on the cognitive (reflective) level we intend God by the mediation of signs and expressions. On page 205 we are told that the most radical intention, the one that puts it in the realm of the unreflected, is of the infinite. And the matter gets its strongest statement on page 206 where consciousness is defined as a drive toward liberation which can follow either the reflective way or the active way.

What I see taking shape in these passages is the suggestion that there is perhaps a religious alternative to obeying the rule of act–expression. It is being hinted that there is a direct way to God. I can think of two ways in which this might be construed. The first, which I think must be rejected, is as follows. The religious act is *really* a direct movement to God which happens to *appear* in the phenomenal realm of expressions. This interpretation would render null and void ninety-nine percent of what Duméry has written about religion. Surely he would not make such a reversal and an unconscious one at that. But there is another way of interpreting these passages.

Duméry himself suggests it in a review of a book on the thought of Pseudo-Dionysius. He judges it to have been Dionysius' achievement to show that Christian behavior can be described in Neo-Platonic language and that the mystical (theologal) life can be understood from the point of view of Plotinian ecstasy (*La tentation*, 147). We have here two modes of religion which require different descriptive languages. Do we also have two modes of religion which can be called the direct way (mysticism, esoteric) and the indirect way (ordinary worship, exoteric)? If we do, we may have a clue for understanding the passages in *Critique et religion*.

Duméry has not given an extensive discussion of mysticism, but there are some references, and the debt to and affinity with Plotinus are openly acknowledged. Those rare moments of mystical ecstasy *are* perhaps best described as a direct movement to God. It seems that in a special sense the religious intentionality reaches its term in those moments for they are the experience of going beyond expressions and determinations. Speech falls away and silence reigns. There is no longer anything definite between the spirit and God. These special experiences demand a special language for their interpretation. But has Duméry made the most helpful choice?

It is one thing to have a philosophy of religion that makes room for mysticism. It is another thing to set mysticism apart from other religious modes or to let the phenomenon of mysticism dominate the interpretation of the other modes. Duméry seems to be doing this latter thing when he suggests that there is a direct, unreflected way to God distinct from the indirect, reflected way.

In order to understand the distinction between direct and indirect, let us take an example from everyday experience. Let us suppose that I move from Madison, New Jersey, to Chicago, Illinois. I go from here to there at a certain time at a certain speed in a conveyance of such and such description. It could be stated simply that I moved, or, also, an exhaustive description of my moving could be offered. Duméry's principle of act–law prescribes that the act and its determinate mode always go together. Moving indicates the action and the description specifies the structures employed. Though it is true that I moved and that it could simply be reported that I moved, it is known by me and others that *if* I moved I had to do it in one determinate way or another. I suggest that there is a parallel to this in the religious action of humans who enact their religious intentionality but always in a determinate mode. And here is the point of criticism: just as it does not make sense to say that there are two ways for me to get from Madison to Chicago, the direct way by simply moving and the indirect way by moving on a certain airplane at a certain time, so it does not make sense to say that there are two ways for a person to be religious, the direct way without the mediation of expressions and the indirect way with them. In both the physical and religious instances of transport, means are used to bring one to a terminus. But having arrived at the terminus does not warrant saying that there is a direct way that can dispense with the means. Nor is it helpful in either case to say that I was *really* moving, though it may have looked as though I were using determinate means.

It may be said in response that I have domesticated mysticism so that its distinctiveness is eliminated. To that I would point out that the mystical way, similar to the way of belief and cult, is still a way. Human mystics follow a path, even a rigorously prescribed one, to the height of ecstasy. The moment of enjoyment passes, and the mystic once again is aware of time and worldly differentiation. Though the peak moment itself is indescribable, it takes its place in a process with a beginning and an end. The whole seems clearly to fit into the act–expression structure.

We have noted before that religious expression is different from other expression, not in its formal structure, but because it intends an object which it cannot comprehend, and yet, in order to fulfill its mediating function, it must somehow point the religious person beyond the expression to the transcendent. This added wrinkle of the doubly relativized expression (in behalf of both parties to the religious transaction) means that both the religious practitioner and the philosophical interpreter must attend to the special complexity of religious experience. Mystical experience is striking in this connection because the ordinary complexity is simplified, purified. The means, the expressions, literally drop away. The question is whether we regard mysticism as realizing the act–expression dialectic at a higher level than ordinary or as a religious possibility of a different, and perhaps normative, kind. Duméry seems to waver between the two possibilities; I favor choosing the former.

I would like to conclude by suggesting a way of understanding the matter which makes a place for all the elements of Duméry's discussion. First, I would hold to the distinction between action (all the realms of concrete, projective life) and reflection (philosophical recovery of the rational structures involved in action). Philosophical reflection would not itself be a way of spiritual liberation, though as a human activity it would have to obey the principle of act–law. Second, within the realm of action called religion, I would distinguish three types of spirituality: the simple, the cultivated, and the mystical. Each type of spirituality or religious life, like all other kinds of human action, would have to obey the principle of act–law. Thus, each kind of religious act would have its accompanying religious expression. The three types might be distinguished according to how they use expression. The person of simple piety would live within the expressions and probably would not have critical awareness of expression as a means or a sympathetic appreciation of expressions other than the ones known to him or her. The person of cultivated piety participates in a wide variety of expressions and can appreciate the validity of the expressions of others. This person is aware that expressions are means to a spiritual end and is able to be self-critical about their use. The mystic also uses expressions and is able, by special gifts and graces, to leave them behind and experience the divine presence in a purer way. If we could regard expressions as the spiritual window for each of these types, the three cases would be as follows. The window for the simple type would be in deep colors, and the design would be a pictorial illustration. The window for the cultivated type would be in lighter colors, and the design would be abstract. The window for the mystic would be tinted just enough so that the mystic would not be blinded, or, perhaps better, the mystic would be in front of the window with closed eyes, bathed in light.

Duméry's occasional references to a direct religious way seem to give an undue prominence to the mystic type. In those passages, his terminology makes the direct or unreflected way coincide with the mystical; his discussion of the reflected way blurs the distinction between religion and philosophy. The proposal sketched above leaves intact the distinction between philosophy and action and still discriminates among the different ways of being religious. I submit that my suggestion better serves Duméry's own philosophical intention and, indirectly, in a way proper to philosophy, the religious intention.

═══════════BIBLIOGRAPHY═══════════

Duméry, Henry. *Critique et religion: problèmes de méthode en philosophie de la religion*. Paris: Société d'Édition d'Enseignement Supérieur, 1957.

————. *La tentation de faire du bien*. Paris: Seuil, 1956.

————. *Le problème de dieu en philosophie de la religion: examen critique de la catégorie d'Absolu et du schème de transcendance*. Paris: Desclée de Brouwer, 1957. English translation by Charles Courtney. *The Problem of God*. Evanston: Northwestern University Press, 1964.

————. *Philosophie de la religion: essaie sur la signification du Christianisme*, Vol. 1–2. Paris: Presses Universitaires de France, 1957.

12

In Praise of Anthropomorphism

FREDERICK FERRÉ

> Who could imagine, replied Demea, that Cleanthes, the calm philo-
> sophical Cleanthes, would attempt to refute his antagonists by
> affixing a nickname to them, and, like the common bigots and in-
> quisitors of the age, have recourse to invective and declamation
> instead of reasoning? Or does he not perceive that these topics are
> easily retorted, and that *anthropomorphite* is an appellation as invid-
> ious, and implies as dangerous consequences, as the epithet of *mystic*
> with which he has honoured us?
>
> Hume, *Dialogues Concerning Natural Religion*[1]

Indeed, as Hume's Demea here hotly contends, the terms "anthro-
pomorphite" and "anthropomorphism" have long been means for
verbal abuse in discussions of theological language. It is the purpose
of this paper to reexamine the justice of this deep-seated antago-
nism to anthropomorphism in discourse about God, and to offer
reasons to praise rather than to bury such speech. Before I conclude,
I shall have occasion to comment on the ethical issues involved in
acknowledging or denouncing anthropomorphic language at the
lower end of the Great Chain of Language, as it links not only God
and man but also man and animals. I shall also make a sharp
distinction between anthropo*morphism*, which I hold is inevitable
and often justified, and anthropo*centrism*, which is not.

I

The main motive for rejecting the use of anthropomorphic language
in connection with God is deep in the tradition of spirituality that
insists on defending the ultimate value of the divine against the
profanity of human traits. The horror of engaging in idolatry, the
misplacement of worship from the sacred to the secondary, is a
long and worthy religious sensibility. Hume skillfully plays on this
theme when he has the skeptical Philo join the orthodox Demea
in ironic alliance against anything tainted with the merely human:

In Praise of Anthropomorphism

"I was from the beginning scandalized, I must own," Philo says, "with this resemblance which is asserted between the Deity and human creatures, and must conceive it to imply such a degradation of the Supreme Being as no sound theist could endure."[2]

Such a motive, rooted in fundamental value intuitions, is easy to respect in view of the grossness of some of the background religious practices and conceptions against which this spiritual revulsion was aimed. Ancient Greek mythology, attributing blatant sexual misconduct and other all-too-human foibles to the gods was offensive to morally sensitive Greeks like Socrates, Plato, and Aristotle; the vulgar ideas and rituals of the Canaanites deeply offended the Hebrew prophets. The incomparable power and majesty of the true focus of worship, as against the feeble constructions of human hands and brains, is well sung by Isaiah:

> To whom then will you liken God,
>   or what likeness compare with
>   him?
> The idol! a workman casts it,
>   and a goldsmith overlays it with
>   gold,
>   and casts for it silver chains. . . .
> Have you not known? Have you not
>   heard?
>   Has it not been told you from
>   the beginning?
>   Have you not understood from
>   the foundations of the earth?
> It is he who sits above the circle of
>   the earth,
>   and its inhabitants are like grass-
>   hoppers;
> who stretches out the heavens like
>   a curtain,
>   and spreads them like a tent to
>   dwell in;
> who brings princes to nought,
>   and makes the rulers of the earth
>   as nothing. . . .
> To whom then will you compare
>   me,
>   that I should be like him?
>   says the Holy One.[3]

This strong religious inclination to insist upon the specialness of the sacred and thus to recoil from any downgrading of the ultimately worthful by classing it with the valuationally secondary is encountered in many traditions and cultures. The Hindu *neti, neti* ("not that, not that") refuses to identify the ultimate with anything proximate.[4] The Christian mystic returns from his or her rapture with warnings and advice against using profane language as though it could give access to the ineffable.[5]

In the various religious traditions of the world, as well, the valuationally based revulsion from degrading the most worthy becomes a logically expressed prohibition against the use of positive predication in language about the most real. Avicenna among Muslim philosophers and Maimonides among Jewish are strong contenders for the doctrine of negative theology, succinctly summarized in *The Encyclopedia of Philosophy* as follows:

According to this doctrine, nothing positive can be known about God, who has nothing in common with any other being. No predicate or descriptive term can legitimately be applied to him unless it is given a meaning which is wholly different from the one the term has in common usage and is purely negative. All statements concerning God considered in himself should, if they are to be regarded as true, be interpreted as providing an indication of what God is *not*. This applies even to the statement that God exists.[6]

Immanuel Kant, from a different theoretical context, gave arguments for the general incapacity of the human mind to cognize the noumenal realm into which God, if there be a God, would need to be classified. But the noumenal realm is defined only "problematically" or "limitatively," by Kant. As he puts it, "The concept of a noumenon is . . . merely *limitative,* and intended to keep the claims of sensibility within proper bounds, therefore of negative use only."[7] In consequence of this, Kant concludes:

Our understanding thus acquires a kind of negative extension, that is, it does not become itself limited by sensibility, but, on the contrary, limits it, by calling things by themselves (not considered as phenomena) noumena. In doing this, it immediately proceeds to prescribe limits to itself, by admitting that it cannot know these noumena by means of the categories, but can only think of them under the name of something unknown. . . .[8]

Søren Kierkegaard pushes the unknowability of God over the

brink of paradox, by declaring that the infinite gap between the finite and infinite requires that God, the Wholly Other, be declared the Wholly Unknowable. "So let us call this unknown something: *God*. It is nothing more than a name we assign it."[9] If this is so, then there is no logical impediment (here is the paradox that delights and stimulates Kierkegaard) to considering God (if wholly unknowable) Wholly *Like* the human, as is affirmed in the Christian doctrine of Incarnation, God-become-fully-man.[10]

II

This paradox has brought us full circle and must suggest that something is wrong with a doctrine that, by means of fierce opposition to anthropomorphism, ends by embracing it in its most complete theological expression. This is not to suggest that something is wrong with the religious sensibility that finds itself impelled to stress the vastness of the qualitative difference between the proper focus of worship and the human world of dullness and compromise. Nor is it to criticize the spirituality that prescribes the systematic emptying of the mind as a method of gaining indescribably valuable religious experiences of unity with the Holy. Nor is it, of course, to fault the doctrine of Incarnation or the religious intuition, lying behind it, that senses the identity of the Cosmic Logos with the Son of Man. These matters are not at issue here.

What I suggest, rather, is that the spiritual motives behind the prohibition of anthropomorphic language about God are ill-served when formalized into a logical doctrine that cannot be followed, finally, without self-destructive consequences. It is only by affirming anthropomorphic discourse, under constraints, that spirituality can in the end be focused and forwarded by the mind.

St. Thomas Aquinas realized the difficulties in the full-fledged *via negativa* of Maimonides. As Thomas writes:

But as regards names of God said absolutely and affirmatively, as *good, wise,* and the like, various and many opinions have been held. For some have said that all such names, although they are applied to God affirmatively, nevertheless have been brought into use more to remove something from God than to posit something in Him. Hence they assert that when we say that God lives, we mean that God is not like an inanimate thing; and the same in like manner applies to other names. This was taught by Rabbi Moses.[11]

The problems with this position, taken as logical doctrine rather than as pious praise for God, are fatal, however. First, Thomas points out, on the basis of the *via negativa* there is no way in principle that a reason could be given "why some names more than others should be applied to God."[12] If "God lives" is meant merely to deny something, why not equally say "God is dead" or "God is a body" or "God is a mushroom" or "God is a polka-dotted balloon," or the like, in a merely negative sense? What does it matter, if nothing whatever is meant positively, what is said or not said in spiritual matters? On what criterion are we to guide our speech in order to avoid error and even blasphemy? Nothing remains.

Next, on this doctrine any terms used for God "would be said of Him by way of being taken in a secondary sense,"[13] but this is demeaning religiously (how can the creature be primary as against the creator?) as well as radically unanchored logically. Any alleged secondary sense would not be interpretable without some primary sense to ground its meaning in the context of the divine.

Third, as Thomas correctly points out, "this is against the intention of those who speak of God. For in saying that God lives, they assuredly mean more than to say that . . . He differs from inanimate bodies."[14]

What, though, can we human beings mean "more" by our words except what we, by human experience, have come to understand? If we mean something at all significant by the affirmation that "God lives"—something more than the denial that God is as inanimate as a stone or as automatic as the tides—then we must draw upon those internal experiences of creativity and joy and vitality that may count, in rare moments, as the peak experiences of human life. If we mean something at all by the words "good" or "wise," cited by Thomas, then the general domains of human goodness—though doubtless greatly magnified—and of human wisdom—though expanded beyond our limited capacities to imagine—must be presupposed.

This is, of course, anthropomorphism. It is, however, not vulgar anthropomorphism, attributing obscene or unworthy traits to the divine. On the contrary, it is precisely by the selection of specific traits acknowledged as eminently worthy that (logically) believers may eliminate the unworthy in connection with the Most High. Without some such positive criterion, as we have seen, anything goes.

Not only so, but even the religious evocation of the Holy itself, in its incomparable grandeur, often relies on the use of frank but unobjectionable anthropomorphic imagery. Isaiah, in the passage cited above, while denouncing the demeaning of God, does not shrink from depicting the Holy One as "sitting" above the circle of the earth, and looking down from a great height at grasshopper-like earthlings, smug with their ludicrous pride. He pictures God, like a nomad patriarch, stretching out the great tent roof of the sky as a dwelling. The passage, of course, despite its vivid imagery, does not itself in the slightest demean God. Without these benign anthropomorphisms, the prophet-poet could never have expressed so well his wonderfully ironic judgment upon vicious anthropocentrism.

We saw earlier that Immanuel Kant was one of the most resolute opponents of anthropomorphic (or any intelligible human) language when applied to the domain he "problematically" defined as the noumenal; but even Kant found it necessary to allow speech reflecting human conceptualities rather than to enforce sheer silence about God. God, for him, was a postulate of pure practical reason and filled the need of assuring that the *summum bonum* (the proper adjustment of happiness to morality) is not beyond final reach. But such assurance, though required for thinking in accordance with the necessities of morality, depends on imagining God as capable of *knowing* our moral worth and *acting* with perfect dependability to arrange the proper balance according to our deserts over the long run, including life beyond this worldly existence. As Kant puts it:

Therefore, the *summum bonum* is possible in the world only on the supposition of a Supreme Being having a causality corresponding to moral character. Now a being that is capable of acting on the conception of laws is an *intelligence* (a rational being), and the causality of such a being according to this conception of laws is his *will*; therefore the supreme cause of nature, which must be presupposed as a condition of the *summum bonum* is a being which is the cause of nature by *intelligence* and *will*, consequently its author, that is God.[15]

But such language is clearly anthropomorphic and, on Kant's earlier argument, quite illicit. How does he handle the problem of talk about "moral character," "intelligence," and "will" in reference to a noumenal being, when even the language of "cause" and "time" have been proscribed as supplied by the mind? His answer is not clear, but in the *Critique of Judgment* he returns to the matter by making a distinction between "thinking" and "cognizing." The need to represent God somehow is practically pressing, forced by thinking in accordance with morality, and therefore a special analogical dispensation is allowed, as follows:

. . . if I wish to *think* a supersensible Being (God) as an intelligence, this is not only permissible in a certain aspect of my employment of Reason—it is unavoidable; but to ascribe to Him Understanding and to flatter ourselves that we can *cognize* Him by means of it as a property of His, is in no way permissible. For I must omit all those conditions under which alone I know an Understanding, and thus the predicate which only serves for determining man cannot be applied at all to a supersensible Object; and therefore by a causality thus determined, I cannot cognize what God is. And so it is with all Categories, which can have no significance for cognition in a theoretical aspect, if they are not applied to objects of possible experience. However, according to the analogy of an Understanding I can in a certain other aspect think a supersensible being, without at the same time meaning thereby to cognize it theoretically. . . .[16]

Even Kant finds it impossible to dispense with (circumspect) anthropomorphic language, then, even though his explanation of how it is logically justified through "a certain other aspect" leaves much to be desired. Little wonder, then, that Ludwig Feuerbach goes all the way in drawing his conclusion:

Where man deprives God of all qualities, God is no longer anything more to him than a negative being. To the truly religious man, God is not being without qualities. . . . The denial of determinate, positive predicates concerning the divine nature is nothing else than a denial of religion, with, however, an appearance of religion in its favour, so that it is not recognized as a denial; it is simply a subtle, disguised atheism. The alleged religious horror of limiting God by positive predicates is only the irreligious wish to know nothing more of God, to banish God from the mind. . . . He who dreads an existence that may give offence, who shrinks from the grossness of a positive predicate, may as well renounce existence altogether.[17]

III

My aim to this point has been to show that positive predication, what has often been denounced as anthropomorphism, not only is *not necessarily demeaning* religiously to the Most High but also is *necessarily not avoidable* logically if the language of either the believer or the philosopher is not to be emptied of all content and all thought about God, however reverently intended, thus to be made impossible.

I have not here attempted to argue for any analysis of how such positive predicates are to be taken. This is a daunting problem, and one with which Thomas Aquinas wrestled hard. His basic sense was right, that we need to thread a way between crass literalism, on the one hand, and self-defeating negativism, on the other. His own proposals for this middle way of analogy are beset with difficulties of their own, as I have on various occasions attempted to point out in detail,[18] but, as Kant also saw, some middle way is needed.

Helpful suggestions sometimes come from unexpected directions, and in this case we might profit from contemplating the issue of anthropomorphic language as it relates not to the higher reaches of mystery, upward towards God, but rather to what we often call the lower orders, towards the animals. There has recently been much sneering about anthropomorphism in connection with animal protectionists' criticisms made against contemporary methods of raising meat-animals in stalls where, for a whole lifetime, they can neither exercise nor so much as turn around, or against egg-production methods in which chickens are kept in small cages in lighted rooms, where round-the-clock laying onto conveyor belts is achieved at the cost of all other normal activities. Critics of this economically profitable tenderizing and mechanizing of animals are told that they are attributing anthropomorphic frustrations to the creatures involved, and that in the absence of any knowledge of animal preferences—or, indeed, whether there are any such things at all as animal preferences—they should refrain from "complaining with their mouths full."[19]

There may be useful parallels here to the arguments over negative theology. From the fact that certain characteristics are well understood in connection with human life, e.g., anguish from imprisonment and forced labor, frustration from inability to participate in normal physical and social activities, etc., it is held that *only* in connection with human life can such characteristics be understood. Swine and poultry are not human; and therefore, we are told, moral criticisms based on anthropomorphic extensions of our concerns to them are without basis or point.

Mary Midgley effectively criticizes the assumptions behind this argument, however, as follows:

. . . the argument . . . apparently runs: Our idea of x . . . is made up of elements drawn from human life: But x is not human: Therefore that idea is only a mirror and tells us nothing about x. Now this argument is not really impressive because it proves far too much. It suggests that the sphere of "human life" can never be extended. Yet it often is extended. Every new thing that we meet has to be understood in terms drawn from earlier human experience. This is inevitable, because "understanding" anything new simply *is* relating it to what we have already experienced, finding a way to bring it within reach of our existing range of concepts. The newness of the new thing has to be assimilated or digested in this way if we are to make it ours. Of course skeptics are right to point out that we make all kinds of mistakes in doing this. But this argument cannot support a more drastic skepticism, because the mistakes can only count as mistakes if we take the correcting insight to be less mistaken.[20]

The animals around us, however, are not even strange "new things" that need to be somehow awkwardly incorporated into our conceptual framework. On the contrary, as Midgley points out, the earliest known contexts for the formation of human languages were the very contexts in which rich and varied interactions with animals were already implicit. What we mean by such terms as frightened, for example, includes as part of its broad range of meaning not only the frightened hunter running from the tiger but also the frightened deer running from the hunter! This does not commit us to the view, of course, that the qualities of the fright of the hunter or of the deer—much less of the bird or the fish—are all identical. Language allows for variety within its range of generality. But it is a strange aberration, allowed only recently by the unprecedented domination by our hypertechnical civilization of all other species, to make the anthropocentric assumption that would restrict the true meaning of all such terms to human beings alone. These are, rather, terms generated in the mixed community—humans and other species—that have been characteristic of the vastly greater part of human experience.[21]

If this is so, then the semantic scruples of the defenders of modern methods in egg-production, for example, turn out to be more *ad hoc* defenses of economic unscrupulousness than eternal truths of logic. It is surely true that we cannot pretend to see the world in all respects confidently from a chicken's point of view, but this fact does not invalidate all ethical concerns about the creatures with whom we interact and whose fate is sometimes in our hands. In the mixed community there are many deep differences between the species, but it would take a weighty argument—and a difficult one to make in view of the evolutionary and physiological evidences—to show that these differences are absolute.

To return once more to the question of God, it is clear that the issue depends here, too, on the extent to which the vast differences between God and man are not merely vast but literally without any foothold for comparison. This extreme position may indeed be claimed, as we saw it was claimed by Maimonides and Kierkegaard, but such claims can be sustained only at an immensely high price for philosophy and—as we also have seen—for religion itself. Many aspects of human personality are doubtless objectionable if attributed to the divine, but must that include as objectionable *every* aspect of human personality, including thinking, planning, loving, willing, and the like? Surely not. As Midgley concludes:

The argument which I have just criticized says that it must do so, simply because personality, emotion and so forth are human. But this means ruling that God—and indeed all non-human life—must be so unlike us that none of it can be understood from a human standpoint at all. This seems to be an arbitrary, groundless dogma.[22]

If religion is to mean anything to human devotees, the supreme focus of their worship must not be beyond linguistic representation as supremely worthy. For this the highest and most valued traits known to the religious community need to be invoked on pain of spiritual emptiness and triviality. If, likewise, the concept of God is to be theoretically important for theologians and philosophers, God must be somehow in relation to all else, on pain of utter irrelevance. This does not make God less holy or awesome. On the contrary, it makes possible the positive affirmation of "holiness" and specification of those other traits that make for legitimate awe.

Human language cannot deal absolutely with absolutes. To this extent humans must realize that when they speak in extremes of God's "absolute" knowledge or power or perfection, they do not speak literally or with full understanding. We know what the word "power," for example, means in human contexts and then we take it as a conceptual model to refer upward, either indefinitely (if we are simply at worship), or until our metaphysical theories interpret the concept for us in its various theoretical relationships (if we are also attempting to think critically in connection with our highest values). As William Paley pointed out,

"Omnipotence," "omniscience," "infinite" power, "infinite" knowledge are *superlatives* expressing our conception of these attributes in the strongest and most elevated terms which language supplies. We ascribe power to the Deity under the name of "omnipotence," the strict and correct conclusion being that a power which could create such a world as this is must be, beyond all comparison, greater than any which we experience in ourselves, than any which we observe in other visible agents, greater also than any which we can want, for our individual protection and preservation, in the Being upon whom we depend.[23]

My main conclusion from this discussion, then, is that yet another religious use of language—one toward which most philosophers have been rather naïvely literalistic—needs to be added to the list of "superlatives," and is more properly to be taken as a poetical compliment to God than as strictly meant: this is the incautious claim, criticized in all the foregoing, that God is "absolutely" other, in all respects, from the rest of reality. It is fitting for an Isaiah to exult in the "incomparability" of Jehovah; it is, however, the destruction of faith and of thought for others to overinterpret this poetic superlative and treat it as a logical doctrine. Human words dealing in humanly understandable qualities, in the last analysis,

. . . are the fire, the vital breath, the oxygen, the salt of existence. An existence in general, an existence without qualities, is an insipidity, an absurdity. . . . Only where man loses his taste for religion, and thus religion itself becomes insipid, does the existence of God become an insipid existence—an existence without qualities.[24]

=======NOTES=======

1. David Hume, *Dialogues Concerning Natural Religion* (1776), ed. Henry D. Aiken (New York: Hafner Publishing Co., 1959) 31.

2. Ibid., 20.

3. Isaiah 40:21–25, Revised Standard Version (New York: Thomas Nelson & Sons, 1952).

4. *Brhad-aranyaka Upanishad*, II, 3, 6.

5. "For, as God is not comprised in any image or form, nor contained in any particular kind of knowledge, the soul, in order to be united with God, must not take hold of any distinct form or any particularized knowledge." St. John

of the Cross, *The Dark Night of the Soul,* trans. Kurt F. Reinhardt (New York: Frederick Ungar Publishing Co., 1957) Pt. I., Bk. 2, Chap. 16, 63.

6. Shlomo Pines, "Maimonides," *Encyclopedia of Philosophy,* ed. Paul Edwards (New York: Macmillan, 1967) vol. 5, 131.

7. Immanuel Kant, *The Critique of Pure Reason,* trans. Max Müller, 2d ed., rev. (New York: Macmillan, 1927) 236. Reprint. *Kant Selections,* ed. Theodore Meyer Greene (New York: Charles Scribner's Sons, 1929) 362.

8. *Ibid.,* 237; reprint. Greene, *op. cit.,* 155.

9. Søren Kierkegaard, *Philosophical Fragments,* trans. David F. Swenson (Princeton: Princeton Univ. Press, 1936) 31.

10. *Ibid.*

11. St. Thomas Aquinas, *Summa Theologica,* Q. 13, Art. 2.

12. *Ibid.*

13. *Ibid.*

14. *Ibid.*

15. Immanuel Kant, *The Critique of Practical Reason,* trans. T. K. Abbott (6th edition, 1909) 223; reprint. *Kant Selections,* Greene, *op. cit.* 362.

16. Immanuel Kant, *Critique of Judgment,* trans. J. H. Bernard (2d ed., 1914), 429; reprint. Greene, *op cit.,* 523–524.

17. Ludwig Feuerbach, *The Essence of Christianity,* trans. George Elliot (New York: Harper and Brothers, 1957) 14–15.

18. See Frederick Ferré, *Language, Logic and God* (Chicago: Univ. of Chicago Press, 1981) chap. 6, "The Logic of Analogy"; and *idem.,* "Analogy in Theology," *The Encyclopedia of Philosophy, op. cit.,* vol. 1.

19. Seen on a farm truck's bumper sticker.

20. Mary Midgley, *Animals and Why They Matter* (Athens, Georgia: The University of Georgia Press, 1983) 127.

21. *Ibid.,* chap. 10, "The Mixed Community."

22. *Ibid.,* 128.

23. William Paley, *Natural Theology: Selections,* ed. Frederick Ferré (Indianapolis: Bobbs-Merrill Co., Inc., 1963) 46.

24. Feuerbach, *op. cit.,* 15.

13

God and the Utopianism of Language

GABRIEL VAHANIAN

By Way of Prolegomena

Voice is a way of being, argues Giorgio Agamben,[1] as though the statement could not be reversed: being is a way of speaking. And yet it is the same author who also points out that "the appearance of a new religion always coincides with a new revelation of language and a new religion means above all a new experience of language."[2] So much so, indeed, that in order for God to be, there must—also—be language (wherein *yes* is *yes* and *no* is *no* at one and the same time as is the *yes* to God at one and the same time a *no* to the idol). There is no religion unless God is tipped into language, or else he is frozen into an idol. Being God, God can only be without being. (Dieu ne peut qu'être sans l'être.) Not this or that, he is *verbum:* Verb is the word. Yet a word not contained by any language.

Indeed, language *contains* no word or else it is a dead language, at best a topic of language.

Like a map, language is no *topos:* it is *outopos,* and for that reason man always lies beyond man as does the ideal or imaginary beyond the real and the real beyond the ideal or imaginary—at their juncture, where experience is experience of a new thing, a new world, a new life. Through the Word, that is, ultimately, through language, man, being both sinful and justified, is that which he is not and is not that which he is. He speaks.

To speak is to have faith. Hemmed in by no language, man is much less hemmed in by the world. Not that he can change worlds but, more precisely and simply, because he can change the world even as, through faith, his life can be changed. Tradition calls this a conversion. But conversion without the reconversion of one's life and of one's world is not enough. Without an eschatology, salvation turns into withdrawal and escape from the world, pie in the sky or gnosis. And that is a denial of that religious dimension par excellence of language, evinced by what I call its utopianism.

God and the Utopianism of Language

A fact means nothing. Meaning occurs not because things are *per se* meaningful but in spite of their meaninglessness; grace abounds in spite of sin.

Likewise, speaking is not merely saying. Nor is it merely doing. It *means*. It signi-fies. But speaking is signified as much as it signi-fies. It is textured into signification. And signification is no classification of do's and don't's, of gods and idols. Just as it could be said that language is iconoclastic if only because it is symbolic, so also it must be said that a sign points less beyond itself than to the subversion of the signified through the signifier as well as of the signifier through the signified.

If words are symbols or even icons, signs are by contrast only words. And what counts is indeed the word, not the name (with or without capital initials).

The word: that is, a bridge across language as though across a bankless river.

Was there ever a word that was not the rival of another? Its contrary? Its simile? "I love you. Neither do I?" *Sacrificium intellectus:* a word leaping onto another to grasp or be grasped by it; or image: of identity at the cost of difference, of difference at the cost of identity.

Identity and difference. The One and the Many. The Same and the Other. As many words as seek only to hem the word in by tracing it back to a place where it could not find place—the body—or by reducing it to a soundless body. Words that rival one another and would hem language in by pretending to lead the way, and bank in the river. Words that, rivaling one another, are therefore waylaid. Words astray that cause us to stray away from being or, rather, from that verbal condition of ours so long as, for the time being, we are what we are not and are not what we are. Only the speechless are frustrated.

The same holds for the classic opposition of faith and reason. Two rivers in the same bed. Like body and soul. Or like God and man. Time and again, tradition, pinning itself down, takes the word for what it means, and wants to go beyond. Beyond the word. Into metaphysics, sort of a premature structuralism for which the soul and the body, God and man, are opposed to one another, lost as they are one in the other. God in man, the soul in the body. The signified in the signifier. Lost, or raptured one by the other. Named one by the other. Though without either's being called into question. Into speech.

The reason that moves mountains is itself nontransferable. Whether reason leads to God, or is reasonable whether it leads to God or to the devil, matters little: it trades on meaning by swapping signs. Yet without signi-fying, like words that lack the word.

To signify: not to be moored so much as to be anchored. Not pinned down so much as penned in. Written out. As is that very word of God for which God—neither signifier nor signified—is nothing but a word, *l'autre de l'autre.*

A word like other words. At least so far as the dictionary is concerned. Or, for that matter, language itself. A noun even. Yet at once proper and common. That which, being no place, can only take place, and takes place only to the extent that it does not replace language—much less the utopianism of the speech thereof when it breaks into words, into a "logic"; that is, an instance at once of revelation and of reason. Of revelation, should reason not shy away from it by reasoning itself out. Of reason, should revelation not sink into revelation.

Reason and revelation: two languages, one and the same logic, one and the same bed—the *logos.*

Logos: neither being nor nonbeing, those twin topics of a logo-centrism held apart by reasons rather than together by reason.

Logos: that is, utopianism of language rather than its sublimation or its concatenation of words into sound and fury. Tipping the body into speech as well as space into time: the timeliness of eternity.

Hence the problem: Not time and being, much less being and non-being, or even time and difference. But time and language. *As* language.

Time: "une parole qui dure" (Maurice Leenhardt)—a word that lasts yet without outlasting itself. And lasts, not so much because as in spite of either the nature of language or its structure: by reason of the utopianism of language, that is, of the fact that language only occurs when and where it is without precedent. I mean, by reason of that utopianism which is not to be reduced to that of nature (metaphysics) or to that of history (structuralism). That is, to that of an apocalypse as the end of time, as though coming from beyond time. Or, for that matter, from beyond language. As though anything could separate us from the Word become flesh—once and for all. Language has no more precedent than does creation or the fullness of time.

* * *

Psalm 116:10 (II Corinthians 4:13): "I believed, and so I spoke."
Lacan: ". . . d'écrit j'ai plus que je n'écrois."

Safouan: "La barre qui figure dans le schéma du signe représente bien une union: seulement, ce n'est pas cette union du signifiant et du signifié qui en est le principe, mais, comme le disait Lacan, leur séparation. Non pas au sens spatial de l'existence parallèle, de chaque côté de la barre, d'un signifiant et d'un signifié. Bien plutôt, ce dernier doit-il advenir et ce que la barre représente, c'est ce qui, avec le signifiant se profile tant comme appel comme résistance au signifié: une barre à franchir."[3]

*   *   *

The argument: Though language is a technique, technique is itself the price of language. Hence, there is no technique outside language, which of course makes sense if the distinction between technique as tool and as method still holds (the former, like a hammer, extends man; the latter affects him within as well as without, even alters him). Technique is thus a metaphor of language rather than that language, serving as a tool, is analogous to technique: God is word, reality is verbal, and verbal is also the human condition. On this view, analogy belongs with the sacred; metaphor with utopia, the sole horizon of which is language (whether about God or about man), just as the sole horizon of both God and man is the Christ.

Language at the Price of Technique

Outside Language No Technique

Whatever its origin—natural or divine—no one ever seems to have fully ignored that language hides a technique.

Better still, no one seems to have ever doubted that, besides consisting of a technique, and in contrast to every other technique that tends to depersonalize or dehumanize, language cancels itself out whenever it departs from its task of personalizing man as well as of humanizing society.

Again, by contrast with technics in general, which are, so to speak, cumulative and owe their efficiency to their further rationalization or standardization, language is really and exclusively a treasure, I mean, a thesaurus: not being cumulative, paradoxically it owes its sole efficiency to the fact that it resists or escapes rationalization. And yet rationalization is only possible through language and works only insofar as it works through language, insofar as language steers clear of its own rationalization. Language is the price—at the price of technique. Not one, at least, to which all other techniques are in debt regardless of their respective achievement. Or, rather, precisely because of their achievements which, as so many "words, words, words," are ultimately put into question by or tested against language. Language is efficient insofar as it is a technique. But efficiency alone is not a sufficient justification of technique. Without language, outside language there is no technique. As Chomsky points out, although we use language in order to communicate, communication itself is a secondary function of language. Grammar and the efficiency of communication are two different things.[4]

Through language, everything can be brought to reason. The least sound, the most furtive gesture, they can all be rationalized. Language even requires it. To wit, George Orwell's counter-utopia, *1984*, where language finally is itself to be given up to the highest conceivable degree of rationalization under the cover of *Newspeak*. As if to show that, if there be any utopia, it must require the excision of language—unless, of course, exactly the opposite is what is being shown! Namely, that utopia can never result from some rationalization or another, much less if as in *Newspeak* language is itself, in the process, being elided, ablated, at the price ultimately of a newfangled *sacrificium intellectus*—that of language. Of the word in the words, of the word with the words, of the word under the words.

Not that utopia is a matter of words alone, whether those of classification or of nomenclature, those distant echoes of some primordial word claiming itself as *archē*, the *sine qua non* of order. In utopia, order is *an-archic*. As is, indeed, grammar itself. And grammar is to language as creation is to nature, destiny (or redemption) to history, and pleroma to gnosis or life after death. Or, for that matter, revelation to reason. And Word to words. In the *Newspeak* of *1984*, language is reduced to words. Forgotten is the fact that language is the condition of the reason only because it is also the condition of faith. Language does not opt between faith and reason, nor does it lie beyond or outside of them. And no more than a poem can lie outside language, can utopia occur without language, through *Newspeak* alone, unless it is a counterfeit. Either language is the horizon of utopia or else speaking in tongues and *Newspeak* are the alternatives. Just as, being the condition of reason, language cannot be corrected by reason,[5] and just as language, the condition of faith, cannot be replaced with glossolalia, so also can no utopia lie in words alone, that is, in the perversion of language. No utopia is worth realizing unless it can and must be subverted by language. Which language, being symbolic, is by the same token iconoclastic. A technique.

Analogy and Metaphor: The Verbal Condition of Man

Language is a technique; I follow Gadamer in pointing out that Aristotle himself had already said so when he defined man as being endowed with *logos,* as one who reasons. He reasons, however, on the grounds as well as to the extent of a language whose *technē* consists in distinguishing the useful from the useless: put differently, in anticipating the future—anticipating it, rather than "fulfilling" it by anticipation if not by proxy.

Language is a technique. But, then, how comes it that, especially if we have known it all along, we should have waited so long— M. Safouan wonders—for linguistics to see the light of day? How is it that, more important, neither the philosophical nor the theological tradition of the West has focussed on the implication, namely, the verbal condition of man?

In spite of Scriptures and the Word of God; in spite of various stories such as creation and the Tower of Babel, the Word become flesh and Pentecost; in spite of Revelation, how is it that the discourse of faith bequeathed by tradition has actually served to avoid if not to cancel the evidence of language, of linguistics?

For his part, Gadamer answers that question by saying: "it was the religious tradition of the West that hindered serious thought about language." Perhaps.

But, then, what kind of religious tradition?

Obviously, I think, a religious tradition still caught up in the meshes of myth. Entirely geared to the sacred. And, worse still, encumbered with all kinds of dichotomy resulting from such bondage on every level: religious and cultural, social and existential. The cleavage of the sacred and the profane has indeed been ultimately the ransom for all the other cleavages that have marred Western thought: faith and reason, subject and object, God and man, being and nonbeing, lower and higher, inside and outside . . .

We've toppled God and eroded the sacred, we denounce objectification and are suspicious of subjectivism. But dualism, we're not quite ready to let go of.

Instead, we fear technology, because it would affect the whole man. And we see it as we do *Newspeak:* a perversion of language.

What if just the opposite were the case? Could it be that through technology language has finally come into its own? Indeed, because technology does affect the whole man, we finally realize that what's needed is a new language, more consonant with a new type of religiosity emerging from the ruins of a sacral universe of discourse allowed by myth—a universe of discourse for which technique is reduced to magic, and speech to some wondrous speechlessness. A universe in which being, that which is, can only lie outside language, a mere tool, a rudimentary technique: utopia definitely lies less "nowhere" than outside this world.

Clearly, the basic dualism of the sacral universe of discourse has until now so affected our thinking and speaking that God-talk is still caught up in it. I will even claim that, under the regime of onto-theology, language was reduced to analogy, shorn as it was of its metaphoric power (like *Newspeak* or, better, like Lucky's speech in Beckett's *Waiting for Godot*). This would need arguing, surely. But I shall simply appropriate for myself a remark of Lacan's when he says that analogy is no metaphor,[6] and adds: analogy rests on Being, on the sacred (or vice-versa), whereas metaphor is geared to the primacy of the word. Analogy turns language into a tool, at best into some annex of the human if not into an instrument of annexation. By contrast, metaphor fails if it does not underscore, indeed score, the verbal condition of reality, whether human or divine.

Just as in Christ there is neither Greek nor Jew, neither male nor female, so also is there in language neither God nor man.[7] Metaphor is iconoclastic, or it is not a metaphor.

Utopia versus the Sacred: From Mask *(Persona)* to Screen (Word)

Concomitant with the rise of technology, the emergence of linguistics and its cognates underlies a radical mutation of our sense for religion, whereby the latter, centered on *logos,* is now beckoned no longer by the sacred but by utopia. Nor is this surprising. If demythologization is a necessity of the word (and especially therefore with faith), so is desacralization. What is needed now is to get rid of dualism, particularly if theology is to be liberated both from the analogy of being and the dialectic of the sacred and the profane.

Even linguistics appears to this day not to be immune from this dualism, though it should or could be. But vestiges are even harder to get rid of than is the real thing. And in our case, although language is nowadays seldom referred to some supernatural reality, the distinction between signifier and signified is still carried on in a way that inevitably betrays dualistic overtones, even if the signified is reduced to the signifier or is brought under the signifier over or across the bar that separates them. Indeed, I am concerned with that famous bar itself. What does it stand for? And am I entirely off the mark in claiming that it harks back to the age-old cleavage of sacred and profane and its variants from letter and spirit to reason and revelation? Not to mention the latest cleavage in vogue at least in some circles: the unconscious and—at the cost of a blasphemy—the other of the other?

Trying to investigate what the bar stands for, one could perhaps also invoke ethnology and the history of religions, and suggest it plays the same role as the mask. A mask meant to conceal a god less than the man who in fact wears it during ritual ceremonies of initiation. As if man himself were meant to hide himself from himself since he is transgressing the hierarchical order of things by being initiated into a higher world, into the world of the unsaid if not unsayable. But if one bears in mind that the unsaid is not necessarily commensurate with the *new*, the *novum (inédit* or *inouï)*, it could perhaps be more readily accepted why the bar between signifier and signified can play the role of a mask. Like the dialectic of presence and absence, the dialectic of said and unsaid harks back to that of identity and difference: it fails, however, in attempting really to come to grips with the *other*, with the otherness of the other except at best in terms of opposition, like the opposition between God and man, being and nothingness, the sacred and the profane. Things are, so to speak, different enough to be complementary of one another, and eventually to the point of rivaling one another without mercy. But there is no idea of things as being compatible one with the other whether they are complementary of one another or not, or determined so to be beforehand.

Likening the bar to the mask may not be quite evident but is not so farfetched as it may sound, and evidence would not be hard to come by, given the structure of our Western mentality and the general conceptuality of our traditional worldviews. It would bear out the contention that the language of the mask is derived from presuppositions tying it to a mythological universe of discourse which is anchored in the sacred. Likewise a good deal of language analysis, even of hermeneutics, betrays to this day a mental atavism dangerously alienated by the erroneous if traditional assumption of salvation as the kernel of religion, as its exclusive kernel.

The evidence, however, would easily point out and comfort the contention that, at least in the Western tradition, Greek as well as Judeo-Christian, religion is pegged on utopia: there is no world but this one in which man can live by faith and which he can and must therefore change. Even magic implies such a perspective! And today grammatology, by contrast with hermeneutics, is definitely motivated by this kind of orientation. From transgression to subversion the distance is the same as that between analogy and metaphor, the myth of man and the human as technique, changing worlds and changing the world, the sacred and utopia. Or between the mask and the screen. And the screen I see as the symbol of a technological civilization in contrast to the mask as the symbol of a mythological civilization. Indeed, ours is already civilization of the screen.

Let's go back to the point that even the bar can be viewed as a screen. By contrast with the mask, for which there is an inside and an outside, a higher and a lower, a subject and an object, the screen does not stand between but behind and before both terms of each couple; it encompasses them. The mask is never dropped. If one term does not wear it the other does. Or else one could not be referred to the other, and vice versa. And there could be no *persona* either. And, likewise, no revelation. Should thus, for instance, the real stand revealed, it could only be from the standpoint of a *persona*, one who is subjected to the real if not, simply, subject to anything and everything that would seem more real than the real. By contrast, the screen works only to the extent that it disappears, and lets be. It alters itself if the *other* must be, and be without having its otherness swallowed up in some dialectic of identity and difference. It does not hide this otherness, nor does it homogenize that which is heterogeneous as does the mask when it reveals by concealing and conceals by revealing. The screen deals with otherness, not with presence and absence as does the mask that hides or, for that matter, unveils. This is nothing else than some *déjà-vu* albeit anamnestically.

Moreover, by contrast with the mask that must be seen, the screen must not. It follows, as strange as it may sound, that the mark of technological civilization lies less with image than with sound, less with analogy than with metaphor. Like analogy, the mask shows, it points *to*. Like metaphor, the screen points *out*, it means: it tips image into word even if we have grown accustomed to designate by writing what previously was called text or if we tend to recognize traditions by reason of their *cultural* rather than *religious* heritage. Heritage in relation to which we act or continue to act as *voyeurs* rather than as *seers*. No wonder! A good deal of text criticism is today more akin to voyeurism than to prophecy. No longer is text a *screen*. Nor does it, like litmus paper (what the French call *révélateur*), reveal yet without hiding anything, whether the author's mind or some unsaid. Instead, it becomes a cliché: is the New Testament a cliché of the Old? Or, in another realm, is nature a cliché of grace? Screening entails no abrogating whether of nature by grace or of God by man.

And could that be the reason why scripture, indeed all scripture, is inspired of God? A God whose radical otherness stands or falls with the no less radical wholeness of man, compatible as they are without being complementary (much less rivals of one another), *encompassed* as they are by one and the same language—of the Word become flesh, of nature turned into creation, of history into destiny, of time into the fulness of time. And of the world into a new world.

I say: where myth was, there should be torah (or *logos*). Instead of *physis*, the Law (or *nomos*). Instead of *archē*, prolepsis. Instead of mother earth, the promised land. Instead of Babel, Pentecost.

Still, I say: no language cancels another without cancelling itself. No scripture abrogates another without abrogating itself. Else it is not inspired of God. Scripture is without precedent just as writing is a *screen*—a trace, of which the origin disappears, through which the origin disappears. Revelation occurs neither at the beginning nor at the end of scripture. A poem does not come before or after language, but in spite of it as well as through it. Where a poem occurs, there is a new thing: language is surpassed by language. Like reason, then, revelation stands or falls with language. And the relation between the signifier and the signified would amount to a game of hide and seek should language be reducible to something either natural or supernatural.

Language and the Christ

In the Old Testament, God is a requirement of torah, not of nature, just as, in the New Testament, he is a requirement of the Christ event, not of history. He is an iconoclastic word about man, just as man is an iconoclastic word about God. Indeed, it has often been pointed out that in Genesis, by contrast with other such stories, man is understood preeminently, if not exclusively, in terms of his relation to God. A God who alone is God. Who is less the One than he is one, and much less an absolute or the craving for an absolute than he is that of which both the absolute and the quest of it fall short—the Other.

Not a stopgap either, as Paul points out when he says that the world is full of gods. In his view, the main thing lies in knowing that in Christ—and only in Christ—nothing can separate us from God if only because only through Christ is God so radically other that man need *not* sink in him, nor he shorn of his humanity as though he were castrated, and thus be alienated from him. Linguists talk of the primacy of the signifier over the signified. Could it be that Paul has already discovered this, yet without understanding it as implying any occultation of the Other by the other in terms of which the self comes into its own? Or, for that matter, as implying that the signified is necessarily eclipsed even while the signifier comes into its own. For in Christ it is not God that dies, but that which masks his otherness whether on the grounds of some pantheistic naturalism or otherworldly monotheism. Or, as Paul puts it, no longer do we know Christ according to the flesh. We can only find him in Scripture.

But, then, does the same not apply to man? In and through Christ his is a verbal condition which is the very condition of God. And by the same token come to an end all types of dualism, from that of the signifier and the signified back to that of the sacred and the profane, the matrix of them all.

Like analogy, the sacred grows out of nature and returns to nature. To the *arché*. In the Old Testament faith is not bound to nature or to any analogy of it but to its metaphor, to torah: religion is not confused with the sacred but is borne by a utopian vision both of the human reality and the reality of the world. (Indeed, the lamb still is mostly viewed sacrificially when in fact, according to another trend, it could and should be viewed eschatologically: e.g., the lion and the lamb lying down together.)

Not *physis* but *techné* and its utopianism is what provides religion with a language, an instrument through which man puts up in the world and not merely with it. (The term "pagan" is not so accidental as all that, either.) To be sure, the sacral universe was not entirely devoid of utopianism. Only, it groped after an unrealizable kind of utopia, thus overcompensating for the scarcity by which man is beset in this world. Today, we have to cope with the reverse problem, which has to do not so much with utopia's being realizable as with the need to choose between utopia and the "final solution." Indeed, they do not mix.

The latter too is realizable. But here as elsewhere realizable need not mean inevitable. Much less, therefore, does a realizable utopia need to imply the alienation of man. I would even argue that utopia is realizable only so long as man remains inalienable. Responsible. Which amounts to saying: outside language there is no utopia. As Lacan writes: "C'est le monde des mots qui crée le monde des choses, d'abord confondues dans l'hic et nunc du tout en devenir, en donnant son être concret à leur essence, et sa place partout à ce qui est de toujours: κτῆμα 'εϛ'αέι

"L'homme parle donc, mais c'est parce que le symbole l'a fait homme."[8] He speaks. Nor does he speak because he has a mouth, but has a mouth because he speaks. He speaks, and a symbol turns him into a man. A symbol: that is not what links him to nature or, for that matter, to history; but what frees him from either. A symbol: that is, the structuring principle of language and its texture; a text, when the real and the ideal converge as do the natural and the artificial (technē), the body and the soul, and as do also the signifier and the signified, the letter and the spirit. All scripture is inspired of God (Paul would say). Or, prodded by a former student to quote Henri Bosco: "All the being of the world, if it dreams, dreams that it is speaking." A symbol.

And therefore a text. To which one goes as one goes to the empty tomb on Easter morning: across the frontier of divine and human; that is, into language—the dawning of truth as emancipation as well as authentication of man. Only thus "wo Es war, soll Ich werden":[9] a new man, without precedent. And who, if it is true that God gave his only Son only because he so loved the world, speaks and thus entrusts the world with God.

NOTES

1. Giorgio Agamben, "Propos . . .," *Bulletin de l'Association freudienne* 2 (1983):27.

2. "Verbum sine verbo," *Le Discours psychanalytique* 6 (1983):65.

3. Jacques Lacan, "Postface," *Le Séminaire* XI (Paris: Editions du Seuil, 1973), 253. Moustapha Safouan, *L'Inconscient et son scribe* (Paris: Editions du Seuil, 1982), 59.

4. Noam Chomsky, "Le langage est le miroir de l'esprit," *L'Année littéraire 1972*, La Quinzaine littéraire (Paris, 1973), 263.

5. Hans-Georg Gadamer, "Man and Language," *Philosophical Hermeneutics*, ed. and tr. David E. Linge (Berkeley: Univ. of California Press, 1976), 59–68 (see esp. 62–63).

6. "Fonction et champ de la parole et du langage (Discours de Rome)," *Ecrits* (Paris: Editions du Seuil, 1966), 262. (=Anthony Wilden & Jacques Lacan, *The Language of the Self* [Baltimore: Johns Hopkins Univ. Press, 1968], 24–25.) Cf. also "L'Instance de la lettre dans l'inconscient, ou la raison depuis Freud," *Ecrits*, 508: ". . . la métaphore se place au point précis où le sens se produit dans le non-sens."

7. "Fonction et champ," 299: "Je m'identifie dans le langage, mais seulement à m'y perdre."

8. *Ecrits*, 276.

9. Lacan, "L'Instance," *Ecrits*, 524, adds: "Quel est donc cet autre à qui je suis plus attaché qu'à moi, puisqu'au sein le plus assenti de mon identité à moi-même, c'est lui qui m'agite?"

A Response to Vahanian

LONNIE D. KLIEVER

Those of us who have followed Gabriel Vahanian's theological work closely over the years will recognize a familiar philosophical and historical landscape surrounding this tightly argued piece on God and language. Assumed as the conceptual horizon of this exploration is his familiar emphasis on the essential utopianism of both the human reality and the biblical faith. The human achieves its own reality only in an "otherness" or "beyondness" which forever remains within reach but beyond grasp. This utopian 'otherness' or 'beyondness' is, of course, what the biblical faith speaks of symbolically as 'God'. For the biblical faith, God is that 'nowhere' (outopos) where human life becomes human. As such, God is God and man is man only as long as they remain other to one another.

Assumed also as the historical backdrop of Vahanian's reflections on language and God is his less well-known distinction between soteriological and eschatological expressions of the biblical faith. Both the human and the divine come to appearance in language, language that is always culturally and religiously particular. The utopian reality of man and God is always expressed in a culture's own religiosity and every religiosity is articulated in a specific cultural framework. This means that a given religious and cultural symbol system may either express or repress true humanity and true divinity. Any given symbol system can spell death or life to man or God!

Vahanian calls each such symbol system a "technique of the human" and notes that each technique is borne by a distinctive "vector of culture." The heart of his theological program centers in sorting out the ways these techniques differ and why their vectors change with the passage of time. He begins by marking a crucial distinction between soteriological and eschatological techniques of the human. Soteriological techniques (religions of the salvation of man) envision God as the condition of man. In soteric religiosity, God's transcendence is exterior to man and the world. Human existence is defined by "scarcity" and "heteronomy" and man's utopian destiny is projected into another world which can only be anticipated through spiritual evasion of this world. By contrast, eschatological techniques (religions of the reign of God) see man as the condition of God. Eschatic religiosity sees God's transcendence as anterior to man and the world. Human existence is marked by abundance and autonomy and man's utopian destiny is realized in this world's becoming other through bodily engagement with it.

Given these distinctions, Vahanian argues that Christianity has been a "soteriological religion" throughout most of its history. Where salvation is seen as liberation from nature, transcendence is understood supernaturalistically. Only a return to the supernatural world above will make up for the mysteries and miseries of life in the natural world. By contrast, when salvation is understood as liberation from history, transcendence is conceived in apocalyptic terms. Only the arrival of the apocalyptic world ahead will resolve the vicissitudes and injustices of historical existence. In other words, both supernaturalistic and apocalyptic soteric techniques rest on mythic conceptions of transcendence. They distinguish man and God, world and kingdom by separating them spatially and temporally. Soteriological religiosity always consigns the utopian reality of man and God to some paradisal past or apocalyptic future. Such utopianism has consisted largely "in changing worlds rather than changing the world."

Vahanian insists that Christianity had no choice but to take the form of a soteric faith because the only cultural vectors available in the Greco-Roman world were mythic. Nevertheless, these supernaturalistic and apocalyptic theisms did mediate the utopian reality of man and God, albeit in an ambiguous way. Belief in another world above or ahead stood guard iconoclastically against all temptations to deify nature or society. But even these misshapen utopianisms have lost their power to bring man and God to appearance in the modern world. All mythic cultural vehicles of transcendence have been dissolved. Modern technology has delivered man from the mythic world of scarcity and heteronomy into the technological world of abundance and autonomy. Modern technology has made man a producer of nature and history rather than their product.

Seen in this light, technology is not the destroyer of humanism and faith so widely feared today. In liberating man from an impersonal nature and history, technology empowers man to humanize both. If man's proper place is neither "residue of nature" nor "afterglow of history," then technology facilitates the "coming man" by extricating him from nature's necessities and history's terrors. In other words, Vahanian sees technology both negating and fulfilling the Christian tradition. By negating Christianity's mythological conception of religion, technology offers at last a cultural vector that can embody a genuinely eschatological faith.

Vahanian makes no claims that this transformation will come about automatically. Technology will foster the utopianism proper to man and God only if it "gets the religion it deserves." That new religiosity will require a new language and a new ecclesiology. Neither has yet appeared, so Vahanian's comments about this linguistic and ecclesial revolution to date are somewhat sketchy. Indeed, the present essay under discussion is his fullest statement to date on a conception of language appropriate to the utopianism of man and God as this utopianism comes to expression in a technological rather than a mythic culture.[1]

Linguistically, Vahanian maps the transition from a mythological civilization to a technological civilization as an axial shift in the way we understand both the nature and the function of language itself. His characterization of this shift is the point at which I want to raise several questions for clarification and further discussion.

1. The Nature of Language—From Analogy to Metaphor

Vahanian insists that language in the mythic universe of discourse could only be conceived of in one of two ways—either magically or analogically. The basic dualism of the sacral universe reduces language either to an occult or instrumental tool. Speech thus becomes some "wonderous speechlessness" which annexes the divine to the human (magic) or the human to the divine (analogy). Certainly this reading is borne out by both the anthropological discussion of magic and the theological discussion of analogy. Whether magic is perceived as a primitive science (Frazier) or as an occult technology (Malinowski), the formulas of magic are techniques for bringing mystery under human control. Similarly, whether analogy is perceived as a language of attribution (St. Thomas) or a language of proportionality (Gilson), analogical discourse is a technique for subjecting the human to mystery's control. In either case, whether the language of magic or the language of analogy, 'God' is not maintained as the Other. Indeed, 'God' becomes Another or Otherwise.

This much seems clear to me. But I am less clear how metaphor overcomes the dualism of the sacral universe of discourse. The scholarly discussion of metaphor is too vast and Vahanian is too sparing in his comments on metaphor for me to gain a clear picture of how the "linguistic turn" he points to is funded by metaphorical as contrasted to analogical language. Conceived in broadest terms, the essence of metaphor is understanding and experiencing one kind of thing in terms of another—a generic definition which suggests that *both* terms of a metaphoric connection are put into question and brought into relief by the metaphor. But, beyond this glimpse of how metaphor succeeds in expressing iconoclastically the verbal condition of both man and God, what more can and must be said to make Vahanian's case clearer? Is it metaphor's much-celebrated multisignification that stands guard iconoclastically against freezing the human or the divine into a datum or evaporating one into a mirrored image of the other? Is it metaphor's anthropomorphic richness that personalizes man and God without separating them into persons? And what are we to make of those theories of metaphor which tie metaphor to mythic consciousness (Ernst Cassirer) or primitive troping (Hayden White)? I realize that elsewhere Vahanian has spoken to such questions by characterizing the language of a technological civilization as bodily and fictile— as a technique that gives man and God an earthly dimension by bridging the imaginary and the real. But I am interested in learning more about the distinctive characteristics of metaphoric language in general and the range of metaphoric discourse in particular (e.g., personalistic or impersonalistic, spatial or temporal) which redeems the biblical promise of an authentic utopianism of the divine and the human in our emerging technological civilization.

2. The Function of Language—From Mask to Screen

Vahanian takes us closer to an understanding of the difference between a mythological universe of discourse and a technological universe of discourse by contrasting language as mask to language as screen. Vahanian never finally reduces God or man to language, though neither God nor man comes to appearance in any way other than language. There is a "bar" between the signifier and the signified, but entire civilizations turn on whether that bar divides or cojoins.

Religious language in a mythological universe of discourse works like a mask to separate God and man. Echoing a rich anthropological and historical literature on masks and masking, Vahanian rightly observes that ceremonial masks conceal the human more than they reveal the divine. To the extent that such masks are revelatory, they reveal the divine by concealing the human. But precisely this dualism of the sacred and the profane has been undercut by the technological revolution which is freeing man from his mythic dependence on and terror of the world. In this emerging technological civilization, religious language is becoming a screen that conjoins rather than a mask that divides man and God.

I am intrigued by Vahanian's contrast of the mask and the screen. His intentions in drawing this contrast seem clear enough—masks point to, screens point out, masks stand between, screens set forth, masks work by remaining in place, screens work by disappearing. Here again we have the claim that a language fully attuned to the utopian reality of man and God maintains their otherness to one another without separation, change, confusion, or division. But I am not fully clear on how language as screen accomplishes this breakthrough. "Masks" and "screens" are obviously metaphors of language. Indeed, "mask" is a metaphor for analogical language and "screen" is a metaphor for metaphorical language. But what kind of screen does Vahanian have in mind in drawing these sharp contrasts? Screen as grid through which we view another context (Max Black)? Screen as surface against which we project our images of man and God (Paul Tillich)? Such questions are surely not raised with the thought of getting *behind* Vahanian's metaphor of the screen so much as getting *inside* that metaphor. Poets, after all, choose particular concrete images to say what they mean, even though the poem is heard in spite of those images as well as through them. I would be helped better to understand Vahanian's views if he said more about the way language screens without masking.

Finally, I suppose the two questions I am raising come down to wanting to hear more about *what* we can say about God and man rather than hearing about *how* we can say it. Vahanian is clear on the formal requirements for such speaking in a technological universe of discourse. But I am not sure how such actual speaking in the language of everyday confession and communion, or prayer and preaching will differ from the ways the church has spoken in the past. May we still use the orientational and structural metaphors modeled on our experience of space and time, of objects and persons to speak of God and man? May we still use the language of scripture which seems nothing if not supernaturalistic or apocalyptic through and through? Is it enough to demythologize and desacralize our *theory* of religious language or must we somehow demythologize and desacralize such language itself? And, if the latter, what concretely will such language sound like and look like? In short, is the shift from analogy to metaphor, from mask to screen, a *metalinguistic* or a *linguistic* shift?

NOTES

1. For other statements on the utopianism of language, see *No Other God* (New York: George Braziller, 1966), 47–63; *God and Utopia* (New York: Seabury Press, 1977), 41–47; "Utopia as Hermeneutic Principle of Demythologization," *Rudolf Bultmanns Werk und Wirkung,* ed. Bernd Jaspert (Darmstadt: Wissenschaftliche Buchgesellschaft, 1984), 286–88.

Reply

GABRIEL VAHANIAN

To the questions, thorny questions inimitably raised by Lonnie Kliever out of comments whose lucidity and sharpness exempt them from being treacherous, *what* indeed can I say and *how* can I say it? Surely his careful, faithful, and yet creative rendering of a theological investigation I have sought to pursue in this and other essays is not meant to conceal only a trap, unless it is one he must himself have fallen into. Kliever's critical acumen is nevertheless as potent in its humiliating identification of soft spots as it is comforting in its endorsement of pathfinding attempts in theological reflection. I am therefore more than pleased in having to cope with a critic as demanding as he is generous, sensitive, knowledgeable.

Kliever knows, and certainly must remember, Augustine's famous injunction to the effect that if we speak about God it is not in order to say something but in order not to say nothing.

What I have been trying to show is that God is not this or that. He is other than this or that. And such otherness is of the kind that can be confronted only through language. According to the biblical, western tradition God is Word and his reality is bound up with speech: God is "language." Rather than "being." And unless being is what comes to being through language, God as being is extraneous to language. Language is then used as a tool. Such usage is quite legitimate in science and other walks of life. In theology, however, language is, to be sure, a tool, but it is not merely a tool. And greater than the shift from myth to technique or from the sacred to utopia is the shift *to* language.

As mask, language "limits" *a* and *b* in relation to each other (e.g., sacred and profane). By contrast, language as screen "de-limits" (e.g., the holy and not yet holy). Unlike the mask, the screen "disappears," as does sin before grace, and man is then *simul* justus *ac* peccator. But then, also, *what*ever can be said and *how*ever it can be said, the significant thing is *that* it can be said.

The sun still rises. It sets. If we can say so, it is only because its rising and setting has at long last become a metaphor and no longer simply looks as though it is a rising and a setting. By contrast with analogy, metaphor does not work by making things look like other things. It is "paschal": it occurs through words. And language, whether its origin is natural or "divine," is metaphoric.

Does then metaphor shun the cleavage Kliever still is fascinated with between "linguistic" and "metalinguistic"? Depending on what he means by metalinguistic, the answer is *yes* if Kliever's cleavage harks back to those of sacred and profane, natural and supernatural, theism and atheism, etc. On the other hand, if metalinguistic does not mean beyond language, and language is not reduced to or exhausted by *langue,* then one could possibly say that the shift is both metalinguistic and linguistic—as, a contrario, Orwell's *Newspeak* would show. Nor should the question minimize the importance of the shift.

A shift similar perhaps to that from the Old to the New Testament, from Israel to the Church: the "language of Scripture" need be no wooden tongue—as in the first place the Bible itself amply demonstrates. Theology comes before so-called biblical theology (the language of Scripture) or else there would have been no New Testament, no new Israel, no new metaphor: the Christ, measure of all things, and in whom there is neither Greek nor Jew. Neither God nor man—except in terms of their radical otherness.

Contributors

Shlomo Biderman   Senior Lecturer, the Department of Philosophy at Tel Aviv University, Tel Aviv, Israel.

Nona R. Bolin   Instructor in Philosophy at Memphis State University, Memphis, Tennessee, U.S.A.

Michael J. Coughlan   Lecturer in Philosophy at St. David's University College, University of Wales, United Kingdom.

Charles Courtney   Professor of the Philosophy of Religion at Drew University, Madison, New Jersey, U.S.A.

Francis X. D'Sa   Director of the Institute for the Study of Religion and Professor of Indian Philosophy and Religions, Jnana Deepa Vidyapeetha, Pune, India.

Frederick Ferré   Professor of Philosophy and Head of the Department of Philosophy at the University of Georgia, Athens, Georgia, U.S.A.

Frank R. Harrison, III   Professor of Philosophy at the University of Georgia, Athens, Georgia, U.S.A.

Martin S. Jaffee   Assistant Professor of Religious Studies at the University of Virginia, Charlottesville, Virginia, U.S.A.

Asa Kasher   Professor of Philosophy at Tel Aviv University, Tel Aviv, Israel.

Lonnie D. Kliever   Professor of Religious Studies and Head of the Department at Southern Methodist University, Dallas, Texas, U.S.A.

Gilbert E. M. Ogutu   Lecturer in Religious Studies at the University of Nairobi, Nairobi, Kenya.

God in Language

Robert P. Scharlemann Professor of Religious Studies at the University of Virginia, Charlottesville, Virginia, U.S.A.

Frederick Sontag Professor of Philosophy at Pomona College, Claremont, California, U.S.A.

Gabriel Vahanian Professor of Theology on the Faculté Protestante of the Université des Sciences Humaines, Strasbourg, France.

Index

Index

Index

Index

86; religious, 42; schematic, 8; of self, 44; and silence, 144; symbol—, 36; transcendent, 13; as triadic, 19. *See also* God, knowledge of
ko'an, 173
Koran. *See* Qu'rān

La tentation de faire du bien (Duméry), 172
Lacan, Jacques, 197, 200, 205
language: as an abstract structure, ix, 14–16, 18, 23; analogical versus metaphorical, 199–200, 209, 211–12, 214; artificial, 34n.29; Buber on, 114–18; as contextual, 14; as culturally specific, 12, 28–29, 98; descriptive adequacy of, 23–4, 26–29, 33n.23, 34n.24; and Dhvani, 44–47; effect of as a medium on knowledge of God, 3, 9, 10, 11, 18, 20, 23, 97–98; generality of, 190; ideal, 153; as information, 35; as instantiating, x, 114, 116–17, 118, 127; and justification of belief, 8, 11; and knowledge, viii–ix, 12, 38, 40; as *logos*, 40, 55, 58n.6; as mask versus screen, 210–12, 213; as a medium, vii, 3, 9, 10, 18, 20, 23, 97, 114, 121, 133–34, 170; natural, 3–8, 10, 11; as *outopos*, 194; and reality, viii, 28, 29, 44–47, 114, 115–18; referentiality of, 9, 10, 132; semiotic foundations of, 15, 27, 28, 29; and silence, 144; symbolic, 42, 54, 199, 205; and technique, 197–99, 200; and theology, 213; and time, 196; as a tool, vii, 213; as transformation, 35; as triadic, 15, transparent, 14; utopianism of, 194, 196, 198–99, 204–05. *See also* God, and language; God, language of; religious language
language-games, 108, 150–51, 159–60, 162
langue, 214

Last Judgment, 150–51, 157–58, 164
law, 8, 203; act—, 162, 177, 179, 180
Lectures on Religious Belief (Wittgenstein), 149, 150, 154, 157, 160, 164
Leenhardt, Maurice, 196
legitimation, 87
Levi, Joshua B., 87
linguistics, 201; meta—, 212, 214
logic, ix, 17, 150, 151, 153, 196
Logic (Hegel), 116, 118
logocentrism, 64–65
logos, 38, 39, 51, 66, 185, 196, 200, 203; language as, 40, 55, 58n.6
Lost in the Cosmos (Percy), 161
Luo people (Kenya): anthropomorphism of, 95; Christianity among, 97–98; conception of God among, x, 90–91, 93–97, 98; language of, 91–92; words for God among, 90–91, 92–94, 95

magic, 209
Maimonides, 184–86, 191
Malinowski, Bronislow, 209
man: age of, 60; in Derrida, 66; Descartes on, 61–63; and God, 195, 197, 203, 204, 205, 207–212, 214
Mary, 51–54
mask, 201, 203, 210, 213
materialism, 12, 168
mathematics, 17, 23
Meagher, John, 173
meaning, 12, 13; of Being, 62, 63, 64; and presence, 66; of propositions, 24, 27; religious, 12–13; significance as soul of, 57–58n.5; Wittgenstein on, 161–62; of the world, 36–37. *See also* significance
Meir, R., 83, 84
Merton, Thomas, 140–42
Messiah, 49
metaphor, 35–36, 40, 46, 57n.2, 67, 199, 202, 209–10, 211
metaphysics, ix, 195, 196; break with, 64, 66, 155–56, 161, 162; logocentrism of, 64–65; of

Index

finitude, 62; Platonist, 60;
  theological, 156–58, 162; and
  writing, 65
Midgley, Mary, 189–91
Mimamsa (school of Hinduism), 102
Mishnah: as Oral Torah, 73–74,
  88n.10; authority of, 73, 76,
  82–83, 86–87; exegesis of, ix,
  75–87; literary traits of, 77, 80,
  81; origin of, 73–74; as pre-text,
  x, 76–87
monotheism, x, 101, 103, 107,
  110–111
morality: reform of, 153; and
  religion, 100–102, 103, 111–12
Moses, 73, 74, 87, 185
mysticism, 13, 170, 178–81, 184
myth, 150–51, 199, 200, 202, 203,
  208, 209, 210

name: sacred, 92. *See also* proper
  name
Nathanael, 49, 50
Natural Theology (Paley), 6
necessity, 26, 124
negative theology, 11, 67–68, 136,
  184–86, 189
Neo-Platonism, 156
Neusner, Jacob, 87n.1
Nietzsche, Friedrich, 60, 63, 69, 161
Noah, 129
nomos, 203
Nya-saye (Luo deity), 90–98

object, 61, 119. *See also* God, as
  object
Ogutu, Gilbert, x
onto-theology, 60, 65, 67, 68, 200
ontology: and epistemology, 63. *See
  also* difference, ontico-
  theological; reduction,
  ontological
opposition. *See* dualism
orthodoxy, 163, 171
Orwell, George, 198, 214
other, xi, 201, 204, 207, 210, 214
overcoming, 63

paganism, 205

Paley, William, 6, 191–92
paradox, 80, 124, 185
Patmos group, 115, 118
Paul, 130, 204, 205
perception, 35, 45
Percy, Walker, 161
performative, 109–110
perlocutionary, 109
Pesikta Rabbati, 74
Peters, R., 103
phenomenology, ix, 31n.10, 63, 161,
  176
Philip, 49
Phillips, Dewi Z., 152, 153, 154,
  162–63, 164
Philosophical Investigations
  (Wittgenstein), 154, 160, 162
Philosophie de la religion (Duméry),
  174
philosophy: post-Cartesian, 18,
  31n.10; and religion, xi, 156,
  169, 176, 177, 181; and
  theology, 60; Wittgenstein on,
  111, 154
phonocentrism, 65
physis 203, 204
Picard, Max, 143
piety, 180
Plato, x, 30n.1, 60–61, 100–102,
  111, 158, 183
Plotinus, 178
poetry, viii, 145, 211
Polanyi, Michael, 31n.10
positivism, 16
pragmatics, ix, 15–16, 19, 29, 32n.12
pragmatism (American), 31n.10
prayer, 110, 163–64, 211
predicates: empirical, 26–27
presence, 61, 65, 66, 67, 68, 118,
  122, 124, 127, 201; of God,
  128–30, 131–32, 138
Problème de dieu, Le (Duméry), 166,
  174
proper name, 9–10, 92, 196; of God,
  10, 20–21, 24, 34n.31, 92, 114,
  122–23, 127, 135, 136, 137,
  138, 152, 185–86
propositions: *a posteriori*, 24–26; *a
  priori*, 24–26, 27–28, 32n.12;
  analytic, 25, 32n.12; empirical,
  25–26; formal, 18; incorrigible,
  17, 18, 24; meaning of, 24, 27;
  synthetic, 25, 26, 27, 28,
  32n.12; truth-value of, 3–6, 17,
  24–27, 30n.7, 32n.12